T0330127

Retirement Provision in Scary Markets

For

Bruce, Elizabeth, Nicholas and Thomas

Retirement Provision in Scary Markets

Edited by

Hazel Bateman

Deputy Director, Centre for Pensions and Superannuation and Senior Lecturer, School of Economics, Faculty of Commerce and Economics, University of New South Wales, Australia

Edward Elgar
Cheltenham, UK • Northampton, MA, USA

© Hazel Bateman 2007

Published by
Edward Elgar Publishing Limited
Glensanda House
Montpellier Parade
Cheltenham
Glos GL50 1UA
UK

Edward Elgar Publishing, Inc.
William Pratt House
9 Dewey Court
Northampton
Massachusetts 01060
USA

A catalogue record for this book
is available from the British Library

Library of Congress Cataloguing-in-Publication Data
Retirement provision in scary markets / [edited by] Hazel Bateman.
    p. cm.
    Retirement provision in scary markets : introduction / Hazel Bateman –
Who's afraid of the big bad bear? or, why investment in equities for
retirement is not scary and why investing without equities is scary / Ronald
Bewley, Nick Ingram, Veronica Livera and Sheridan Thompson – Assessing the
risks in global fixed interest portfolios / Geoffrey Brianton – The role of
index funds in retirement asset allocation / David R. Gallagher –
Retirement wealth and lifetime earnings variability / Olivia S. Mitchell,
John W.R. Phillips, Andrew Au and David McCarthy – How have older workers
responded to scary markets / Jonathan Gardner and Mike Orszag – Financial
engineering for Australian annuitants / Susan Thorp, Geoffrey Kingston and
Hazel Bateman – Smoothing investment returns / Anthony Asher – Ansett's
superannuation fund : a case study in insolvency / Shauna Ferris – Pension
funds and retirement benefits in a depressed economy : experience and
challenges in Japan / Masaharu Usuki – The structure and regulation of the
Brazilian private pension system / Flavio Marcilio Rabelo.
    Includes bibliographical references and index.
    1. Pension trusts–Management. 2. Stock exchanges. 3. Uncertainty. 4. Risk. I.
Bateman, Hazel.

HD7105.4.R48 2006
331.25′2—dc22

2006002840

ISBN 978 1 84376 906 4

Typeset by Cambrian Typesetters, Camberley, Surrey
Printed and bound in Great Britain by MPG Books Ltd, Bodmin, Cornwall

Contents

Contributors

Anthony Asher, Australian Prudential Regulation Authority, Sydney

Andrew Au, University of Pennsylvania, Philadelphia

Hazel Bateman, The University of New South Wales, Sydney

Ronald Bewley, Commonwealth Securities, Sydney

Geoffrey Brianton, Merrill Lynch Investment Managers, Melbourne

Shauna Ferris, Macquarie University, Sydney

David R. Gallagher, The University of New South Wales, Sydney

Jonathan Gardner, Watson Wyatt LLP, Surrey, UK

Nick Ingram, Commonwealth Securities, Sydney

Geoffrey Kingston, The University of New South Wales, Sydney

Veronica Livera, Commonwealth Securities, Sydney

David McCarthy, Imperial College, London

Olivia S. Mitchell, Pension Research Council, Wharton Business School, University of Pennsylvania, Philadelphia

Mike Orszag, Watson Wyatt LLP, Surrey, UK

John W.R. Phillips, Social Security Administration, Washington, DC, USA

Flávio Marcílio Rabelo, Escola de Administracao de Empresas de São Paulo

Sheridan Thompson, Commonwealth Securities, Sydney

Susan Thorp, University of Technology, Sydney

Masaharu Usuki, NLI Research Institute, Tokyo

Preface and acknowledgements

This book was motivated by consideration of the economic, financial and social implications of the increasing reliance on funded private provision for retirement. Most of the contributory chapters were workshopped at the conference 'Retirement Provision in Scary Markets' held in Sydney, Australia in July 2003. The successful staging of this conference, the tenth in a series of annual colloquia of superannuation researchers held in Australia, was due to the hard work and dedication of the academics and administrators associated with the Centre for Pensions and Superannuation at the University of New South Wales. Special thanks must go to the Director of the Centre for Pensions and Superannuation, Professor John Piggott, for ongoing support and encouragement, as well as to Clea Bye for her excellent conference organization.

An edited volume such as this would not be possible without the hard work and cooperation of the contributory authors. I would like to thank all of them for their overwhelming support, from initial planning through to the conference itself, and then the rewriting and editing required as the conference papers evolved into book chapters. Acknowledgement must also be made to the conference discussants and participants, whose comments and suggestions helped to shape the final manuscript. Nadine Caisley deserves special mention for reading the entire manuscript as it neared completion.

Finally, I would like to thank my family for their understanding and patience, particularly my daughter Elizabeth who provided unending moral support while preparing for her own HSC exams.

Hazel Bateman
University of New South Wales, Sydney
November 2005

1. Introduction

Hazel Bateman

Over the past few decades there has been a global move towards private provision for retirement through individual defined contribution plans, at the expense of publicly provided and employer-sponsored defined benefit arrangements. As a consequence, workers and retirees are increasingly exposed to uncertainties in financial, economic and labour markets. These uncertainties have materialized in the form of extreme stock price volatility, discontinuous labour market participation, regulatory failure and macroeconomic instability. The broad aim of this book is to identify these potentially scary aspects of pre-funded private provision for retirement, relate specific country experiences and offer possible solutions. Overall, private funded retirement income arrangements are seen to be resilient to a wide range of scary market scenarios.

RETIREMENT INCOME TRENDS AROUND THE WORLD

In developed and less developed countries alike there is an ongoing trend towards greater emphasis on private retirement income arrangements. In the developed world, this has been largely due to financing shortfalls associated with generous, less than fully funded, public pensions in the face of population ageing (OECD 2005a; Commission to Strengthen Social Security 2001; Feldstein 2005; Takayama 1998). Also important has been the goal to increase living standards of the elderly (Bateman and Piggott 1997). In the developing world the trend has been driven by a slightly different set of factors, including rapid industrialization or a desire to increase economic growth, combined with inadequate, low coverage or corrupt formal retirement income arrangements (World Bank 1994; Holzmann and Hinz 2005).

Chile was the first country to make funded private arrangements the dominant form of retirement income provision when the pay-as-you-go (PAYG) public pension was 'privatized' in 1981. This marked the beginning of a trend which continues to this day. Switzerland and Australia followed in the mid-1980s, with the introduction of mandatory funded private arrangements to supplement their public pension schemes. Voluntary participation in private pensions increased in the UK with the introduction of 'contracting out' in the mid-1980s, whereby many defined benefit public pensions were converted into private defined contribution arrangements; and in the USA and Canada, private pension coverage increased to around 50 per cent of the workforce following the introduction of tax preference for Individual Retirement Accounts (IRAs), 401(k)s (an employer sponsored defined contribution pension plan named after section 401k of the Internal Revenue Code sub-section that regulates it) and Registered Retirement Savings Plans (RRSPs).

Over the past two decades, funded private retirement income arrangements have also gained prominence across most of Latin America, many OECD countries (including Sweden and Poland), a number of transition economies (including Hungary and Kazakhstan), Asia (including Hong Kong, South Korea and Japan) and many developing economies (see Holzmann and Hinz 2005; Bateman et al. 2001).[1] In the USA there has been an ongoing debate about the pros and cons of the 'privatization of social security'. Despite numerous proposals and reports, legislative action is yet to be taken (see Diamond and Orszag 2004; Commission to Strengthen Social Security 2001; Feldstein 2005).

VULNERABILITY TO SCARY MARKETS

Under privately provided retirement incomes based on defined contributions, income in retirement is directly related to the size of the periodic contributions, the net rate of return on these contributions and the length of the contributory period. However, when translating this simple formula into practice, many more variables come into play. These include the length and continuity of labour force participation (which affects the ability to make contributions and the timing of these contributions), the amount of the periodic net contribution (which may be affected by statutory minimum requirements, the capacity to make voluntary contributions and the existence of incentives for voluntary contributions, taxes on contributions, wages growth and any contribution or entry fees), and net returns (influenced by asset allocation, asset returns, taxation of investment income and capital gains, investment fees, administrative expenses, market structure, governance and the regulatory framework).

As a result, private provision for retirement is particularly vulnerable to scary markets in the form of fluctuations in economic, financial and labour markets, long-term socioeconomic and demographic trends, market failures in the retirement saving industry, and the ability of governments to adequately regulate this industry.

Recent economic, financial and labour market indicators, for five of the countries examined in the following chapters, are summarized in Table 1.1. The indicators examined are GDP (gross domestic product) as a measure of macroeconomic performance and stability, CPI (consumer price index) as a measure of the purchasing power of retirement incomes, interest rates and share price index movements as indicators of asset returns, and the unemployment rate as an indicator of the state of the labour market.

Macroeconomic stability, as proxied by GDP growth rates, has been only moderately scary over the past 15 years for most of the countries examined. In Australia, real GDP growth ranged from a low of –0.6 per cent per annum in 1991 to a high of 5.3 per cent per annum in 1994, while in Brazil, the annual GDP growth rates have ranged from a low of 4.8 per cent in 1990 to a high of 5.9 per cent in 1994. However, movement in the CPI, the indicator responsible for determining the real value or purchasing power of retirement savings, appears scarier, ranging from a high of 2948 per cent per annum in Brazil in 1990, to a low of –1.0 per cent per annum in Japan in 2002. All countries considered here show some variation in rates of unemployment, moderate variation in interest rates, and extreme variation in share price indexes. The greatest variation has been experienced by Brazil for all three of these indicators.

To provide an indication of scary stock markets, annual share price index movements in Australia, Japan, the UK and the USA are summarized in Figures 1.1 to 1.4.

Another potentially scary phenomenon is the demographic trend of population ageing. Table 1.2 shows the increase in the old-age dependency ratios across all five exemplar countries. We know that an ageing population will lead to a smaller future labour force and raise questions about the ability of

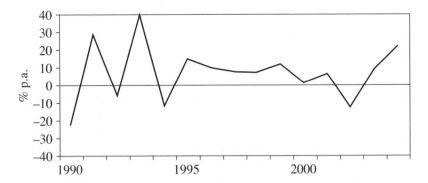

Sources: ASX 200, *Reserve Bank of Australia Bulletin*, various issues.

Figure 1.1   Australia share price index, per cent per annum

Table 1.1 Scary economic and financial conditions (1990–2004)

	Australia	Brazil	Japan	UK	USA
GDP% p.a.					
Highest (year)	5.3 (1998)	5.9 (1994)	5.3 (1990)	4.0 (2000)	4.5 (1997)
Lowest (year)	−0.6 (1991)	−4.2 (1990)	−0.3 (2002)	−1.4 (1991)	−0.2 (1991)
CPI % p.a.					
Highest (year)	7.3 (1990)	2948 (1990)	−3.2 (1991)	7.5 (1991)	5.4 (1990)
Lowest (year)	0.3 (1997)	3.2 (1998)	−1.0 (2002)	0.8 (2000)	1.5 (1998)
Unemployment %					
Highest (year)	10.5 (1992)	3.7 (1990)	5.4 (2002)	10.4 (1993)	7.5 (1992)
Lowest (year)	5.5 (2004)	12.3 (1993)	2.1 (1991)	4.8 (2004)	4.0 (2000)
Interest rates % p.a.*					
Highest (year)	14.2 (1990)	49.9 (1995)	7.4 (1990)	12.1 (1990)	7.7 (1990)
Lowest (year)	4.8 (2001)	17.1 (2004)	1.0 (2003)	4.2 (2003)	1.0 (2003)
Share price % yr on yr**					
Highest (year)	40.3 (1993)	3275 (1993)	34.8 (1999)	17.2 (1993)	33.5 (1995)
Lowest (year)	−22.4 (2003)	−17.6 (2002)	−38.7 (1990)	−24.5 (2002)	−23.4 (2002)

Notes:

*   Interest rates: Australia (Treasury Bills), Brazil (money market rate), Japan (government bond), UK (government bond, short term), US (Treasury Bill).

** Share price index: Australia (S&P/ASX 200), Brazil (industrial share price index), Japan (Nikkei-225, until 2001; thereafter TOPIX), UK (FT Industrial Ordinary until 2001; thereafter FTSE 100), USA (Dow Jones Industrial until 2001; thereafter S&P 500).

Source: International Monetary Fund, *International Financial Statistics* at http://ifs.apdi.net/imf/about.asp and International Monetary Fund, *World Economic Outlook* at http://www.imf.org/external/pubs/ft/weo/weorepts.htm.

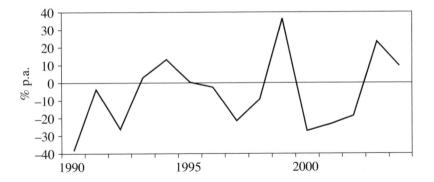

Sources: Nikkei-225 (to 2001); thereafter TOPIX, *Reserve Bank of Australia Bulletin*, various issues.

Figure 1.2   Japan share price index, per cent per annum

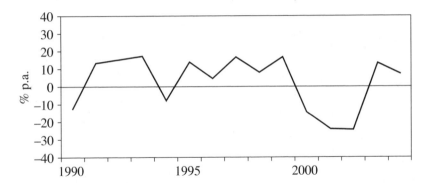

Sources: FT Industrial Ordinary (to 2001); thereafter FTSE 100, *Reserve Bank of Australia Bulletin*, various issues.

Figure 1.3   UK share price index, per cent per annum

governments to fund public pensions. However, we are less certain about the long-term implications for financial markets and asset returns (Disney 1996; Poterba 2001). Some empirical studies suggest that equity prices will weaken at the expense of bond prices once the baby boomers in the major OECD economies move from accumulation to decumulation. However, it is also argued that this will be offset by increased saving elsewhere in the world.

Other potentially scary aspects of a greater reliance on private provision for retirement include the increased importance of a sound regulatory structure. It is possible that too little or inappropriate regulation may increase the

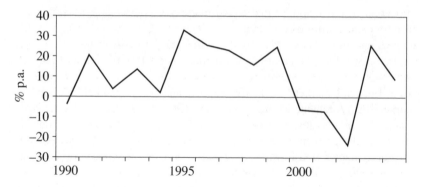

Sources: US Dow Jones Industrial (to 2001); thereafter S&P 500, *Reserve Bank of Australia Bulletin*, various issues.

Figure 1.4   USA share price index, per cent per annum

Table 1.2   Scary population trends – old age dependency ratios

	Old-age dependency ratio			Very-old persons ratio		
	2000 %	2005 %	Increase	2000 %	2005 %	Increase
Australia	20.4	47.0	26.6	23.3	34.0	10.7
Japan	27.7	64.5	36.9	21.9	42.2	20.3
UK	26.6	45.3	18.7	25.0	37.3	12.3
USA	21.7	37.9	16.2	26.5	36.1	9.6

Source: OECD (2003), Table 1.

likelihood of institutional failure, while over-regulation may force down net rates of return.

Finally, an important implication of the trend towards private defined contribution pension plans is the shift in risk bearing from the government and employers to individuals. Therefore, to the extent that markets are scary, the impact is felt directly by workers and retirees.

STRUCTURE OF THE BOOK

The contributory chapters to this book address a broad range of scary and potentially scary scenarios. The first three substantive chapters focus on asset allocation. The perceptions that equity markets are too volatile to be included in retirement portfolios and that fixed interest assets are low risk are challenged, and the role of index funds in lifecycle investment portfolios in an environment of heightened financial market uncertainty is explored. The next two chapters turn to labour markets. Two issues are considered – the impact of scary financial markets on labour supply, and the impact of scary labour markets on retirement income adequacy. Chapters 7 and 8 consider scary financial markets during decumulation. Two quite different solutions are offered to the problem of ensuring adequate, yet smooth, retirement income streams. Chapter 9 follows with a discussion of the impact of corporate collapse and regulatory failure on employer-sponsored pensions, while Chapter 10 tackles the issue of fundamental pension reform in a depressed economy with a rapidly ageing population. Finally, Chapter 11 discusses pension reform in the context of extreme macroeconomic and financial volatility. The author concludes with the observation that the proposed regulatory reforms are almost as scary as the underlying macroeconomic conditions.

Overall, the contributory chapters consider a broad range of scary scenarios for a number of representative countries, and offer many novel solutions.

Chapter 2, by Bewley, Ingram, Livera and Thompson, is motivated by the perception that current equity market returns are more volatile now than in the past and that this may be leading retirees and their advisers to steer clear of equities. The main question under investigation is whether the unusual and unprecedented events of the past few decades, such as the Asian financial crisis or the threats of terrorism, have caused a permanent increase in the volatility of equity markets. This leads the authors to question the right mix between risky and riskless investments in retirement.

Using statistical analysis and simulation methods, Bewley et al. find that, when considered over the long term, there has not been an upward shift in market volatility of Australian equities. In fact, Sydney residential property is found to have a much higher probability of suffering losses over the short term than Australian equities. However, the analysis does uncover increased volatility in individual stocks in the period since the 1997 Asian financial crisis, which suggests the need for effective diversification strategies. The authors argue that equities are an essential component of an investment portfolio for both retirement savers and retirees, and conclude that the scariest thing about investing for retirement is not the risk associated with equities, but the risk of not including equities in an investment portfolio.

The inclusion of fixed interest in a retirement savings portfolio is considered by Geoffrey Brianton in Chapter 3. Although fixed interest portfolios have been considered a 'safe' asset, the number of risks in a typical one has increased over the past decade, due to an increase in corporate debt relative to government borrowing. As a result, fixed interest has shifted from being invested predominantly in domestic and government-issued securities to portfolios that have a global spread of investments and an increasing reliance on credit. This has occurred in the context of more integrated international capital markets, a move to a low-inflation global economy and a withdrawal from the debt markets by many government issuers. Consequently, the standard measures of duration and convexity are no longer sufficient to measure and control risk in portfolios that contain exposure to a number of yield curves, currency risk and credit risk.

In the light of these developments, Brianton argues that while the changes have meant that the number of investment risks in a typical bond portfolio has increased significantly, this does not axiomatically translate into riskier portfolios. Provided risks are understood and well managed, global bond portfolios do not carry greater risks. The chapter concludes by highlighting the uncertainty surrounding the retirement of the baby boomers and whether they will shift their wealth to bonds as they move from accumulation to consumption. The impact this may have on future asset prices has been keenly debated (see OECD 2005b).

A partial solution to actual or perceived increases in the risks associated with equities or fixed interest is the subject of Chapter 4. Here David Gallagher discusses the use of index funds as a low-cost alternative to direct investment in equities and fixed interest, particularly in times of heightened financial market uncertainty. He notes that this trend has arisen for a number of reasons, including the empirical research which has highlighted the overall underperformance of active managers – in both conventional and scary markets. As a result, pension funds and retirement savers alike are becoming increasingly sensitive to active managers being unable to generate at least the returns of the underlying indexes across asset classes. This chapter provides a background to the rationale for indexing, discusses the alternative approaches to indexing and evaluates the various challenges facing index portfolio managers.

The associated issue of scary labour markets is introduced in Chapters 5 and 6. In Chapter 5, Mitchell, Phillips, Au and McCarthy consider the effect of scary labour markets, in the form of earnings variability, on people's preparedness for retirement. The metric considered is accumulated wealth at retirement and the reference economy is the USA. The authors note that past research has demonstrated that the average US household on the verge of retirement would need to save substantially more in order to preserve consumption in old age. And, while several socioeconomic factors have been suggested that might explain the shortfalls, the prior studies have not assessed the role of earnings variability over the lifetime as a potential explanation for poor retirement prospects.

To address this issue, Mitchell et al. evaluate the effect of earnings variability on retirement wealth using information supplied by respondents to the

Health and Retirement Study (HRS). This is a rich and nationally representative dataset on Americans on the verge of retirement, and is matched with administrative records on lifetime earnings. Particular findings include that workers with higher lifetime earnings levels experience lower earnings variability, and that retirement wealth is more sensitive to earnings variability for non-married individuals than for married individuals. Overall, earnings variability is found to have interesting and powerful effects on retirement assets, being detrimental to both short-term retirement saving and wellbeing in retirement.

In Chapter 6, Gardner and Orszag investigate how older workers actually responded to the scary equity markets in the period 1999–2002. Over this period, the FTSE All-Share Index in the UK declined by 42 per cent, the S&P 500 in the USA declined by 38 per cent, and stock prices in Europe declined by around 40 per cent and in Hong Kong by over 40 per cent. While such declines in stock markets were not unprecedented, this time was a little different because, more than ever before, equity markets were being used to finance retirement.

Bodie et al. (1992) were the first to examine retirement decisions jointly with asset allocation. This initial work has been extended over the past decade and the main predictions of the academic literature include that: the proportion of assets invested in equities should increase with the ratio of human capital to financial capital; individuals with flexible retirement dates should hold more assets in equities; a decline in financial wealth should induce more work; and socioeconomic variables are also important drivers of retirement decisions.

Using a survey of 4500 individuals in the UK who were approaching retirement, or who were semi-retired or retired, Gardner and Orszag conducted a natural experiment to see how the changes in world equity markets affected their retirement plans and asset allocations.

Nearly 50 per cent of individuals reported that their savings had 'declined a lot' and around 20 per cent that they had 'declined a little'. The study indicated that 25 per cent of older working individuals had pushed backward their retirement date, compared to their plans two years previously. This was somewhat surprising since, particularly among this cohort, defined contribution pension plans are not the dominant from of private pension provision.

On the other hand, for those individuals who had already retired, there was little correlation between the degree of loss and the likelihood of returning to work. This provides some support to the theories in which the retirement decision is modelled as irreversible.

However, Gardner and Orszag also found that individuals who have more control over their retirement date are no more likely to have been more exposed to the equity market, which is in contrast to predictions about asset allocation in Bodie et al. (1992) referred to earlier.

The next two chapters turn to the impact of scary markets in the retire-ment/decumulation phase. Two different approaches to protect retirement income streams against volatile asset returns are offered. In Chapter 7, Thorp, Kingston and Bateman use financial engineering in the form of a consumption floor to address the question of optimal decumulation and asset allocation of retirement savings. In Chapter 8 Anthony Asher develops a smoothing algo-rithm using a set of forward contracts of different durations in order to smooth benefit payments in retirement.

The analysis by Thorp et al. in Chapter 7 creates a crucial link between the policy-based analysis of retirement income streams which is frequently centred on a desired subsistence consumption path or replacement rate, and the theoretical analysis which depends on assumptions about agents' preferences for consumption and risk. The conventional treatment of these preferences is via the constant relative risk aversion (CRRA) model, which implicitly sets this consumption floor to zero. Thorp et al. take an alternative view that util-ity from consumption is better measured relative to some reference level, and consider risk management in terms of protecting a consumption floor using a HARA (hyperbolic absolute risk aversion) utility formulation. Maintaining a consumption floor, while allowing for exposure to volatile returns once that consumption floor is ensured, is a way of protecting retirement savings against volatile asset markets.

Using simulations and numerical experiments calibrated to the Australian retirement income arrangements, Thorp et al. demonstrate that to ensure a constant subsistence rate of consumption over a reasonably long retirement, annuitants need more conservative portfolio strategies than are commonly advised. On the basis of their results, Thorp et al. note that since protecting oneself from longevity and investment risk places such stringent restrictions on portfolio allocations and consumption paths, the simulations could be used to make a *prima facie* case for annuitization. They then investigate the opti-mum time between retirement and annuitization.

Chapter 8 continues the theme of incomes in retirement with a discussion of smoothing algorithms. The context here is that with the switch from defined benefit to defined contribution schemes, investment risk has been transferred from sponsor to member and benefits paid are not necessarily predictable or smooth. The risks are relevant both before and in retirement: before retire-ment, as asset price volatility affects the retirement accumulation; and after retirement, as asset price volatility directly transfers to retirement income volatility. A strategy favoured by most defined contribution plans and their members is to use asset diversification in order to provide an optimum mix of security, inflation protection and participation in the equity premium. This chapter discusses an algorithm which works by smoothing volatile investment returns using a set of forward contracts of different durations to produce a more acceptable income flow. Under the proposed algorithm, the smoothed return is similar to that obtained by 'lifestyle' disinvesting from equities, and buying zero-coupon fixed interest assets as maturity approaches. However, the approach provides for gearing in the initial years (which would allow recapture of the equity premium) and is likely to result in lower costs, as the transactions would be internal to the fund.

The focus now moves from scary economic, financial and labour markets to the implications of corporate collapse and regulatory failure. In Chapter 9, Shauna Ferris discusses of collapse of Ansett, then Australia's largest domestic airline, and the impact this had on the superannuation entitlements of Ansett employees.

Most Ansett employees had belonged to a defined benefit fund, the Ground Staff Superannuation Plan. Before the collapse of Ansett this plan had reported to members that it had assets of about $580 million. However, only a few months later, when Ansett collapsed in September 2001, the trustees announced a shortfall of more than $100 million. The trustees sought additional funds from the Ansett administrators to cover the benefit liabilities, but the administrators denied the liability and fought to avoid making any payment to the fund. Unfortunately, the law was not clear and the case spent two years in court, with legal costs in excess of $6 million. In the end, a negotiated settlement was reached in which the fund received nothing and the members were left with a shortfall which had grown to almost $150 million. On average, members would receive less than 80 per cent of their benefit entitlements.

The Ansett story highlights how superannuation funds based on both defined benefit and defined contributions are vulnerable not only to scary economic, financial and labour markets, but to corporate and regulatory deficiencies as well.

The two final chapters turn again to scary macroeconomic conditions and financial markets. However, the context here is not only the impact on the retirement benefits of members in existing schemes, but the problems policymakers may face when trying to reform retirement income arrangements in difficult macroeconomic and financial circumstances.

Japan is considered first in Chapter 10. While the Japanese economy, along with the USA, UK and other developed economies, entered into recession in the early 1990s, the Japanese economy remained depressed for around a decade after the other economies recovered. At the same time, the rapid ageing of the Japanese population was becoming more prominent, with the labour force itself beginning to decline from the early 1990s. In addition, urgent public and private pension reform was becoming inevitable due to the underfundedness of both public and private pensions. In this chapter Masaharu Usuki discusses how companies have adjusted their pension plans, and how the government has modified its policy stance to cope with this scary macroeconomic, financial, demographic and retirement benefits scenario. Responses included measures taken by pension plans, their sponsors and government: more sophisticated asset management by plan sponsors, changes in benefit design (through the reduction of benefits, conversion of defined benefit plans into cash balance plans, introduction of defined contribution plans and plan terminations), and changes in government regulations (including deregulation of asset management, changes to funding rules and the introduction of new types of funded pension plans). Overall, the responses have meant that the impacts of unanticipated declines in asset prices and economic activity have been shared across workers, profits and retirees.

The final chapter considers the case of pensions in Brazil. Brazilian pension reforms are quite similar to those taking place in the USA, UK and Australia. However, unlike these countries, the Brazilian pension reforms are taking place against a backdrop of extraordinary macroeconomic volatility and uncertainty. In this chapter, Flávio Rabelo introduces the current Brazilian pension system and discusses the proposed reforms, while highlighting the enormous difficulties associated with pension reform in a volatile, developing economy. Rabelo concludes with the observation that despite the extreme economic and financial market volatility in Brazil, almost as scary is the increasing trend towards more, and more complicated, private pension regulation.

CONCLUDING COMMENTS

Overall, the chapters in this volume address a myriad of scary scenarios, including volatile asset markets, problematic labour market trends, population ageing, corporate collapse, regulatory failure, and depressed and volatile macroeconomies, across a broad range of countries – Australia, Brazil, Japan, the UK and the USA. Partial solutions to scary markets are advanced, including the standard response of asset diversification, as well as financial engineering, smoothing algorithms and risk sharing. The issues raised, and solutions offered, have universal application.

NOTES

1. For a more complete list see Holzmann and Hinz (2005), ch. 7 and Bateman et al. (2001), Appendix 2.

REFERENCES

Bateman, H. and J. Piggott (1997), *Private Pensions in OECD Countries – Australia*, Labour Market and Social Policy Occasional Papers, No. 23, Paris: OECD.

Bateman, H., G. Kingston and J. Piggott (2001), *Forced Saving: Mandating Private Retirement Incomes*, Cambridge: Cambridge University Press.

Bodie, Z., R.C. Merton and P. Samuelson (1992), 'Labour supply flexibility and portfolio choice in a lifecycle model', *Journal of Economic Dynamics and Control*, **16**: 427–49.

Commission to Strengthen Social Security (2001), *Strengthening Social Security and Creating Pension Wealth for all Americans*, Final Report, Washington, DC.

Diamond, P.A. and P.R. Orszag (2004), *Saving Social Security: A Balanced Approach*, Washington, DC: Brookings Institution Press.

Disney, R. (1996), *Can we Afford to Grow Older? A Perspective on the Economics of Ageing*, Cambridge, MA and London: MIT Press.

Feldstein, M. (2005), *Rethinking Social Insurance*, NBER Working Paper 11250, March.

Holzmann, R. and R. Hinz (2005), *Old Age Income Support in the 21ˢᵗ Century – An International Perspective on Pension Systems and Reform*, Washington, DC: World Bank.

International Monetary Fund, *International Financial Statistics*, http://ifs.apdi.net/imf/about.asp

International Monetary Fund, *World Economic Outlook*, http://www.imf.org/external/pubs/ft/weo/weorepts.htm

OECD (2003), *Policies for an Ageing Society: Recent Measures and Areas for Further Reform, Economics Department*, Working Paper No. 369, Paris: OECD.

OECD (2005a), *Pensions at a Glance: Public Policies Across OECD Countries*, Paris: OECD.

OECD (2005b), *Ageing and Pension System Reform: Implications for Financial Markets and Economic Policies*, report prepared at the request of the Deputies of the Group of Ten by an expert group chaired by Ignazio Visco, Banca d'Italia.

Poterba, J. (2001), 'Demographic structure and asset returns', *Review of Economics and Statistics*, **83**: 565–84.

Reserve Bank of Australia, *Reserve Bank Bulletin*, various issues.

Takayama, N. (1998), *The Morning After in Japan: Its Declining Population, Too Generous Pensions and a Weakened Economy*, Tokyo, Japan: Maruzen Co. Ltd.

World Bank (1994), *Averting the Old Age Crisis: Policies to Protect the Old and Promote Growth*, New York, Oxford University Press.

2. Who's afraid of the big bad bear? Or, why investing in equities for retirement is not scary and why investing without equities is scary

Ronald Bewley, Nick Ingram, Veronica Livera and Sheridan Thompson[1]

INTRODUCTION

Few would deny that the turmoil experienced in the political and financial arenas in recent times has changed people's perceptions of the world. Examples of these unusual events include the stock market collapse of 1987, the worldwide problem of terrorism, the Asian financial crisis and the financial collapse of several global conglomerates, to name just a few.

The impact of these events on investment performance is a cause of much concern to all investors. The financial press is saturated with opinions on the current state of investment markets. Some proclaim the arrival of the bear market to end all others. Others advocate that the time for investment is ripe, claiming that markets have nowhere to go but up. These alternative views have certainly increased the confusion and scepticism of investors regarding equity markets, particularly of those investors who recall more stable times from the past.

While the impact of these events on the performance of investments is a matter of concern for all investors, it is particularly so for those in or facing retirement. These days we are actively encouraged to provide for our own retirement, with government social security offering only the bare minimum. Thus the impact of these turbulent times on our financial security in retirement is a matter of grave concern. Whereas those who have many years to go before retirement have the opportunity to recuperate from any unexpected losses in their investments, retired individuals may not.

The fear that equity markets are altogether too volatile, particularly in recent times, for retirement investments have led some retirees and their advisers to steer clear of equities as much as possible. Retirees have come to rely on conservative lifetime annuities and other seemingly low-risk investments such as property. However, these low-risk investments, while offering a stable stream of income, may not provide retirees with enough funds for the lifestyles they desire.

Retirees may find themselves altering their expenditure patterns significantly in fear of running out of funds, thus failing to take the fullest advantage of their lifetime savings. Or they may continue with the lifestyle they are accustomed to and gradually erode their investment capital without further reinvestment. On the other hand those retirees with investments that are weighted too heavily towards risky markets face the possibility of crystallizing losses from their investment funds.

To those who have worked hard in their careers for many decades, anticipating a comfortable lifestyle in retirement, the thought of not having sufficient funds in their twilight years is a daunting one. In addition to the usual investment risk of not meeting investment goals, retirees face the additional burden of longevity risk, or the risk of outliving their funds. Usually emphasis is placed on the former type of risk, with little thought given to the possibility that the pool of funds and stream of income received will not sustain the increasingly higher life expectancies we can enjoy.

In this chapter we attempt to address the challenge of mitigating the two main types of risk facing retirees: investment risk and longevity risk. These risk management issues are translated into striking the right balance between risky and less risky investments in retirement. Investment asset allocation during retirement has the particular challenge of ensuring that retirees are not put into an overly aggressive investment position with excessive investment risk, leaving them vulnerable to equity market fluctuations. The other part of the retiree investment challenge not often considered by conventional retirement plans is the danger of an asset allocation that is overweight towards fixed interest and other low return investments. Such a strategy may fail to realize the potential of the retiree's funds to provide the income for their desired lifestyle.

In the context of the particular circumstances and issues of investments during retirement, we address three pertinent questions. First, is the world more volatile now than before? Second, are equities really all that risky? Third, how do the answers to these two preceding questions affect the right mix between risky and riskless investments in retirement?

Our first task is to separate fact from fiction when it comes to the question of whether we live in a more volatile investment world now than before. In answering this question, we perform an objective statistical analysis of the data. The results clearly depend on the period being analysed. Our longer-term view refutes the popular belief that all equity markets have undergone an upward shift in volatility.

However, importantly our analysis shows that while broad markets have not become more volatile, component stocks or industries have. This change in the balance of volatility means that effective diversification strategies are now even more necessary for investors than before.

The common perception when comparing equity markets with perceived lower-risk investments such as fixed interest or property is that equity markets suffer long and sustained periods of loss before recovery that are not similarly experienced by other investments. We provide a number of representations of the past experience in various asset classes that give a different view of asset market behaviour. For example, surprisingly, some property markets have experienced longer periods of sustained loss than Australian equities, debunking the myth of their infallibility.

We also assert that the same arguments of diversification that are applicable to investments during the working period of an individual's life also apply to the retirement period. If retiree investors are prepared to invest for a reasonably long period of time, our portfolio analysis suggests that excluding equities will be to the considerable detriment of many retiree investors. Equities offer significant diversification benefits because of the low correlation between the asset classes.

We estimate that the rewards offered by equity investments are significant enough to overcome the higher risk accompanying them. Our multi-period asset allocation analysis shows that equities should be included in retirement investments, especially in the beginning phases of retirement, unless the retiree has only small savings to commence this strategy. Equity investments should be balanced with adequate fixed interest and cash investments that offer a secure and stable income stream and diversification of risk. We demonstrate these effects using a number of hypothetical retirement scenarios.

IS THE WORLD MORE SCARY?

Casual inspection of equity market returns might suggest that they are more volatile now than in the past. Experience has shown that asset markets experience temporary periods of higher volatility surrounding an adverse event. However, these short-term clusters usually subside with time and volatility returns to its normal level. The challenge is to identify those equity market reactions that are strong enough to signal a significant permanent change from the short-run clusters that occur and modify an investment strategy accordingly.

We consider a number of issues in regard to this question. The first is whether the unusual and unprecedented events of the past decades, such as the Asian financial crisis or the threats of terrorism, caused a permanent increase in equity markets' volatility. We then investigate Australian equity market volatility in more detail by decomposing it into market-level, industry-specific and firm-specific volatility. Our findings on the Australian market are then compared with the findings of the Campbell et al. (2001) study on the US market.

Finally in this section we ask, how bad can a bad experience in equity investments be? And, how does such a negative experience in equities compare with that in other investments?

Are Equities more Volatile?

In analysing whether or not asset returns have become more volatile with recent events we consider, by way of example, Australian equities (ASX 200), listed property trusts (LPTs) and international equities. International equities are represented by the S&P 500 for the USA and the Morgan Stanley Capital International (MSCI) Index for global equities. Both international indexes are expressed in Australian dollars. Monthly returns of the four assets for the last ten years are shown in Figure 2.1.

This figure confirms a number of stylized facts about the asset class series. Month-to-month returns appear to fluctuate randomly around some average value, making short-term prediction futile. However, there is a limited degree of predictability in the volatility of these series. Returns appear to experience short-term bursts of abnormally high or low volatility in certain periods, followed by a return to more average volatility levels.

The two international equity series appear to have higher (long-run) volatility since 1997, coinciding with the post-Asian crisis period. It is unclear from a visual inspection whether Australian equities and listed property trusts show an increase in long-run volatility.

The CommSec test for detecting structural breaks in long-run volatility has the advantage of not having to impose a particular hypothesized break point. Instead every possible data point is considered. Where the test statistic at a particular point breaches its critical value, it is highlighted as the point at which a possible permanent change occurs.

Each of the series shown in Figure 2.1 was tested for structural breaks. In results not shown, structural breaks in long-run volatility were found in both of the international equity market volatilities. To ensure that the detected change in volatility was not a result of a volatility break in exchange rates, we subjected the AU$/US$ exchange rate series and the international indexes expressed in US dollars to the same volatility break test. Structural breaks were detected in all three series.

The listed property trust series also showed evidence of a small but significant change in volatility since the Asian crisis period. However, the Australian

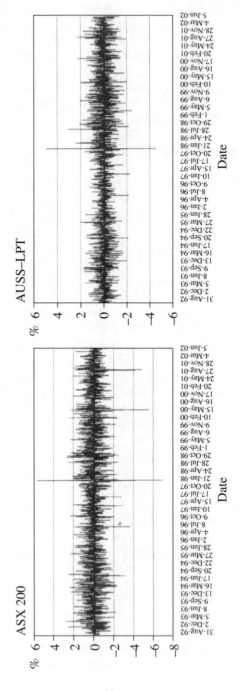

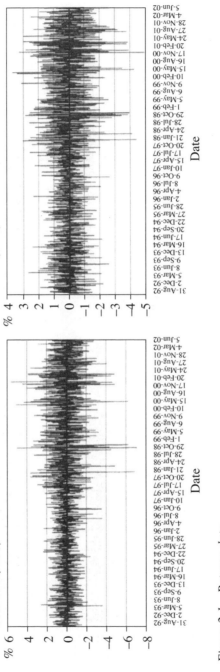

Figure 2.1 Returns data

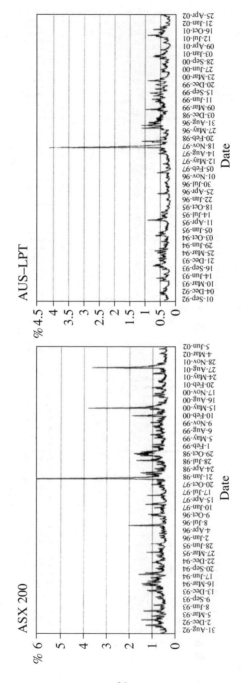

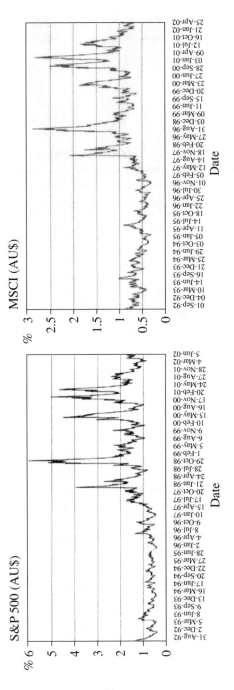

Figure 2.2   Estimated volatility

equity market appears to have been immune to the effects of the Asian crisis. No significant break was detected for the ASX 200, even though the LPT index is a component of it. This conundrum is explored more fully in the next section.

We estimate the monthly volatility of each of the series using the CommSec method, which is based on a Generalized Autoregressive Conditional Heteroskedasticity (GARCH) process. It allows for the possibility of structural breaks. Our estimates are given in Figure 2.2. The short-run clusters around a permanent long-run break are clear for all but the ASX 200. The absence of a break in the ASX 200 is striking.

The fact that the short-run clusters are of limited duration means that risk to the investor only depends upon the long-run level of volatility, provided that investors are prepared to hold the assets for more than a few months. The puzzling resilience of Australian equities to a structural break in volatility is now examined in more detail, with a longer-term perspective.

A Decomposition of Risk

Having found no evidence of a significant permanent change in volatility in Australian equities as a whole, but some evidence of a break in a component, that is, LPTs, we examine this equity volatility question more thoroughly.

Total equity volatility can be expressed as the sum of the parts attributable to the overall market, the representative industry and the representative firm, following Campbell et al. (2002). In this way we are better able to analyse any changes in volatility that may have occurred in the component parts that happen to cancel out in the aggregation to Australian equities as a whole. This cancellation effect may occur because of changes in the correlation structure of these components.

Campbell et al. (2002) devised a theoretical method for defining component measures of market, industry and firm risk that sum to the excess return volatility of a typical firm. Their method defines a firm's total excess return (excess returns relative to a risk-free measure) volatility as the variance of the component daily returns, that is, the market-, industry- and firm-specific parts. They use the daily data within each month to estimate monthly volatility.

Campbell et al.'s study of the US equities market concluded that the volatility of individual stocks in the USA has been trending upwards, but the market and industry components were stable. However, their data period ended in 1997, before the Asian financial crisis took effect. Our Australian equities study starts in 1985 because there are no comparable data before that year. However, at the other end of the sample, we have almost five more years of data than Campbell et al. This extension to the sample is particularly important because the Asian crisis occurred in the last few months of the Campbell et al. sample.

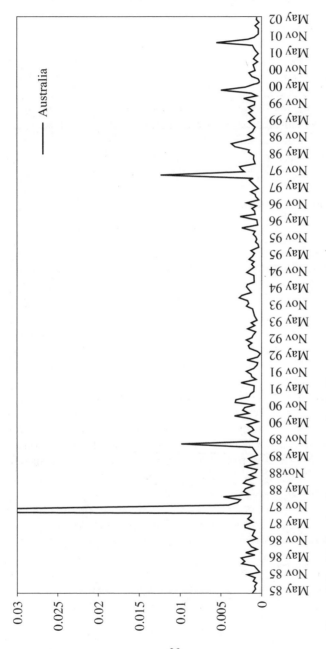

Figure 2.3   Market-level component of volatility

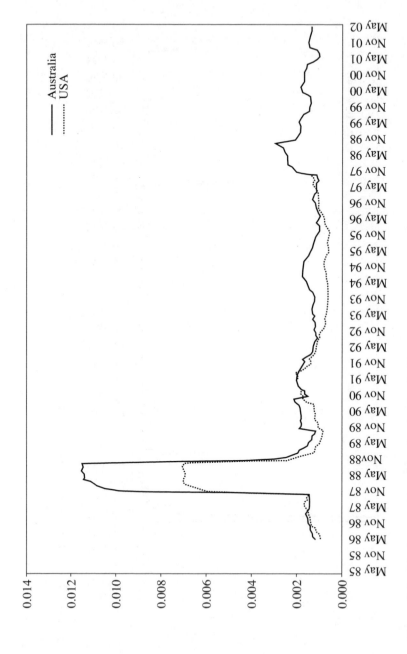

Figure 2.4   Moving average of market-level volatility

The raw monthly market volatility component is shown in Figure 2.3. This is similar, but not identical to, what would have been obtained by analysing the ASX 200. The main difference is that the Campbell et al. methodology uses fixed weights within each month.

The October 1987 peak is off the scale, at a value 0.073, but this volatility cluster subsides to normal behaviour within six months. The October 1989 shock dissipated within a month, while the October 1997 Asian crisis shock dissipated within four months. Thus our analysis shows that the shocks that affected the Australian market in recent years, while causing temporary increases in volatility, were not persistent enough to create any permanent increase in riskiness. We do not find evidence of an upward trend in overall market volatility.

The absence of a trend in the Australian market volatility can best be seen in the 12-month (lagged) moving average shown in Figure 2.4. The Asian financial crisis appears to have lasted longer in this representation, partly because of the length of the moving average and partly because of the subsequent volatility spikes. Nevertheless there is a distinct return to the levels of the mid-1990s. The correspondence between Campbell et al.'s estimates for the USA and ours is striking.

The raw industry-level volatility component is the weighted average of industry-level risks. We see from Figure 2.5 that the post-1997 volatility clusters significantly contribute to a large and permanent change in the lagged 12-month moving average of the industry-specific effects.

Comparable US data from Campbell et al. are also shown in Figure 2.5. Interestingly, the estimates from the two countries are similar in 1996 and 1997. There is a slight difference in the trend before that time and there is much less risk around 1987 in the USA than in Australia. Without comparable data for the USA after 1997, it is difficult to draw strong conclusions about the similarities or differences between industry-level risks in the two countries. However, we do conclude that industry-level risk in Australia has been trending upwards in recent years. Unlike Campbell et al., we did not detect any trend in firm-specific volatility (not shown).

These structural changes within different industries have important implications for diversification strategies within equities. With the exception of a few industries, the relative volatilities between industries (not shown) do not appear to be distinctly different when we consider the entire sample period. However, since the Asian crisis, relative volatility between industries has changed. This suggests greater inter-industry diversification benefits since 1997 than previously.

How Bad is Bad?

The preceding quantitative analysis of the changes in equity risk gives little

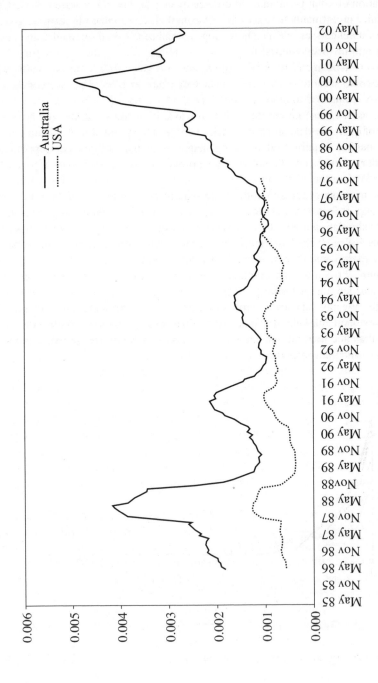

Figure 2.5   Moving average of industry-level volatility

indication of what the actual experience of weathering the peaks and troughs of equity investments may feel like. As another measure of the relative riskiness of asset classes, we ask, how long is a bad run? A bad run is measured as the length of time required for an asset to recoup losses after accounting for inflation. This measure gives us an idea of how long retirees might be expected to weather losses if they include equities among their investment strategy, compared to other asset classes.

We assess these probabilities in two ways. First, we scrutinize the last 19 years of quarterly data and count each run of loss. The probability of each asset class having experienced a losing sequence historically is computed by considering every possible quarterly start date of investment over the past 19 years. We computed the probability of an asset class experiencing a run of losses, in terms of the amount of time required in quarters for the asset class to recoup its loss to a level equal to, or higher than, its starting value. Second, we use simulation methods to predict future losing runs. These probabilities of loss are based on the assumption that asset returns from quarter to quarter are independently and identically normally distributed.

Figure 2.6 shows the cumulative probability of each asset experiencing particular lengths of losing periods over the last 19 years of monthly historical data. We have chosen a number of asset classes representative of a variety of investment markets. They are Australian and international fixed interest, Australian and international equities, direct property and listed property trusts. Since residential property is considered by many investors to be a safe and

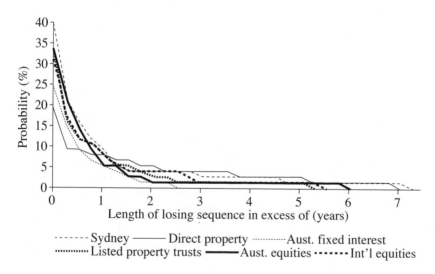

Figure 2.6   Probability of losing sequences

highly profitable investment, we have included Sydney residential property (inclusive of rents) as an asset class. All data are in real terms.

Figure 2.6 may be interpreted as follows. Consider the case of Australian equities as an example. Based on historical data, we find that Australian equities had a 33 per cent probability of making a loss for at least one quarter before making a profit or breaking even. Australian equities experienced losses for one year or more before regaining losses 6 per cent of the time. The probability of Australian equity investments taking four years or more to break even or make a profit is much lower at 3 per cent.

Unsurprisingly, Figure 2.6 shows that there is a much lower probability of sustaining a long period of losses than facing losses for one or two quarters. Even those investments made at the worst times rebound within a maximum of eight years over the last 19 years. The asset classes with the lowest probabilities of experiencing losses for one year indicate the best investments for very short-term investors.

Figure 2.6 also reveals an interesting comparison of the relative performance of the asset classes. Sydney residential property had the highest probability of making a loss for at least one quarter after investment at 40 per cent of the time followed by Australian equities at 33 per cent of the time. Direct property investments had the lowest incidence of losing value before recouping losses at 18 per cent of the time.

Despite the preference for residential investments among many investors, particularly retirees, our calculations show that the Sydney market experienced a downturn for seven years following the 1989 first quarter peak before rebounding. Similarly, despite having the highest probability of a profitable short-term investment, some direct property investments experienced losses for seven years before rebounding. In contrast, the longest period over which Australian equities experienced a loss before regaining the initial investment value was six years. The longest losing sequence for international equities was five and a half years.

We now repeat the preceding analysis, which was on historical data, to project the likelihood of prolonged losses in the future through simulations. Under the assumptions of our model, returns are assumed to be identically and independently normally distributed, allowing for unexpected exogenous shocks that are not part of the underlying process. In our analysis of historical performance we included the impact of the quarter including the 1987 stock market crash in our estimates of average returns but not variances. We do not believe that the crash is likely to be repeated within a 19-year period.

Our simulation results are reported in Figure 2.7. They show that the probability of having to bear losses in equities is much lower for prolonged periods than it is for shorter periods such as one or two years. Sydney residential property has a much higher probability of suffering losses over the short term than Australian equities. We estimate a 35 per cent chance of Sydney property sustaining a loss for one year or more, compared to less than 25 per cent for Australian equities. While we estimate that there is a 5 per cent chance of sustaining a loss in Australian equities for seven years or more, this is very similar to the probability for residential property. The estimated probabilities of losing sequences approach zero asymptotically.

Our results based on historical data and simulations suggest a result that is contrary to traditional retirement strategies, which underweight equities due to their perceived higher risk. In terms of the length of time the investment has to be held for until it yields a profit, we find that equities in fact fare better than residential investments.

Over the past 19 years the longest run of losses in Australian equity investments was six years, compared to seven for property investments. Both historically and based on simulated projections, we find that international equities are slightly riskier than Australian equities. They generally require longer holding periods than Australian equities in times of bear markets. Overall our analysis on probabilities of loss advocates that, if held for a sufficient period generally exceeding five years, equities can offer retiree investors significant benefits without incurring excessive risk.

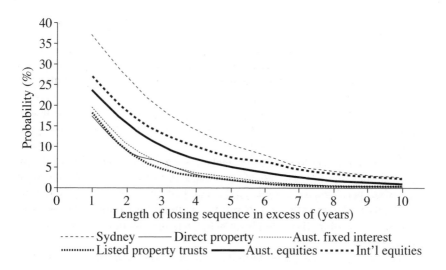

Figure 2.7   Projected probability of losing sequences

IS THERE LIFE WITHOUT EQUITIES?

Retiree investors should and do approach equities and all other risky investments with caution. Experience shows us that equity markets have higher risk than many other asset classes. Our analyses of the actual experiences in investments in the past 19 years have shown that, at the very worst periods in equity market cycles, investors would have had to wait six years before recouping their money. However, other investments such as some investment property are equally risky.

A retirement strategy with low investment risk based solely on cash and fixed interest investments has the benefit of giving investors a steady income stream with little or no uncertainty. But such an investment strategy can be costly, even in, or especially in, retirement. At a time when investors require the maximum benefit from their investments, the compensatory benefit of including equities as part of a diversified strategy can far outweigh the cost.

We first consider the investment choices available to an investor who chooses to exclude equities completely, in the form of Australian shares, LPTs or international shares. Figure 2.8 shows the estimated portfolio efficient frontier obtained by combining Australian fixed interest, direct property and Sydney residential property only ('without equities') based on the risk/return characteristics of the representative asset classes over the last 20 years. In this first case we assume that the retiree investor does not wish to invest in any international assets or domestic equities.

We see that Australian equities and Sydney residential property have very similar risk/return characteristics, providing the highest return for a given amount of risk. The impact of the recent significant downturn in international equities on the estimated returns is apparent.

The estimated frontier is the outer envelope of all possible combinations of the three assets. For each level of risk the portfolios estimated to yield the highest return are those on the upper outer layer of portfolios. The frontier is bound from above and below by the highest and lowest risk/return asset classes, which are Sydney residential property and direct property, respectively.

The shaded line in Figure 2.8 gives the estimated efficient frontier including Australian equities. The shaded and black lines are not very distant from each other because Australian equities and Sydney residential property are very similar in risk and return. However, including Australian equities in a diversified portfolio offers significant benefits to the investor, in terms of both risk and return.

The gains from including Australian equities are most apparent for less conservative investors. Consider an investor who is willing to accept 12 per cent annual volatility on their investments. The return on a portfolio excluding

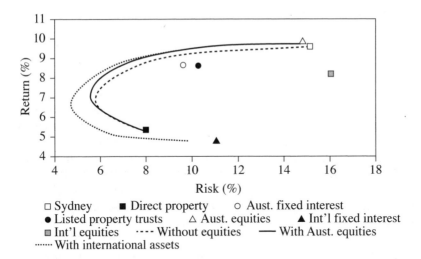

□ Sydney   ■ Direct property   ○ Aust. fixed interest
● Listed property trusts   △ Aust. equities   ▲ Int'l fixed interest
▣ Int'l equities   ···· Without equities   —— With Aust. equities
······ With international assets

Figure 2.8   Estimated efficient frontiers

Australian equities is approximately 9.5 per cent per annum. Then consider an investor who includes Australian equities in their portfolio. By moving to a portfolio on the shaded frontier that includes Australian equities, the investor can get an equivalent amount of return for more than 2 per cent less risk. For a conservative investor who is only willing to bear 6 per cent volatility, once again, including Australian equities offers less risk for an equivalent return.

The benefits of diversification become very apparent when we compare the portfolio outcomes including and excluding Australian equities. Even though it is the asset class with the highest risk, we see that even for the most conservative investor, including Australian equities offers significant diversification benefits in terms of lower risk. The ability to reduce risk for a desired level of return is an advantage offered by Australian equities that is highly desirable to retiree investors, who would wish to bear as little risk as possible.

International equity investments have been a cause for much concern over the past three years, having sustained significant losses during that time. Even though they have staged a small recovery, many investors are giving international equities a very wide berth. However, the low correlations between asset classes mean that even international investments can be beneficial to investors when combined with other asset classes.

Compare the shaded estimated frontier in Figure 2.8, which includes Australian equities but excludes international assets, with the dashed line, which also includes international equities. We see that both the shaded and dashed estimated frontiers are bound at the right by Australian equities, which is the highest risk/return asset. For the less conservative investor, including international equities offers no additional benefit. However, for a more conservative investor who is only willing to bear 6 per cent volatility, including international assets offers an equivalent return but for a much lower risk level of 5 per cent per annum.

The result of our analysis is that including international assets offers the greatest benefit to more conservative investors, despite their status as inferior asset classes when considered individually. Although international assets have a lower level of return and higher risk, the fact that they have low correlations with the other asset classes means that they can offer significant diversification benefits to conservative investors.

WHY ARE RETIREES DIFFERENT FROM OTHER INVESTORS?

History shows that the financial industry has been known to have its actions dictated by the perceived shifts in equity markets. There have been numerous occasions when the industry has come under criticism for 'chasing returns' and taking advantage of favourable short-term experiences to push clients into more aggressive risk profiles. However, investors are also culpable by demanding higher returns to meet their growing need for self-funded retirement into increasingly longer life expectancies.

Certainly the boom period in equities during the 1990s was accompanied by increasing allocations to equities in balanced funds for investors both in and nearing retirement in Australia. This problem is not unique to Australia. For example, the same pattern was followed by the financial industry in the UK in the early 1970s.

The recent industry lobbying of the government for the introduction of growth-based allocated pensions is another symptom of succumbing to short-term market fluctuations, coupled with the increasing demands of retiree investors. While a useful addition to the range of products available, these products present a potentially dangerous zone if all retirement funds are placed into one such fund without adequate liquid assets.

Adverse world events may have led investors to be more wary of equity markets now than in the past. However, we have argued that equity risk has not in fact increased and that equity allocations should be retained as part of a diversified strategy. Comparing investment choices with and without equities, we have found considerable evidence in favour of including equities. Australian and international equities provide increased returns as well as significant diversification benefits.

Even though equities have not changed significantly in nature, it cannot be denied that the needs of investors, particularly retiree investors, have changed markedly. We are increasingly forced to make sufficient provisions for our retirement or face the prospect of relying on the diminishing benevolence of the social security system.

We are also living longer now than before. If a typical person attends a tertiary institution until the age of 23, then works until the age of 60, that leaves a working life of approximately 37 years. This typical scenario presents the challenging possibility of having a retirement period longer than a person's working period. An individual would have to accumulate sufficient funds and invest prudently enough to fund a longer spell in retirement than in their working life.

Life expectancy is often cited as the age to which retirees need their resources to last. However, there is a close to 50 per cent chance of outliving the actuarially determined life expectancy. We suspect that this is too high a longevity risk for most. Instead, resources must last until some later date at which longevity risk is more acceptable, say only a 20 per cent chance of outliving resources. We call this the 'required' period.

The increasing reliance on self-funded retirement, coupled with the increasing periods over which such funding is required, sets retirees apart from other investors. Another factor distinguishing retiree investors is the tax environment they face. For example, tax can be largely avoided with allocated pensions, which gives a strong incentive to retirees to rely on such products. For our analysis we choose to ignore the many complexities of the Australian superannuation taxation system. We comment in passing that the prospect of further government-led change to the taxation system may be scarier to retirees than the riskiness of equity markets!

Given the particular requirements of retiree investors to balance investment risk and longevity risk, two popular investment vehicles for retirees are lifetime annuities and allocated pensions. Lifetime annuities invested in conservative assets offer a relatively low return, but are guaranteed by the life company to continue for life (that is, there is no risk of outliving funds). On the other hand, allocated pensions offer more equity-oriented assets, but retirees face investment risks.

Too low an equity allocation means that returns may not be sufficient to allow the portfolio to last the required period. Thus there is a strong case for equities, especially in the early years of retirement when the required period for the portfolio is longer than in the latter stages of retirement. We have shown that the maximum estimated number of years that downturns in equity markets are expected to last is about five or six years. This gives strong support to the inclusion of equities in retirement investments.

Conversely the equity allocation can be too high. Intuitively, if returns are negative in the early years, this can dramatically affect the portfolio's ability to support the desired lifestyle for the required period. This impact can be particularly hard if too many growth assets are held when markets perform negatively to the point where growth assets have to be sold to pay for the current retirement lifestyle. This situation is doubly bad because growth assets are being sold at a bad time in the market, when their potential to support a long retirement may be lost. The damage is done and the required period and/or desired lifestyle cannot be met.

Given the consequences of a poor retirement investment strategy for the retirees of today and tomorrow, what then is an appropriate allocation to equities in retirement and for how long should it be maintained? We address this question in the next section, using simulation techniques to hypothesize the likely outcome of several alternative investment scenarios, under various retirement conditions. Our simulations provide indicative results that shed some light on the practical consequences of having equities among retirement investments.

DO EQUITIES REALLY ADD VALUE IN RETIREMENT?

Our analysis shows that the scariest thing about investing in retirement is not the risk associated with equities but the possibility of outliving our funds, or longevity risk. On one hand, equities may very occasionally have bad runs of six years or more, which would put a significant strain on retirees' funds. On the other hand, however, is the very real possibility of living for 30 or 40 years after retirement. Thus retirement investing strategies have to walk the thin line of conservatism to avoid financial collapse through over-aggressive investments while providing for increasingly longer lifespans.

To give an idea of what the experience of investing in retirement might be like for representative types of retirees, we have conducted a number of simulation experiments. We simulated the experience of investing and spending in retirement under four scenarios. These scenarios were formulated with assistance from a number of advisers who are well versed in the experiences of advising retirees. Although stylized, they give an indication of the impact of equity investments in retirement.

Our simulations of the retiree experience are based on a number of assumptions. We assume that the retiring age is 60. We do not assume a particular life expectancy. Instead we allow for the possibility of a very long lifespan of 100 years or more, which may not be unreasonable. We have assumed four levels of income/wealth for retirees.

We have divided the total number of years in retirement into three phases, according to our perceptions of likely expenditure patterns. The first ten years of retirement are characterized by the highest annual expenditure, as this is the period in which retirees will be most likely to undertake travel and other extracurricular activities. In the second ten years, expenditure is lower per annum than in the first ten. In the last phase of retirement, we assume that the largest portion of income is necessary for health care expenses. Excluding health care, we assume that retirees have few additional expenses. Therefore, the third phase of retirement has the lowest per annum expenditure. We assume that the investment asset allocation remains constant over each phase. The details of the assumptions used are given in Table 2.1.

For simplicity we assume that each retiree has the choice of investing in a combination of two investment assets: a riskless asset such as cash and an equity asset that is risky. We assume an average annual real return of 10 per cent and a standard deviation of 14 per cent for the equity asset. These correspond with the 20-year historical average return and standard deviation figures for Australian equities. Drawing values from a normal distribution with these mean and standard deviation parameters simulates the return on equities in each year.

The riskless asset is assumed to have a known real return of 3 per cent. If each investor only invested in the riskless asset, he or she would run out of funds at the age of 66 under Scenario I, 72 under Scenario II, 84 under Scenario III and would not run out of money over a reasonable lifespan under Scenario IV.

Our task is to evaluate the benefit of investing in equities over the different phases of retirement. The criteria for a favourable investment strategy are that the retiree does not outlive available funds and can maintain a desired lifestyle.

As a measure of the gain of including equities in retirement investing, we measured longevity risk or the possibility of outliving retirement funds, given a certain asset allocation between the risky and riskless assets. If a retiree runs out of his/her own funds, he/she would have to rely on social security payments or sell other assets not considered in this portfolio. We calculated the probability of running out of funds at each year after retirement, given a certain asset allocation.

The expenditure for each year is accounted for at the end of a particular year, after which the remaining investment funds after drawdown are carried forward to the next year. The remaining funds then earn a particular investment return for that year, which is accumulated to the fund at the end of the year. All figures are in real (inflation-adjusted) terms.

We simulated a number of alternative asset allocations for Scenarios I to IV. We have assumed that the proportion of equities in each phase remains constant, but is allowed to vary across the hypothesized phases of retirement. We do not account for any fees or taxation issues.

To simplify the scenarios, given the myriad of possible combinations of the two assets, we have assumed that the proportions of equities held in each phase of retirement are 80 per cent, 40 per cent and 0 per cent, with the

Table 2.1 Retirement simulation scenarios (excluding inflation)

	SCENARIO I: Low income	SCENARIO II: Middle income	SCENARIO III: High income	SCENARIO IV: High net wealth
Lump sum at beginning of retirement	$100 000.00	$250 000.00	$500 000.00	$1 000 000.00
Phase 1: 60yrs–70yrs				
Duration (yrs)	10	10	10	10
Annual expenditure	–$20 000.00	–$25 000.00	–$35 000.00	–$50 000.00
Phase 2: 70yrs–80yrs				
Duration (yrs)	10	10	10	10
Annual expenditure	–$15 000.00	–$20 000.00	–$25 000.00	–$35 000.00
Phase 3: 80yrs onwards				
Duration (yrs)	10	10	10	10
Annual expenditure	–$10 000.00	–$15 000.00	–$15 000.00	–$30 000.00

remaining proportion invested in the riskless asset. We have deliberately chosen three extreme positions of equity allocation of 0 per cent, 40 per cent and 80 per cent in order to highlight the resultant differences in outcome.

A buffer minimum allocation of 20 per cent to the riskless asset has been allowed, to provide some amount of guaranteed financial security to retirees. This minimum riskless allocation provides some allowance for drawdowns to be made in periods of negative market performance without having to liquidate equity assets.

A 0 per cent allocation to equities in any phase of retirement is the most conservative and a 40 per cent allocation to equities is considered moderate. We assume that retirees are more likely to wish to be more conservative in the latter years of retirement than in the former. Thus we have eliminated those combinations where the proportion of equities in the latter phases is higher than in the former phases.

The scenarios and allocations reported in this chapter are not in any way to be regarded as advice as they do not take into account the particulars of actual individuals. Rather than recommending actual allocations to equities, our simulations are intended to provide indicative results as a point of comparison between alternative investment strategies.

Figure 2.9 shows the cumulative probability of a low-income individual reaching zero wealth in the years following retirement, for the various proportions of equity investments in the three phases. Each line in the graph represents a different combination of the proportions of equity investments in the three phases. For example, '80: 40: 0' indicates that there is an allocation of 80 per cent equities/20 per cent riskless assets in the first phase, 40 per cent equities/60 per cent riskless assets in the second and 0 per cent equities/100 per cent riskless assets in the last phase.

Regardless of the allocation to equities, the results for low-income individuals are bleak. For an individual who has a comparatively low lump-sum amount at the beginning of retirement, yet wishes to maintain some standard of living, our simulations show zero wealth at 60 to 70 years, regardless of the asset allocation.

This result occurs because of the low investment fund pool combined with rapid drawdowns in the early part of retirement. An investment in equities must be held for a reasonable period that is sufficient to accumulate gains. Because of the rapid drawdown of funds in the first few years of retirement, the pool of funds invested deteriorates at too rapid a pace to allow income to be maintained into the second and third phases. Unfortunately retirees with only a small lump sum available at the start of retirement will probably have to rely on social security payments and/or be willing to accept a lower than desired lifestyle.

The outlook for a middle-income retiree with a $250 000 lump sum available

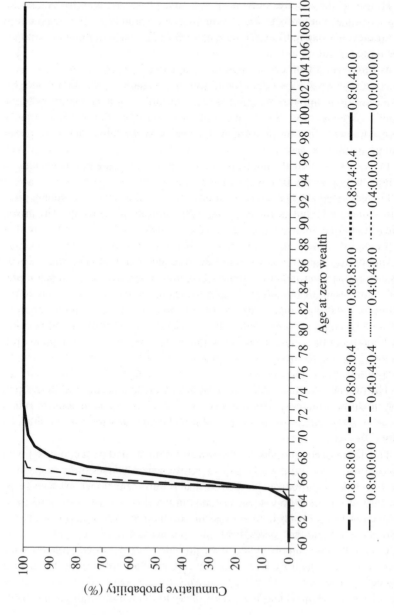

Figure 2.9 The cumulative probability of zero wealth in retirement – low-income retirees

at retirement, shown in Figure 2.10, is more promising. In this situation, our simulations show that in the first decade of retirement, retirees can maintain their desired lifestyle with little risk of running out of money, regardless of which investment strategy they adopt.

However, the asset allocation of the first phase becomes crucial in the second phase. The probabilities of running out of funds while maintaining a certain level of expenditure increase at a very rapid pace in the second phase. For retirees with no allocation to equities in any phase, our experiment indicates zero wealth with certainty from the age of 72.

For a retiree with a 40 per cent allocation to equities in the first phase, but no allocation in the next two phases, the probability of zero wealth increases rapidly. The next most detrimental strategy is to have a 40 per cent allocation to equities in the first two phases, but no allocation to equities in the last phase. The probability of zero wealth is considerable, yet decreases significantly for an individual who takes an aggressive stance on equities in the first phase of retirement but no equities in the latter two phases.

For strategies with a significant allocation to equities, the incremental probability of running out of funds is very low from age 85 onwards. The probability of equities sustaining a bad run over an investment period of more than 15 years is minimal.

Comparing the performance of the alternative investment strategies in Figure 2.10, a clear pattern emerges. The simulations advocate an aggressive allocation to equities in all phases of retirement for middle-income retirees, to minimize the probability of running out of funds. For middle-income retirees, the probability of economic death in any phase of retirement is lowest when the majority of funds are invested in equities over the whole retirement period. As the allocation to equities in each phase increases, the probability of running out of funds at each age decreases.

The probability of running out of money at any age declines as the proportion of equities increases because even with the longest estimated bad run of six years, equities provide the potential for gains in the long run that far outweigh their riskiness.

For high-income individuals, shown in Figure 2.11, who choose to invest in risk-free assets only with no exposure to equities, the risk of running out of funds increases dramatically. By the age of 85, the drawdowns on their funds are far greater than the low interest accumulated by investing in a risk-free cash asset. The probability of zero wealth in the first 15 years of retirement is insignificant, regardless of the investment strategy.

Even for a lifespan of 90 years, the probability of economic loss does not exceed 15 per cent for any strategy, excluding that which does not contain any equity investments. However, allowing for the possibility of a long lifespan of 100 years, individuals are least likely to run out of funds if they invest

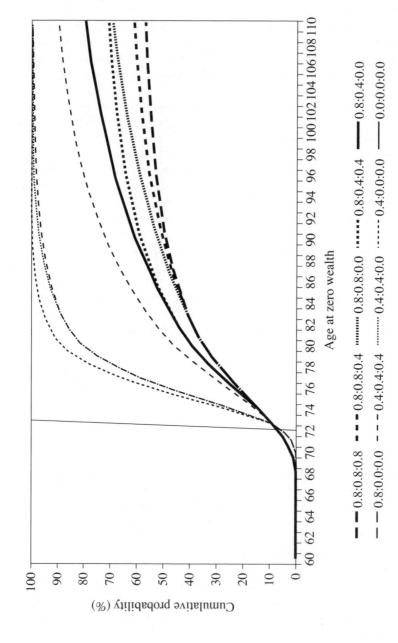

Figure 2.10   The cumulative probability of zero wealth in retirement – middle-income retirees

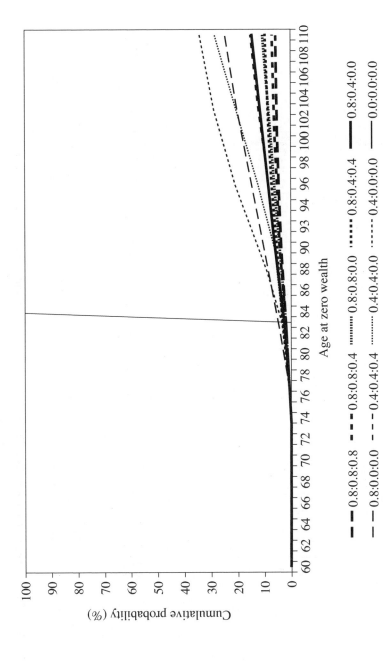

Figure 2.11   The cumulative probability of zero wealth in retirement – high-income retirees

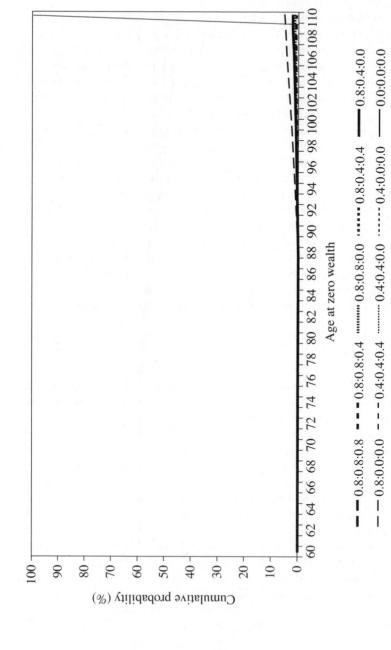

Figure 2.12   The cumulative probability of zero wealth in retirement – high-net-wealth retirees

a significant portion of their funds in equities. Retirees are most likely to face financial difficulties when they do not undertake any equity investments in the latter phases of their retirement.

For retirees classified as 'high net wealth' retiring with a considerable lump sum of $1 000 000 or more, our simulations shown in Figure 2.12 indicate that the chance of running out of funds at any time in their retirement is extremely low. Where such a large sum is invested, despite frequent drawdowns, the capital invested is sufficient to earn the income necessary to maintain the chosen lifestyle. The long investment period coupled with the large fund overcomes any losses in the equity portion of the investment.

The lessons from our simulation analysis are very much in favour of including equities as part of a sensible investment strategy, over an individual's entire retirement period. Regardless of the size of the lump sum available, retirees are estimated to be least likely to outlive their funds if a significant portion of their funds are invested in equities. The potential long-term profits from equities outweigh their risks, including the risk of a prolonged bad run.

However, the assumptions made on the lump-sum amount invested at the start of retirement and the annual drawdowns are crucial to this result. If these values are such that the drawdowns erode the investment capital at a pace that is too rapid, the investment capital will not have sufficient opportunity to accumulate gains. Given a healthy lump-sum payment and a sensible lifestyle, the probability of encountering financial difficulties during a lifespan is low.

CONCLUSIONS

We have reviewed some of the important issues facing the investment strategies for retirees. The main focus of our analysis was the role of equities as part of retirement investment strategies.

We find that compared with the other asset classes, equities are, surprisingly, not that risky. In particular, our analysis showed that the reputed 'safe haven' of investment, the property market, has been more susceptible to prolonged periods of poor performance than equity markets. These comparative risk measures, combined with their profitability in the long run, make equities a viable alternative to property and a worthy component in a diversification strategy.

Our duration analysis shows that runs of loss over five years, after allowing for inflation, are possible for most asset classes, but are sufficiently rare to make their returns worthwhile. Of course a cash buffer is desirable to weather any temporary downturn and good diversification strategies are essential.

The results of our simulations confirm our findings that equities should be included as part of a diversified investment strategy with a long-run view.

Except for the low-income scenario, our simulations indicated that including equity investments throughout retirement offers superior returns to those strategies that avoid equities.

In conclusion we assert that the underlying long-term value of equity markets is resistant to temporary bear markets. This resilience means that retiree investors should include equities in their investments to take advantage of the benefits offered by them.

NOTE

1. This chapter does not necessarily reflect the views of CommSec nor the Commonwealth Bank of Australia.

REFERENCE

Campbell, J., M. Lettau, B. Malkiel and Y. Xu (2001), 'Have individual stocks become more volatile? An empirical exploration of idiosyncratic risk', *Journal of Finance*, **56**(1), 1–43.

3. Assessing the risks in global fixed interest portfolios

Geoffrey Brianton

INTRODUCTION

The last few years have been a challenge to the superannuation industry. Negative returns, and in some cases double-digit negative returns, have raised questions about the safety and stewardship of superannuation assets. This experience has turned attention to the role of bonds within portfolios. Bonds, the forgotten asset class during the seductive bull run in equity markets in the 1990s, are coming into focus again.

The recent attention to the reliability of returns could represent a secular shift back to bonds. Many defined benefit (DB) pension funds have moved heavily into bonds, and the ageing demographics of the developed world will potentially feed the demand for capital-stable, income-producing investments.

The bond markets themselves have changed over the last decade; corporate debt has increased relative to government borrowing. This has pushed bond portfolios from the safety of 'riskless' government bonds into the risky domain of corporate bonds. Against this back-drop, interest rate markets have moved from being inflation driven and parochial to globally integrated and set in a low-inflation environment.

Domestic bond portfolios, primarily invested in sovereign debt, have been transformed into global portfolios with a focus on corporate debt. These changes have meant that the number of investment risks in a typical bond portfolio has increased significantly. This does not axiomatically translate into riskier portfolios. Provided risks are understood and well managed, global bond portfolios do not need to carry greater risks.

CHANGES IN THE BOND MARKETS

For some companies with a DB pension fund, the size of their pension schemes and the volatility of the fund's surplus can make their overall profitability more dependent on the performance of the pension fund rather than the performance of their core business. For example, the estimated

45

asset–liability shortfall of General Motors pension scheme is US$16 billion – a figure roughly equal to the market capitalization of the entire company.

For a DB fund, where the future obligations of the fund are more or less known, bonds can be used as an investment strategy to match those liabilities – an approach known as immunization. Boots in the UK were one of the first to switch their DB fund into bonds in a profile that matched their ongoing liabilities. The move towards immunization has been encouraged by accounting standards such as FASB 87 (Financial Accounting Standards Board) (in the USA) and, more recently, FRS 17 (Financial Reporting Standard) (in the UK). These accounting standards require changes in the surplus of a DB fund to be included in the company's profit and loss on a marked-to-market basis.

Arguably, shifting from equities to bonds is trading off shorter-term stability against a longer-term increase in the funding costs. Over a 10- or 20-year time horizon it is difficult to argue that an immunized bond portfolio will produce a better return than a portfolio with a significant allocation to equities. But, for the companies themselves, it can mean a return to a focus on their core business rather than an unwelcome push into becoming a life assurance company. Other DB funds have followed Boots in their shift into bonds.

Figure 3.1 shows long-term rates since January 2000 for the UK. The decline in rates is typical of rates throughout the major markets. Significantly, long-term rates (as indicated by the 30-year swap rate) have been lower than ten-year rates for much of this period. Anecdotally, this is as a prolonged effect of the introduction of the FRS 17 standard.

Figure 3.1   Declining longer-term interest rates

In Australia, most superannuation funds are accumulation funds. There has not been a pronounced shift to immunized bond portfolios. However, the ageing demographic of superannuants will tend to increase the role of bonds. As they shift from accumulating assets to consumption, equities will become a riskier investment, and capital-stable, income-producing assets, such as bonds, will become more attractive. The extent of this shift remains to be seen. Doomsayers have forecast a generation-long shift from equities to bonds, leading to asset price deflation that will eat away at the retirement provisions for Generation X following the Baby Boomers' wake.

The extent to which demographic shifts and moves from DB funds towards immunization will increase the demand for bonds is unclear. However, changes on the supply side over the last decade have been pronounced and have caused a fundamental shift in the way in which bond portfolios are constructed.

In Australia, government borrowing has been in decline since 1996 (see Figure 3.2). The mooted sale of the government's remaining share of Telstra would have raised sufficient revenue for Treasury to redeem all government bonds. This provoked a debate on whether the Australia government should be debt free and whether the Australia economy needs a sovereign risk debt market. In the end, the sale of Telstra failed to gain sufficient political support and the structure of the nation's balance sheet with no net debt was not revealed. This is not the first time this issue has been visited. In 1989/90 the government undertook reverse bond tenders and the end of the treasury market was forecast. This was unwound as the Federal Budget moved into deficit for several years.

Source: Citibank, *The Yield Book*.

Figure 3.2 Government borrowing in Australia (real borrowing in US$ bn (June 2003 base))

The trend among the English-speaking nations has been to reduce government debt, but within continental Europe and Japan, government borrowings have been on the rise (see Figure 3.3). The net effect is that government debt has remained roughly stable (in real US dollar terms) over the last decade. Recently, budget deficits, while not quite fashionable, are certainly more common. Japan is running a budget deficit of over 7 per cent, France and Germany near 4 per cent and the USA approaching 5 per cent of GDP. It is likely that global government debt will increase over the next few years.

In Australia, Commonwealth Treasury estimates have the budget moving back into a structural deficit over the next decade due to demographic changes (assuming taxes are held as a constant proportion of GDP). This will occur even in the absence of reduced economic growth. It is likely that the Australian government debt market is at a cyclical low rather than at the end of its lifespan.

While government debt has waned then waxed over the last decade, corporate bonds issues have been steadily increasing, particularly over the last few years (see Figure 3.4). The vast majority of the growth in the corporate market has been in US dollar-denominated bonds. Corporate bonds denominated in euros comprise the second largest portion of the market, with sterling and yen bonds representing only 2.6 and 0.7 per cent of the market respectively.

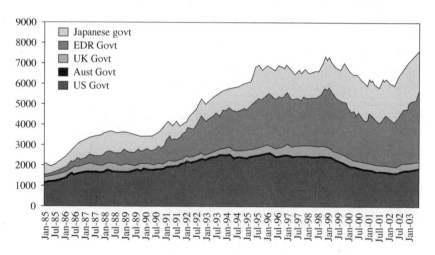

Source: Citibank.

Figure 3.3   Government debt market capitalization (real borrowing in US$ bn (June 2003 base))

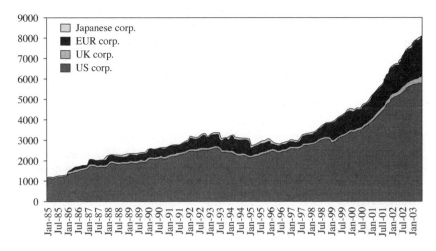

Source: Citibank.

Figure 3.4 *Corporate debt market capitalization (investment grade)(real borrowing in US\$ bn (June 2003 base))*

CREDIT RISK AND DIVERSIFICATION

The cyclical behaviour of the government bond market and the strong growth in the corporate market have resulted in the global investment grade bond market now being roughly the same size as the sovereign debt market. For bond market investors this means that credit risk is no longer a garnish – it is part of the main meal. Also, declining interest rates have led investors to venture further into the corporate debt market in search of additional yield.

It's not true to say that sovereign debt is entirely riskless. Governments do default on loans, and if you take a generous sample of history, many, if not most, governments have defaulted at some point. However, governments, with their ability to print money, tax, imprison or call in an army, will generally have last-lender standing in any currency. So the move into corporate debt introduces a more common, less dramatic type of risk – a company that cannot pay its bills. To cover this increase in risk, corporate bonds trade at a higher yield. The obvious question is whether this increase in yield is sufficient to cover the risk.

Table 3.1 shows the conditional return for a hypothetical five-year BBB-rated bond over a one-year time horizon based on the estimated probability of its credit rating changing over the year. The transition probabilities are based

Table 3.1 Conditional one-year return of a five-year BBB bond

Rating	Probability (%)	Annual return (%)
AAA	0.0	8.8
AA	0.2	8.6
A	3.1	8.1
BBB	92.2	7.0
BB	3.5	1.5
B	0.6	–2.4
CCC	0.1	–16.8
Default	0.3	–49.1
Expected return		6.6
Expected loss		0.4

Sources: JP Morgan, Credit Metrics, S&P.

on Standard and Poor data over the last 20 years. In 92 per cent of cases the bond will remain rated BBB and *ceteris paribus* the bond will return 7 per cent. If the credit rating of the bond was to fall to BB (a 0.5 per cent probability), the bond's resale value would fall and the total return over the year would be 1.5 per cent.

The probability of a default is quite small but the effect is quite dramatic, with the expected 'recovery rate' (the proportion of their capital recovered by creditors) for a BBB bond being less than half. In the event that the bond is upgraded, the return is higher than 7 per cent due to the capitalized value of the improvement in the bond's credit rating.

Weighting each return outcome by its probability, we can estimate an overall expected return for the bond. Comparing this expected return with that of an unchanged BBB bond gives an estimate of the expected loss due to the credit risk of the bond. In this case it is 0.4 per cent. This measure of expected loss is more complete than just expected loss due to default, as it takes into account changes in the value of the bond due to changes in credit quality.

For a BBB bond the increase in yield over sovereign debt (the credit margin) has typically varied between 1 per cent and 3 per cent (see Figure 3.5, which shows BBB margins for US corporate bonds over the last 20 years). The increase in return is significantly and consistently higher than the expected losses.

This calculation will vary, depending on the extent to which the market is rewarding or penalizing bonds for credit upgrades or downgrades. However, the conclusion that, over time, credit margins generously compensate for credit risk is robust.

On this simple analysis it would appear that taking credit risk is well

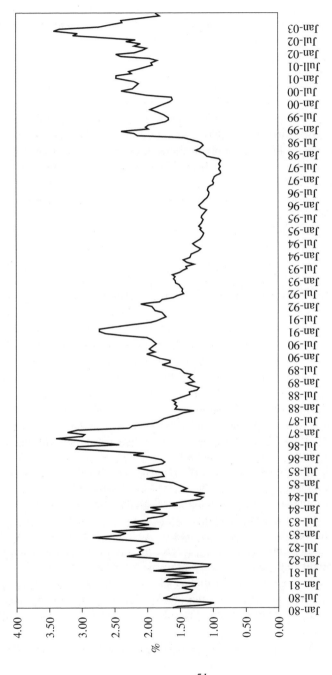

Source: Citigroup.

Figure 3.5 BBB margins for US corporate bonds (duration-adjusted spread to Treasury bond for 7–10-year BBB bonds)

51

rewarded. This overlooks the asymmetric nature of the risk. A corporate bond gives a very high probability of a small increase in return and a small probability of a large, in some cases complete, investment loss. To holders of Enron and WorldCom bonds, a small expected loss turned into realized losses of 100 per cent – a devastating result for any portfolio with anything more than a small weighting to these issues.

A bond portfolio moving into credit needs to tread carefully and diversify the risk of default as far as possible. For bond investors in a small market such as Australia, this presents a problem. The Australian market is dominated by the financial sector, which comprises about a third of the entire market. Other sectors such as media and telecommunications have only a handful of different issuers. For investors trying to pursue higher returns there can be a temptation to ignore the need for diversification and aggressively pursue higher-margin securities. In a narrow market like Australia this will lead to a dangerously concentrated portfolio.

The lack of depth and breadth in the Australian market prevents portfolios from creating a significant exposure to credit that is sufficiently diversified.

MACRO AND MICRO CREDIT MANAGEMENT

For investment managers, the growth in credit-based, global bond portfolios has meant a much broader skill set is required to manage the bond component of a portfolio. A decade ago, duration management (that is, management of the portfolio's yield curve exposure) was the main and sometimes only active management strategy within a bond portfolio.

Duration management largely requires consideration of a relatively small number of variables, typically short-, medium- and longer-term rates. However, credit requires a much deeper analysis. The Lehman Global Aggregate Index (one of the most common benchmarks used for global bond portfolios) covers over 6000 securities. It is a much more labour-intensive task to have understood the credit risk of these securities than it is to research the interest rates that underpin them. Broadly speaking there are two approaches to managing credit – macro and micro.

A macro approach focuses on the pricing of credit and the extent to which overall credit margins are increasing or decreasing. Figure 3.3 can be viewed as a 'macro' credit indicator as it shows the overall margin of BBB bonds rather than the behaviour of an individual stock. A micro approach focuses on the individual bonds and whether the market is correctly pricing their prospects for upgrades, downgrades, default or changes in the underlying company.

The distinction is quite significant, as the macro and micro approaches imply different investment styles and different means of rewarding risk. A macro credit manager would argue that there is no economic argument for stock selection risk to be rewarded over time, whilst diversified credit risk should be rewarded and has, historically, had a very attractive risk/reward trade-off. The macro manager would focus on the overall position of the credit cycle, investing in credit, but looking to retreat to sovereign or highly rated issues during recessions and periods of high uncertainty. Credit decisions would be implemented by investing in a broad range of securities, thereby minimizing the exposure to stock risk.

A micro or stock selection approach would tend to neutral allocations in any particular credit band or country and attempt to add value by selecting the stocks within the band that they perceive as better value. The difficulty faced by a manager looking to add value via stock selection is the previously mentioned asymmetric nature of an individual bond's return. An undervalued AA bond has only a limited upside if the view proves to be correct, but a large potential downside if it is incorrect. The best way of mitigating this risk is to take many small bets rather than a few large ones.

Consequently, both macro credit managers and stock-picking managers have, for different reasons, an interest in seeking a broad universe of bonds. This is the central logic behind the growth in global bond portfolios with broad-based global benchmarks such as the Salomon Brothers World Broad Investment Grade Index (World Big) and the Lehman Global Aggregate Index.

The need for global diversification of credit exposure has been well recognized by Australian superannuation funds. Bond mandates with global investment grade bond benchmarks and/or scope have been the fastest-growing area in debt market investment management in Australia.

CONCLUSION

The growth in the corporate bonds market relative to government bonds has pushed bond portfolios into increased credit exposures. In turn, this has led to the need to diversify this exposure across the broad canvas of the global bond market. Given the demands on bond markets for retirement income in the coming decades, this is a healthy development. Investment managers have been pressed to widen their skill set, and this has significantly increased the economy of scale required to manage bond portfolios. Bond portfolio management is predominately an industry for firms with a global footprint.

It is difficult to know how the various forces acting on bond markets will play out over the next decade, and how this will affect those looking for a secure retirement and those looking to build their wealth for their retirement in the future.

There is a scary scenario. Over the next two decades, the Baby Boomers, the wealthiest generation in history, will be switching from accumulation to consumption and will seek to sell their (arguably) inflated assets and shift their wealth to bonds. In doing so they could create a dual problem, pushing down the yields on bonds – shrinking their own income – and at the same time inducing asset price deflation that erodes the wealth of their successors – Generation X.

This scenario is pessimistic. A more sanguine outlook would note that demographic shifts and economic growth rates will not be uniform across the globe, and the supply of bonds, both government and corporate, is likely to continue to increase. With capital markets operating on a global basis, increases in the supply of bonds can be directed to increased demand. Certainly, the provision of retirement incomes for the Baby Boomers and building wealth to provide for the retirement of subsequent generations will continue to present a challenge to policy makers and the capital markets.

4. The role of index funds in retirement asset allocation

David R. Gallagher

INTRODUCTION

Pension fund trustees have exercised significant management and fiduciary responsibilities in activities on behalf of pension fund members. Some important tasks undertaken by trustees are the implementation and monitoring of the plan's portfolio strategy and performance. Therefore, once the pension fund has decided on the strategic asset allocation to be adopted, manager and/or investment selection is critical. In this respect, trustees are required to make choices about whether the plan will exercise either active, enhanced index, or passive fund management (or some combination of the three). Active management is built on the premise that capital markets are not perfectly efficient, and that information gathering and synthesis can lead to superior investment returns relative to the market. At the other end of the spectrum, passive fund management seeks to replicate the returns of the underlying benchmark, which means that outperforming the market is not the goal of the strategy. Enhanced index management is largely passive management, although quantitative techniques are permitted such that the strategy attempts to generate small alpha (that is, outperformance of the market) in a risk-controlled setting.

Investment markets to date have been most commonly associated with active investment management. Indeed, a significant majority of assets managed by pension funds, institutions and retail investors are founded on active management principles. However, indexing has been growing in significance as an alternative and lower-cost investment strategy designed to capture the returns of a particular asset class. This trend has arisen for a number of reasons, perhaps the most significant being the empirical research that has highlighted the overall underperformance of active managers (on average) after expenses. In the context of retirement provision in scary markets, pension funds will be significantly sensitive to active managers being unable to generate at least the returns of the underlying indexes across asset classes. Underperformance will result in the fund having difficulties in achieving the plan's investment objective over the long term.

The size of assets benchmarked to well-known broad market benchmarks is significant. Indeed, more than US$1 trillion of index mutual fund assets are benchmarked to the S&P 500 Index in the USA. In addition, indexing has become an ever-increasing component of investment management, particularly for pension fund investors. Exchange-traded funds, or ETFs as they are more commonly known, represent an alternative and increasingly popular indexing product. The difference between open-end index mutual funds and ETFs is that the latter are closed-end funds which trade as listed securities on an exchange, and whose performance and volatility move in alignment with the underlying basket of stocks in which the security is tied.

Indexes represent a statistical methodology which summarizes the behaviour, that is, risk and return, of a pre-defined group of securities. More specifically, indexes permit quantitative analysis that measures the change in value of a basket of securities over time. Asset classes such as equities, bonds, property and cash markets are generally easily identified through the availability of well-known benchmark proxies. These benchmarks enable investors to better understand the risk-and-return dimensions of the underlying securities comprising the market index. However, indexes vary according to the depth and breadth of stocks included in the list of constituents, as well as variation in the preferences of investors as to which stock universe most appropriately relates to their investment objectives.

Some of the best-known index providers include Standard and Poor (S&P), Dow Jones, Morgan Stanley Capital International (MSCI), Russell, and the FTSE Group. While indexes help to define the overall performance of national markets, benchmark indexes are also commonly available which explain the performance of industry sectors, such as energy, industrials, health care and financials, and securities based on stock size (where market capitalization is decomposed into large-cap, mid-cap and small-cap). In addition, indexes have varying histories, where the oldest benchmark of common US stocks (the Dow Jones Industrial Average) date back to the late 1800s.

Indexes are constructed and maintained almost exclusively as market capitalization weighted benchmarks, where the weight attributable to each constituent security is on the basis of the size of securities within the investible universe. Therefore, under this index methodology, the increase in value of one security, *ceteris paribus*, leads that stock to become increasingly significant in explaining changes to the overall index. The other important feature of a closed-end benchmark index which adopts a market-cap-weighted index is that rebalancing is significantly more critical (and cumbersome) where other index methodologies are adopted, such as equal or price-weighted constituents. Perhaps the three most significant operating requirements for any successful index is that the stocks included in the benchmark are 'investible' (that is, liquid and available to investors to legally own), they are representative of the market that the index is seeking to reflect, and the benchmark maintenance procedures cause minimal disruption to the smooth operation of the index. In other words, the benchmark composition needs to reflect securities that can be easily replicated by investors; the securities should be liquid, the index methodology should be transparent, and the index provider should consistently maintain the stock universe in a manner that minimizes turnover. Recent times have witnessed changes to index weight determination using a 'free-float methodology'. Here the proportionate share of a security comprising the benchmark is not only considered in terms of market capitalization and liquidity, but also in terms of the available quantity of stock freely available to be traded. The free-float approach therefore avoids giving a greater benchmark allocation to stocks that have a larger quantity of investors holding stocks for strategic ownership purposes (such as Murdoch family's ownership in News Corporation).

The remainder of this chapter discusses indexing in the context of pension fund investors. The asset class spectrum is discussed next, followed by the types of investment vehicles through which investors attempt to capture the returns available from security markets. The relative merits of active versus passive investment management are considered. A review of the approaches used by index fund managers to replicate the benchmark is then presented, together with a discussion of the various challenges faced by index portfolio managers in their pursuit of the returns and risks of the underlying benchmark. The final section concludes.

THE ASSET CLASS SPECTRUM

An asset class represents a group of financial assets. In theory numerous asset classes may exist. However, in investment markets, asset classes are typically defined in broad terms on the basis that the securities comprising the asset class have some degree of commonality in their characteristics. In the Australian investment markets, the six largest and easily identifiable asset classes are Australian equities, international equities, Australian bonds, international bonds, property and cash. Table 4.1 documents the size of the major asset classes which comprise the Australian investment industry.

Australian investors have the highest exposure to domestic and international equities asset classes, with domestic bonds representing the third largest asset class in the market. The category 'other investments' identified in Table 4.1 includes private equity or venture capital, tactical asset allocation investments and infrastructure-type investments.

Asset classes may be divided into two broad categories – growth assets and defensive assets. Growth assets include equity and property investments,

Table 4.1   Size of Australian asset class sectors managed by investment managers (at 30 June 2001)

Asset class	A$ billion	(%)
Panel A: Growth asset classes		
Australian equities	211.16	29.43
International equities	140.22	19.55
Property	77.51	10.80
Panel B: Defensive asset classes		
Australian bonds	123.81	17.26
International bonds	28.54	3.98
Cash	85.37	11.90
Panel C: Other assets		
Other investments*	50.78	7.08
Total	717.41	100.0

Note: *Other assets include capital guaranteed assets, tactical asset allocation assets, life insurance policies and infrastructure investments.

Source: Rainmaker Information.

where returns derived from such investments comprise income and changes in capital value. Defensive assets on the other hand are defined as income returns from investments in bonds and liquid securities. Defensive asset classes exhibit a degree of stability in the underlying value of an investor's initial investment. That is, highly liquid money market securities and bonds derive interest income from the underlying capital value, where the capital value remains fixed. In the case of bonds held to maturity, the principal component or initial investment is redeemable at maturity. Debt instruments provide the investor with a legal claim to repayment of the principal value at a future date.

In addition, growth and defensive asset classes may be distinguished in terms of their historical returns, *ex-post* volatility, and the level of asset class correlation existing between sectors. Table 4.2 presents the returns, volatilities and correlations between asset classes. Standard industry benchmarks are used as asset class proxies. Table 4.3 identifies and defines these indexes. Benchmark indexes are defined as a statistical measure that enables changes in the value of a group of securities comprising a particular asset class to be calculated. They therefore allow market participants to measure the returns and risks of a portfolio of securities to serve as a yardstick or reference point when comparing alternative portfolios.

Table 4.2 Historical annual returns, volatility and correlations (13-year period January 1988–December 2000)

Asset class	Return (% p.a.)	SD (% p.a.)	Correlation (%)						
			AEQ	IEQ	DP	LP	AFI	OFIH	Cash
AEQ	11.6	13.8	100.0	33.8	0.2	52.2	34.8	17.1	0.1
IEQ	12.8	15.1	–	100.0	–3.9	27.8	17.6	31.1	–3.1
DP	5.8	4.6	–	–	100.0	–1.1	–12.6	–10.0	15.5
LP	11.6	10.1	–	–	–	100.0	41.8	28.0	–0.7
AFI	11.5	4.9	–	–	–	–	100.0	58.6	26.0
OFIH	11.3	3.3	–	–	–	–	–	100.0	27.2
Cash	8.4	1.1	–	–	–	–	–	–	100.0
CPI	3.3	2.2	–	–	–	–	–	–	–
AWE	3.9	2.5	–	–	–	–	–	–	–

Source: Mercer Investment Consulting.

59

Table 4.3   Benchmark indexes employed as asset class proxies

Asset class	Code	Benchmark index
Australian equities	AEQ	S&P/ASX 200 Accumulation Index*
International equities	IEQ	MSCI World (ex-Australia) Index in (net dividends AU$ reinvested)
Direct property	DP	Mercer Direct Property Index
Listed property	LP	S&P/ASX Listed Property Trusts Index
Australian bonds	AFI	UBS Warburg Composite All Maturities Bond Index
Overseas bonds	OFIH	Salomon Smith Barney World Government Bond Index Hedged in AU$
Cash	Cash	UBS Warburg Bank Bill Index
Inflation	CPI	ABS Consumer Price Index
Average weekly earnings	AWE	ABS Average Weekly Earnings (All Males)

Note: *ASX All Ordinaries Accumulation Index was used before March 2000. The difference in market capitalization coverage between the S&P/ASX 300 and the S&P/ASX 200 is less than 3 per cent.

While future returns and the volatility of asset classes are unknown, historical data provide investors with some degree of insight into the level of returns derived and the risks associated with each of the asset classes.[1] Consideration of historical data assists investors to forecast likely future scenarios.

Table 4.2 reveals that international equities recorded both the highest return and standard deviation in the 13-year period than any other asset class sector. As expected, growth asset classes exhibit higher standard deviations (or risk) than is the case for defensive asset classes. However, the problem of evaluating returns and risk over static periods is two-fold. First, such an approach does not allow analysis of returns and risks over different periods of time. The second disadvantage is that all observations are treated equally and therefore there is no scaling to apply greater weights to the most recent data. To better understand the relative returns and risks over varying time periods within the 13-year period evaluated, Figures 4.1 and 4.2 show the five-year rolling returns and standard deviations for each of the major asset classes.

INVESTMENT VEHICLES AVAILABLE TO INVESTORS

Pension fund trustees are required to decide on the implementation strategy to

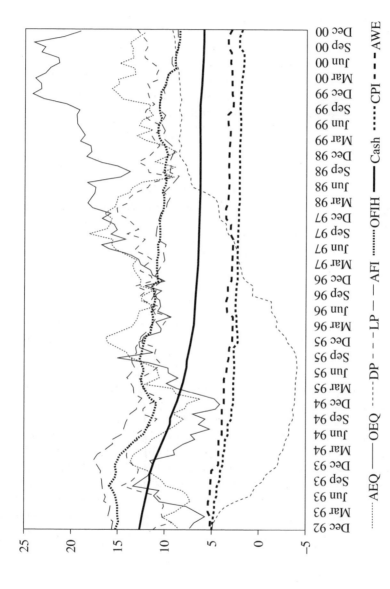

Figure 4.1 Five-year rolling annual returns (% per annum)

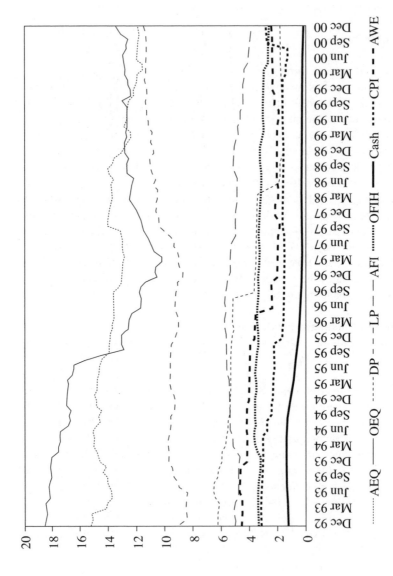

Figure 4.2   Five-year rolling annual standard deviations (% per annum)

······ AEQ —— OEQ ····· DP - - - LP - - - AFI ······· OFIH —— Cash ······ CPI - - AWE

be adopted in executing the investment strategy on behalf of fund members. Accordingly, the trustee must make decisions as to what type of investment vehicle is appropriate for the pension fund, and, if necessary, whether the fund's assets are to be delegated to professional external managers.

Fund Structures

Public and private portfolios

A managed fund is an investment product made available to investors by professional investment managers. It is through managed funds that investors are able to access the investment services offered by fund managers. Managed funds are typically collective or pooled investment vehicles offered to investors as unit trusts (public portfolios); however, investment managers may also provide investment services to large institutional clients through an individually managed or discrete (private) portfolio.

A managed fund represents the combined assets of investors who have subscribed to the fund. With this pool of liquid assets, investment managers allocate funds across different securities and asset classes in accordance with the investment objective of the fund. Managed funds offered as unit trusts are established under a trust deed that governs the operation of the fund. The trust deed also dictates the means by which the unit trust can receive and redeem investments made by investors.

Features of managed portfolios

Managed funds are attractive to investors for a variety of reasons. These include:

- Diversification benefits: investments made in pooled investment vehicles make it easier to spread small monetary investments across a large number of asset classes and individual financial securities than would be possible without such a vehicle.
- Economies of scale: transaction costs incurred by managed funds in physical transaction securities are likely to be much lower through collective investments than would be the case through smaller, private transactions. In addition, dividend imputation may allow managed funds to more efficiently utilize franking credits on domestic shares.[2]
- Access to investment skill: investors may not have the necessary time or expertise (either locally or globally) to invest their capital in both a prudent and profitable manner.
- Portfolio administration services: investors may find the administration services provided, including record-keeping, accounting and taxation services to be a valuable additional service.

Types of Managed Funds

Investment managers provide investors with access to a multitude of different types of managed investment products. These products can be differentiated on the basis of three main criteria: the investment objective; the spectrum of asset classes and securities comprising the managed fund; and the type of investor to whom the product is tailored.

The investment objective or strategy to be implemented by a portfolio manager is the most significant differentiating feature of a managed fund. The investment strategy documents how the funds invested will be managed, including the investment style that will be followed. Managed fund assets are invested using (1) an active investment philosophy, (2) a passive or index approach or (3) an investment objective that is largely passive in structure, but incorporates some active strategies, such as enhanced index or quantitative strategies.

Essentially the active and passive investment philosophies are diametrically opposite to one another and their use will depend on investors' preferences and beliefs as to whether capital markets are efficient.

Actively managed funds

Active investment managers believe that returns in excess of the underlying benchmark index are achievable through the use of security-specific and macroeconomic information. The identification of mis-priced securities (security selection) and altering the portfolio's asset allocation in anticipation of market movements (market timing) are the two most common methods active managers use in their attempts to outperform benchmark indexes.

Index managed funds

Index fund managers subscribe to the view that markets are broadly efficient and that, over time, index-mimicking portfolios will outperform the average active fund. Index managers also cite potential advantages in that their funds are offered at a lower cost to investors compared to active funds, and that a passive strategy minimizes the crystallization of capital gains tax liabilities.

Enhanced index funds

Enhanced index funds attempt to earn returns above the benchmark index. However, the achievement of active returns requires minimizing the fund's tracking error – standard deviation of the difference between the fund's return and the target benchmark's return. Enhanced index funds represent a blended strategy between an active and index approach. The enhanced-passive approach is predominantly structured as an index strategy with small tilts relative to the underlying index. The objective generally involves the following enhancement strategies:

- Investing in companies through initial public offerings (IPOs) ahead of an IPO's inclusion in an index.
- Internal 'crossings' with other funds actively managed by the same investment manager. Securities may be acquired at more favourable prices than may exist in the market.
- Receiving dividends in the form of shares by participating in dividend reinvestment plans (DRPs). The attractive feature of DRPs is the issue of shares at a discount to the current market price. DRPs can also provide cost benefits to the manager by minimizing the required trading in index securities. The costs of order execution are minimized.
- Very small sector bets within industries and stocks relative to the index.
- Employing derivatives, such as futures and options contracts, to take advantage of short-term market movements.

Exchange-traded funds

Exchange-traded funds (or ETFs) are relatively new investment vehicles that trade as listed securities on a securities exchange. ETFs are listed unit trusts or 'shares' representing investment in a basket of other listed securities. An ETF's market value is determined with respect to the market values of the individual securities comprising the basket. Because ETFs are equivalent to the purchase or sale of a security linked directly to an underlying index, these products represent an alternative to investing in index funds managed by professional investment managers. ETFs provide investors with an efficient and diversified security that tracks market indexes. Indeed, ETFs in the USA levy lower expenses than open-end mutual funds. ETFs are also beginning to be used by investment managers as substitutes for futures contracts or in addition to derivatives.

The first ETF was launched in Canada and was listed on the Toronto Stock Exchange (TSE) in 1989. This Canadian ETF tracked the largest 35 TSE listed stocks. ETFs then became available in the USA in 1993 with the introduction of the Standard & Poor's Depository Receipts (SPDRs), or Spider, traded on the American Stock Exchange (AMEX). Spiders represent an investment in a value-weighted portfolio of common shares comprising the S&P 500 Index, with the objective of providing investors with identical returns to the S&P 500. Spiders pay dividends equal to the proportional weight of stocks that actually declare dividends. The launch of the Spider was quickly followed by other ETF issues, Diamonds based on the Dow Jones Industrial Average, World Equity Benchmark Shares (WEBS) and iShares issued by Barclays Global Investors, and the NASDAQ listed Cubes (derived from their ticker symbol QQQ) tracking technology stocks. ETF assets offered in the USA have approximately doubled in the year to December 2000 to US$70 billion, which are invested across 80 ETF securities. In Australia, ETFs have only recently been issued and are traded on the Australian Stock Exchange. Salomon Smith Barney was the first to introduce an ETF in 2001.

THE ACTIVE VERSUS PASSIVE DEBATE

The debate about active versus passive management has continued to evolve for more than four decades. Literature around the world confirms the inability of active mutual funds to outperform passive benchmarks or indexes such as the S&P 500 on a risk-adjusted basis after expenses (Jensen 1968; Elton et al. 1993; Malkiel 1995; Gruber 1996; and Edelen 1999). The findings of Australian studies are generally consistent with the international evidence (Bird et al. 1983; Robson 1986; Hallahan and Faff 1999; Sawicki and Ong 2000). An interesting paradox is that the significant majority of assets professionally managed on behalf of investors are actively managed, which means that the average investor is underperforming the benchmark after expenses are deducted! In addition, research also shows that these findings have largely been time independent, including the high proportion of fund managers' products underperforming the benchmark on a relatively persistent basis (see Malkiel 1995).

While capital markets efficiency theory says that these findings of underperformance (after expenses) should not be unexpected, a number of papers have attempted to explore capital market anomalies (such as momentum, seasonality, size, post-earnings announcement drift and turn-of-the-year effects) which might provide sufficient evidence that market efficiency does not hold in absolute terms. Behavioural finance has also sought to explain some of these issues, given that investors are not rational 100 per cent of the time.

Indeed, a number of mutual fund studies have attempted to explore why active mutual funds have not outperformed risk-adjusted benchmarks. The first reason, noted by Sharpe (1991), is concerned with the definition of the benchmark, and why the average investor must earn a return equal to the benchmark. The reasoning is that the performance of the index equals the weighted-average return of both active and passive investors before investment expenses. Sharpe's (1991) law concerning the aggregate return to investors equating to the market return must hold. Therefore, by definition, active management must be a zero-sum game.

Other factors that have been postulated as reasons for underperformance by active managers include the size of their management fees (relative to index funds), their inability to identify mis-priced stocks and to successfully time the market, and their higher relative trading costs and market impact costs relative to index funds. Also relevant is the large size of the funds under management, which makes it difficult for an active manager to quickly and efficiently alter the portfolio's composition.

This is not to say that active management is all bad. However, the empirical evidence suggests that a significant proportion of active fund managers have been unable to provide investors with superior returns to the market index. In many ways, the higher degree of scrutiny now applied to underperforming active managers, who levy higher expense ratios compared to index-linked products, has ensured that pension fund investors in particular have considered alternative strategies that can minimize their expenses incurred, while also helping their funds to achieve the investment objectives mandated by their pension plan.

STRATEGIES FOR INDEX TRACKING AND TRACKING ERROR MANAGEMENT

Index management, at face value, appears to be a very simple investment strategy that requires an investor to simply hold all index constituents in the exact same weights as the underlying benchmark. In reality, however, the implementation of an indexing strategy is not necessary straightforward. As discussed below, index management leads to the portfolio manager incurring frictions in index replication against an index which is a paper portfolio that can be altered instantaneously and without cost. Therefore, given the frictions that are experienced by index portfolio management, the inevitable fact is that index funds will be unable to deliver investors with identical returns to the benchmark. Accordingly, a passive portfolio manager's objective must then be to implement an investment strategy which seeks to constrain the tracking error (that is, a quantitative measure of differences in the performance between the fund and benchmark over time) of the fund such that investors achieve returns which closely approximate the target benchmark at minimal cost.

The choice of index replication technique adopted by a passive portfolio manager depends on a number of criteria. However, the overriding objective for a passive fund manager is to achieve an optimally configured portfolio that minimizes the costs incurred, but also minimizes the tracking error volatility. There is an inverse relationship between tracking error accuracy and cost. An investor utilizing passive funds must recognize that perfect replication is not achievable, and will ultimately depend on the design of an index, the underlying liquidity of stocks comprising the benchmark, the size of the investment portfolio being managed, and the replication technique adopted. Liu et al. (1998) highlight three methods commonly adopted in indexing by professional money managers – full replication, stratified sampling and optimization. Each is discussed in turn below.

Full Replication

Full replication involves a passive portfolio manager holding each stock in the index in the same weight as the target benchmark index. Depending on the liquidity of stocks comprising the index, and the extent to which index changes and corporate actions require a benchmark adjustment, full replication techniques should lead to investors incurring minimal tracking error relative to other non-replication techniques. However, they can be more costly to implement.

Stratified Sampling

Stratified sampling relies on a passive portfolio manager holding a subset of stocks to the benchmark. However, the subset of stocks held are required to have factor risk exposures which together will mimic the index. Two important risk factors considered important in the process are the size of the stock in the benchmark (that is, stocks with bigger weights in the benchmark have a higher degree of dominance) and the sectors comprising the index. Stratified sampling relies on estimates of the variances, covariances and correlations of returns for index-securities, such that the subset of securities selected in the index-mimicking portfolio will exhibit similar risk/return properties to the benchmark. However, given that the factor inputs cannot perfectly predict the future relationship between stocks, tracking error in performance will be unavoidable when non-replication techniques are employed.

Optimization

Similar to stratified sampling, quantitative risk modelling is the more rigorous of non-replication techniques for building index-tracking portfolios. The key objective in portfolio optimization is to select a subset of securities that are expected to approximate the underlying benchmark's performance and risk, using a highly quantitative technique which attempts to find the minimum tracking error volatility portfolio that can be achieved at minimal cost.

ISSUES IN INDEX TRACKING AND MANAGEMENT

Market Frictions

Since the aim of index funds is to replicate the performance of an index, then the difference between the return on a benchmark index and the return on an index funds' portfolio (or tracking error) can be used to evaluate their performance. Tracking error in the performance of index funds is likely to arise from the difficulties inherent in management of passive portfolios. Theoretically, the management of an index portfolio is straightforward, requiring passive fund managers to hold each constituent index security in the same proportion to the benchmark (known as a 'full replication' strategy). In reality, index funds will experience considerable difficulty in replicating the target index, because the index represents a mathematical calculation that does not take into account market frictions. The calculation of an index ignores market frictions in the sense that when the security weights within the index change, the index implicitly assumes that rebalancing of securities to reflect the new market weights can occur costlessly, instantaneously, and at prevailing market prices. However, index funds face a number of market frictions in attempting to mimic the index portfolio, or more specifically, returns on the index. These frictions can ultimately result in tracking error in performance.

Transaction Costs

Explicit costs associated with trading in securities markets, including broker-age fees and stamp duty, can influence the ability of passive funds to replicate index performance. The index itself is calculated as a 'paper' portfolio, which assumes transactions can occur costlessly (see Perold 1988). In reality, passive funds incur explicit costs associated with transactions relating to client capital flows. For example, cash-flow movements cause flow-induced trading for passive funds, requiring new cash to be invested across index securities or part of the portfolio to be liquidated. Apart from cash-flow-induced trading, index funds also trade regularly for a variety of other reasons associated with strat-egy implementation. Because index funds are required to trade, explicit trans-action costs are incurred. These costs erode the value of the index fund by the amount of the explicit costs and lead to tracking error in performance measured after management expenses.[3]

Funds also incur implicit transaction costs in trading, including bid–ask spreads and the price impact of trading. These costs will also cause tracking error in performance measured before management expenses. Transactions by passive funds can cause temporary demand-and-supply imbalances, which imply that they are not able to trade instantaneously at prevailing market prices. Overall, this implies that client-related cash-flow movements and the implicit costs of trading, such as bid–ask spreads, are likely to be related to the magnitude of tracking error.

Index Volatility

Another factor likely to be related to tracking error is the volatility of the underlying benchmark index. If the composition and weighting of stocks held by an index fund perfectly match those of the index, changes in the value of the index fund portfolio should match changes in the benchmark index. However, at any point in time, the composition of the portfolio of a passive fund is unlikely to be perfectly aligned with the index portfolio for a number of reasons. For example, most index fund managers are likely to use some form of proxy portfolio because the smaller, less liquid, stocks in the underlying index are more difficult to acquire. Other funds explicitly aim to hold an imperfect proxy portfolio with the objective of minimizing the costs of assembling a portfolio to track the underlying index. New client cash inflows may also take time to be invested in the funds' desired portfolio, especially those involving less liquid stocks. As a result, unsystematic movements in the stocks underlying an index that are not in a passive fund manager's portfolio will result in tracking error. Similarly, unsystematic movements in the overweight stocks in a fund manager's portfolio relative to the index portfolio will also cause tracking error. Consequently, higher benchmark index volatility is likely to be associated with higher tracking error.

Dividends

Tracking error can also arise from dividends paid by stocks in the index. When a listed company in an index goes ex dividend, the index effectively assumes that the dividend is reinvested in the stock from which it is derived on the ex-dividend date. However, investors (including passive funds) experience a significant time delay, which normally extends into weeks, in receiving cash in relation to a dividend. As a consequence, tracking error can occur for two reasons. First, transaction costs are associated with reinvesting the dividends once received, and these erode the value of the passive funds portfolio. In contrast, the index assumes that the proceeds from the dividend payment are reinvested costlessly at the prevailing market price.

Second, the fund manager must wait for receipt of cash in relation to dividends before being able to reinvest it. Hence there is likely to be a positive relationship between the level of dividends paid by stocks in an index and passive fund tracking error.

Index Constituent Changes and Corporate Actions

Tracking error may also be related to changes in the composition of the benchmark index. These include periodical index adjustments related to company additions and deletions, capitalization changes and corporate restructuring. Fund managers may need to trade in order to adjust their portfolios to properly track the index following such changes. Transaction costs are also incurred in this trading, further increasing tracking error. Depending on the relative size of the stocks entering and exiting the index (in terms of market capitalization), these changes may also require a number of costly odd-lot transactions in order to match the rebalanced index. The index manager also faces the additional challenge of executing orders at the best possible prices and in a manner that minimizes the crystallization of capital gains tax liabilities to avoid significant erosion of returns. In the case of corporate restructuring, tracking error can also arise when index securities are involved in a merger or takeover by another company outside the index. For example, a timing delay may exist between the date on which the index fund receives the cash settlement and the date when the target firm is removed from the index.

Price Pressure in Stock Prices Due to the Demand for Immediacy in Trading

Periodical changes to the index can also make it difficult (and costly) for a passive fund to replicate the benchmark index.[4] Beneish and Whaley (1996) identify that 'front-running' by market participants, who acquire index securities ahead of their inclusion in a benchmark, can have an undesirable impact on index funds.[5] Ultimately, changes in the composition of the index require passive funds to trade, which can result in transaction costs and tracking error. Overall, changes in the composition of the index are also expected to cause tracking error.

Index Replication Strategy

The magnitude of tracking error may differ across index managers depending on the portfolio management approach used to replicate returns on the index. The index replication policy adopted by a passive portfolio manager will in large part be determined by the number of stocks in the benchmark, a stock's relative size (that is, the market capitalization weight) and the underlying liquidity of the stocks in the index. The liquidity of stocks in the basket will have a significant impact on the implicit transaction costs incurred by passive funds, as well as the ease with which accurate pricing of stocks can be achieved (that is, the avoidance of stale prices from infrequent trading). Essentially, the availability of a futures contract underlying the cash market benchmark will help to minimize tracking error.

Full replication strategies require that index funds hold *all* securities in the basket index in the same proportion as represented in the index. Stratified sampling and optimized portfolios on the other hand are non-replication strategies designed to mimic the index through investment in a *subset* of index securities, while at the same time ensuring the portfolio has similar risk-and-return

characteristics as the index.[6] Non-replication strategies aim to minimize transaction costs compared with full replication strategies. However, the trade-off
is potentially higher tracking error arising from the performance of excluded
securities which comprize the underlying index. Optimized portfolios are
constructed using highly quantitative, multi-factor risk models aimed at minimizing tracking error through an understanding of the covariance between
factors driving asset returns (Liu et al. 1998 and Olma 1998). The expectation,
ceteris paribus, is that tracking error will be systematically lower for full replication index funds compared with non-replication index funds.

Index Design and Maintenance Rules

Frino et al. (2004) highlight the important role that index providers and
committees have in ensuring that passive portfolio managers are able to efficiently replicate benchmark indexes. Indeed, in the case of any action which
will affect the index divisor, such as changes in the constituents of the
benchmark, share issuances, share repurchases and spin-offs, the manner in
which the index treats such activity, as well as the timing of these amendments, has been shown to explain exogenous tracking error in the performance of index-linked mutual funds. Great care needs to be exercised by an
index committee when maintaining the benchmarks under their control. This
includes maintaining an index that is organized in a fair, consistent and
transparent fashion.

Index Exclusivity Effects

A recent paper by Haberle and Ranaldo (2004) presents interesting empirical
evidence about the constituents of indexes often forming an 'exclusive' benchmark, and they argue that the selection rules for inclusion/exclusion constitut-
ing these indexes is essentially another form of active management. Their
evidence, for a wide sample of well-known and cited equity benchmarks globally, shows that the exclusive-type indexes outperform all-inclusive indexes on
a risk-adjusted basis. Therefore, exclusive benchmarks are argued to have
attributes consistent with momentum-based strategies, where 'winners' have a
higher probability of becoming members in exclusive-based benchmarks, and
for market-cap-weighted indexes, these better-performing stocks constitute an
even greater weighting in the benchmark.

Scale

Index fund management, in contrast to active management, benefits from
economies of scale. Evidence in the finance literature (Frino et al. 2004)

shows that large funds tracking a benchmark experience lower tracking error in their performance than smaller funds. Larger funds are also more easily able to adopt full replication strategies compared to smaller funds, conditional on a number of factors (including the liquidity of the benchmark).

EXTERNALITIES IN INDEX FUND MANAGEMENT

Index strategies represent a low-cost, buy-and-hold, rules-based method of portfolio management. Stocks held by passive funds are determined on the basis of the security's membership of a benchmark, and then weighted in the portfolio according to their representation in the underlying index (that is, a full replication strategy). There is no need for fundamental analysis to be undertaken in determining whether the stock represents 'fair value', and the decision to buy or sell is dictated entirely by an index committee. Indeed, it is this very aspect of investing that has generated significant debate and propaganda about the viability and appropriateness of index funds. John C. Bogle, founder of Vanguard Investments in the USA, one of the indexing pioneers of the 1970s, faced significant criticism about whether index funds were a legitimate strategy in promoting efficient, well-functioning and highly liquid capital markets.

The buy-and-hold indexing approach means that there are a number of issues that investors need to consider in determining whether the benefits of indexing (lower cost, lower turnover, lower taxation and so on) outweigh the controversial aspects of passive portfolio management. Each of these externalities is briefly discussed below.

Corporate Governance

Indexing (using full replication) does not involve selecting stocks based on any other criteria than whether the security is a constituent of the benchmark. Therefore, contrary to an investor allocating scarce resources (that is capital) to those areas in the economy that are most productive, indexing requires that assets are allocated using a mathematical and rules-based approach. To this end, passive fund managers are limited in the ways they might otherwise discipline poor company management (other than by voting as shareholders, if indeed they decide to participate at all in the voting process). Given that the full replication indexation approach allocates assets to all constituents depending on their relative benchmark weighting, a passive manager is unable to sell their ownership in the company if corporate performance has been adverse for shareholders.

Winners versus Losers

Based on the work of Haberle and Ranaldo (2004), indexing might be perceived to be a momentum-based strategy. In market-capitalization-weighted benchmarks, the larger stocks are given greater weights in the benchmark. It follows that as stocks perform strongly, their relative weight in the benchmark becomes greater, *ceteris paribus*. This means that if markets do not behave in a rational manner, and if stock prices move to levels that appear 'stretched' (or overpriced) in terms of their valuation, an indexing strategy will require a new investor to allocate a disproportionate level of total wealth to stocks that might well experience price reversals in the short term. Another example in the case of poorly performing stocks is that if a stock is expected by the market to file for bankruptcy, but remains a constituent of the benchmark, then an index approach will still require new money to be allocated to the stock irrespective of any rational or subjective view about whether the company will continue to operate into the future.

Investor Choice and Socially Responsible Investing

While there is a variety of benchmarks available to investors, including sub-indexes based on stock size and value/growth dimensions, *broad* market indexes do not cater for investors who hold social and/or moral beliefs. This is because an indexing strategy requires that pension fund trustees invest assets in a manner that is not consistent with their preferences. In other words, investors wishing to follow a passive approach and who also have strong religious, environmental, or other socially determined priorities will still be required to own stocks that are otherwise inconsistent with their wishes. Depending on the index and the preferences of the investor, an example of stocks that may not be consistent with socially responsible investing include those with poor workplace practices, poor environmental policies, or who manufacture or provide services that are not deemed to be either safe or desirable in the community. Examples of the latter relate to tobacco, alcohol, gambling, armaments/weapons manufacture, animal testing and the mining of uranium.

CONCLUSION

This chapter highlights the important role of index-oriented investments for pension funds. While index funds have been available for more than 30 years, their rapid growth has only been relatively recent, particularly since the 1990s. The primary driver of index fund growth among investors is the relative underperformance of actively managed funds documented in the literature. This should not be surprising when a benchmark, by definition, represents the weighted average sum of all investment opportunities of index constituents; hence, on average, for every winner their must be a loser (relative to the benchmark). In addition, investors have been attracted to passive investment strategies given their lower-cost structures, increased tax efficiency and wide diversification.

While index investment strategies appear simple in theory to implement, there are a number of complexities which makes perfect replication of the underlying benchmark unachievable. Therefore it is the role of an index fund manager to adopt an index replication technique that attempts to minimize tracking error in performance, while also ensuring that the fund does not engage in excessive trading and portfolio turnover. In essence, there is an inverse relation between tracking error volatility and fund trading costs. The choice of index replication technique adopted, and the tracking error tolerance permitted by the fund manager, will depend on both endogenous factors (manager's portfolio process) and exogenous factors (the nature of the indexes' liquidity as well as the rules governing amendments to the benchmark constituents). The role of an index manager is therefore to achieve returns (and risk) commensurate with the market index, conscious of the fact that market frictions, and the nature of the index representing a paper portfolio, will make exact replication of the index return impossible. Overall, evidence suggests that, on average, index funds achieve their risk-and-return objectives over the long run.

Indexing also results in investors acting in a manner that may lead to negative externalities being present in their investment arrangements. Largely these arise because an indexing approach is a rigid and rules-based methodology, and does not require an investor to act in a rational manner. Accordingly, indexing raises concerns relating to the strategy of allocating assets without regard to the investment prospects of the index constituents and the capability of exercising effective corporate governance responsibilities.

The future of indexing should witness continued growth in both the size of assets and the number of accounts delegated to passive portfolio managers. In addition, increasing economies of scale, and advances in portfolio management configuration practices, which attempts to more optimally blend active and passive portfolio management, should ensure an increasingly important role for index-linked products among pension plans globally.

NOTES

1. For this reason the evaluation period does not include data from 1987, as the October equity market crash would potentially distort the analysis.
2. Dividend imputation entitles investors in Australian companies, paying profits out as franked

dividends, to a reduction in the amount of their personal income tax. This is achieved by accounting for the corporate tax that has already been paid on profits. In other words, an investor who is taxed at their top marginal tax rate is only assessed for tax on the difference between the corporate tax rate and their top marginal tax rate if the dividends are fully franked.

3. Management expenses cover costs incurred by the fund manager associated with custodian services, trading and administration. They also include the profit earned by the fund manager.

4. The ASX rules governing the inclusion and exclusion of securities from the All-Ordinaries Index are made with regard to a stock's liquidity and market capitalization. Full replication funds may experience increased difficulties as a result of index changes, given that smaller capitalized securities have a higher probability of not meeting the All-Ordinaries Index liquidity rules.

5. For example in the USA from October 1989, Standard and Poor's pre-announced changes to the S&P 500 Index, where the index change became effective five days after the announcement. This amendment was designed to make it easier for index funds to acquire the new securities ahead of their inclusion in the index. However, because index funds rebalance portfolios on the day the change becomes effective, this allows risk arbitrageurs the opportunity to sell the stock to index funds at a premium. The Australian Stock Exchange (ASX), in a similar manner to Standard and Poor's, pre-announces changes to the All-Ordinaries Index, however the length of time between the announcement of the change and the actual index amendment depends on the size of the stock.

6. These characteristics include size, industry and dividend yield and other risk attributes such as those identified by BARRA.

REFERENCES

Beneish, M. and R. Whaley (1996), 'An anatomy of the S&P Game: The Effects of Changing the Rules', *Journal of Finance*, **51**(5): 1909–30.

Bird, R., H. Chin and M. McCrae (1983), 'The performance of Australian superannuation funds', *Australian Journal of Management*, **8**: 49–69.

Edelen, R. (1999), 'Investor flows and the assessed performance of open-end mutual funds', *Journal of Financial Economics*, **53**(3): 439–66.

Elton, E., M. Gruber, S. Das and M. Hlavka (1993), 'Efficiency with costly information: A reinterpretation of evidence from managed portfolios', *Review of Financial Studies*, **6**(1): 1–22.

Frino, A., D. Gallagher, A. Neubert and T. Oetomo (2004), 'Index design and implications for index tracking: Evidence from S&P 500 Index funds', *Journal of Portfolio Management*, **30**(2): 89–95.

Gruber, M. (1996), 'Another puzzle: The growth in actively managed mutual funds', *Journal of Finance*, **51**(3): 783–810.

Haberle, R. and A. Ranaldo (2004), 'Wolf in sheep's clothing: The active investment strategies behind index performance', UBS Global Asset Management, Working Paper.

Hallahan, T. and R. Faff (1999), 'An examination of Australian equity trusts for selectivity and market timing performance', *Journal of Multinational Financial Management*, **9**(3–4): 387–402.

Jensen, M. (1968), 'The performance of mutual funds in the period 1945–64', *Journal of Finance*, **42**(2): 389–416.

Liu, S., A. Sheikh and D. Stefek (1998), 'Optimal indexing', in A. Neubert (ed.), *Indexing for Maximum Investment Results*, Chicago, IL: GPCo Publishers.

Malkiel, B. (1995), 'Returns from investing in equity mutual funds 1971 to 1991', *Journal of Finance*, **50**(2): 549–72.

Olma, A. (1998), 'Implementing equity index portfolios', in A. Neubert (ed.), *Indexing for Maximum Investment Results*, Chicago, IL: GPCo Publishers.

Perold, A. (1988), 'The implementation shortfall: Paper versus reality', *Joural of Portfolio Management*, **14**(3): 4–9.

Robson, G. (1986), 'The investment performance of unit trusts and mutual funds in Australia for the period 1969 to 1978', *Accounting & Finance*, **26**(2): 55–79.

Sawicki, J. and F. Ong (2000), 'Evaluating managed fund performance using conditional measures: Australian evidence', *Pacific-Basin Finance Journal*, **8**(3–4): 505–28.

Sharpe, W. (1991), 'The arithmetic of active management', *Financial Analysts Journal*, **47**(1): 7–9.

5. Retirement wealth and lifetime earnings variability

Olivia S. Mitchell, John W.R. Phillips, Andrew Au and David McCarthy[1]

INTRODUCTION

To better understand the determinants of retirement preparedness, it is important to obtain extensive and detailed household information on people's pension, social security, housing and other forms of financial wealth. One excellent source is the Health and Retirement Study (HRS), which we use in this chapter to assess the factors driving retirement wealth among older Americans. Previous research showed that the median US household on the verge of retirement held about two-fifths of its retirement wealth in the form of social security promises, one-fifth in employer pension promises, and the remainder in housing and other financial assets. Prior studies also indicated that the typical older household had not adequately prepared for retirement, in that substantial additional retirement saving would be needed to smooth old-age consumption. Factors associated with greater retirement wealth accumulations included having committed to 'automatic saving' mechanisms such as company pensions and having to pay off a mortgage. This chapter extends the literature by focusing on the nexus between household retirement wealth and the variability of workers' lifetime earnings. In particular, we use the HRS linked with administrative earning records data supplied by the Social Security Administration to evaluate the relationship between lifetime earnings variability and retirement preparedness.

Our research is relevant to researchers and policymakers for several reasons. First, potential pension or social security reform proposals might have very different impacts on retiree wellbeing, depending on how specific reforms link workers' earnings profiles to their retirement benefits. For this reason, it is useful to evaluate how earnings variability (EV) differs across people of various income levels and socioeconomic characteristics. Second, while theoretical models have begun to explore correlations between financial assets and human capital, little analysis explores how labor earnings variability empirically translates into retirement wealth accumulations in the real world. Third, we explore whether retirement wealth is more powerfully associated with earnings variability *per se*, holding constant other demographic, social and economic characteristics of workers and their families, and also whether retirement wellbeing is particularly vulnerable to earnings fluctuations at particular points in the worklife cycle. In view of current macroeconomic volatility and associated unemployment and wage cut patterns, this topic should be of particular interest to pension system designers.

In what follows, we first briefly review prior studies regarding retirement wealth profiles for older Americans and describe the nature and scope of retirement saving. We then discuss the alternative measures of lifetime earnings variability used in this study and describe what the data show. Last, we demonstrate how these EV measures are related to retirement wealth measures, holding constant other socioeconomic, health status and preference factors in a multivariate statistical analysis.

PRIOR STUDIES

Our previous research used the nationally representative Health and Retirement Study linked to administrative records on earnings to explore how patterns of retirement wellbeing in the older US population are associated with differences in the length of worklife and pay levels.[2] The initial HRS cohort was first interviewed in 1992, when it was on the verge of retirement, that is age 51–61 (spouses of any age were also interviewed). Using these data, Mitchell and Moore (1998) and Moore and Mitchell (2000) measured important saving shortfalls for this cohort, concluding that the median older household would need to save 16 per cent more out of annual income each year in order to maintain consumption levels after retirement at age 62. The targeted additional saving rate was cut in half, to 8 per cent of annual income, if retirement were delayed to age 65.[3]

Subsequent analysis demonstrated that several factors played a role in retirement wealth accumulations (Mitchell et al., 2000a). These included respondents' and spouses' educational attainment, lifetime earnings, marital and children status, and ethnicity. Overall, socioeconomic variables accounted for a substantial portion of the saving deficits for retirement. In addition, health and preference proxies accounted for 20–25 per cent of explained variance in retirement wealth accumulation, and in particular, households having longer financial planning horizons were likely to be closer to saving targets. Various other factors, including depression, memory problems and earlier-than-predicted mortality, did not appear to be strongly associated with saving shortfalls. Finally, the analysis indicated that both spouses' economic status, health status and preference proxies should be taken into account to understand married couples' preparedness for retirement. Subsequent analysis by Levine et al. (2000a and b, 2002) examined how married women's earnings contributed to HRS household wellbeing in retirement. Overall, spousal effects accounted for about one-half of the explained variance in saving shortfall patterns for married households.

One key issue left unexamined in prior research is whether the timing and variability of workers' lifetime earnings patterns are powerfully related to retirement asset accumulation. Dynarski and Gruber (1997) showed that idiosyncratic earnings variation had little effect on *pre-retirement consumption*, but there has been little analysis of how fluctuations in pay might influence *post-retirement wellbeing*.[4] In the present chapter, therefore, we explore how aspects of lifetime earnings variability influence retirement wealth levels. The outcomes of special interest include levels of retirement wealth, such as social security, pension and other financial assets.

DATA, RESEARCH DESIGN AND METHODS

The HRS, along with its companion employer pension and social security earnings and benefits records, affords a unique opportunity to analyze the influence of lifetime earnings variability on retirement wealth. In addition to containing rich health and demographic information, the linked HRS data file provides a comprehensive picture of workers' lifetime earnings patterns. These are obtained from Social Security Administration records of workers' taxable earnings from 1950 to 1991, provided with respondent consent. We use these lifetime earnings records to generate measures of lifetime earnings fluctuations for sample respondents as well as their spouses, and then we link these to Mitchell et al.'s data file to examine retirement wealth.

The variables used in our analysis involve measures of retirement wealth and workers' earnings variability. Here we focus on the latter, since retirement wealth measures are described elsewhere (Levine et al., 2000a, 2002; also see the Data Appendix). Slightly different earnings information was available from the Social Security Administration, depending on when the data were collected.[5] For the entire period 1950–91, earnings up to the social security tax ceiling were available; using these we compute workers' average indexed monthly earnings (AIME) as per social security formulas, which averaged $1400 per month for an annual earnings level of approximately $19 500 (all dollar figures are expressed in 1992 dollars). In addition, for the period 1980–91, so-called 'W2' earnings were also available, which include labor compensation above the taxable social security earnings ceiling. Figure 5.1 indicates how often annual earnings were at the taxable cap, which for women was only 2 per cent of the years between ages 20 and 50, as well as for each

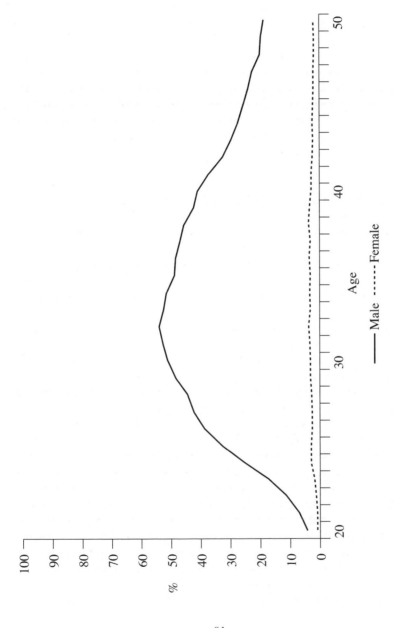

Figure 5.1 Percentage of respondents with capped earnings by age and sex

decade of life (20–29, 30–39 and 40–49). Men were more likely to have capped earnings, with the percentage at 27 per cent during their twenties, 50 per cent in their thirties and 27 per cent in their forties. To mitigate the impact of such capping, we use the higher of the social security and W2 values for years that both reports are available, and for other years (that is, before 1980), we run year-specific Tobits to generate predicted earnings for those at the cap that year.[6] Finally, we create measures of lifetime earnings variability.

One way to represent lifetime earnings variability relies on a concept familiar from financial markets, namely the standard deviation of lifetime earnings. For this chapter, we employ this measure normalized by own average earnings, which is the coefficient of variation (COEFVAR). One COEFVAR measure covers the entire period between the worker's twentieth and fiftieth birthdays, which we call 'lifetime COEFVAR'. In addition, we also compute the coefficient of variation over each decade of the worker's life, when the individual was in his twenties, thirties and forties (respectively COEFVAR20, 30 and 40). These decadal EV measures help identify patterns of earnings variability at different ages, which allow us to determine whether the timing of variability affects retirement wealth accumulation.

Of course, if we were to only use COEFVAR, this would presume that earnings variability has a symmetrical impact – that is, an earnings drop or an increase of the same size would have the same effect on key outcomes of interest. Since this is not *a priori* clear, we also develop an asymmetric EV measure which focuses only on earnings declines. We call this the 'expected hit' to earnings (EXPHIT), which allows us to evaluate whether earnings drops have a stronger negative effect on retirement wellbeing than do symmetric fluctuations *per se*. Lifetime EXPHIT captures the real wage loss in the event that it occurs over the worker's lifetime, multiplied by the probability that he or she experienced a loss (normalized by own average earnings). In this sense, it is a shortfall measure akin to those used in insurance and risk analysis. Decadal measures are also derived (EXPHIT20, 30 and 40), measuring, respectively, the conditional expected earnings drops when the worker was in his or her twenties, thirties and forties.

Descriptive statistics for these EV measures are provided in Table 5.1. Focusing first on the symmetric term, it is interesting that lifetime COEFVAR is larger than unity, but the measure is larger for younger workers and it shrinks by a third later in life. Thus earnings variability measured by COEF-VAR declines with age. Turning to the asymmetric measure, the expected earnings loss conditional on having an earnings hit (EXPHIT) averaged about 18 per cent of lifetime earnings overall. The decade-specific measures are larger during the worker's twenties and forties and smaller during the worker's thirties. In other words, the asymmetric EV measure displays less of a clear age decline than the symmetric one. We also offer a correlation matrix of the

Table 5.1 Earnings levels and variability measures for HRS respondents (weighted data)

COEFVAR40	0.623	0.707
EXPHIT	0.177	0.176
EXPHIT20	0.183	0.369
EXPHIT30	0.146	0.257
EXPHIT40	0.201	0.284

Correlation between variability measures

	COEFVAR	COEFVAR 20	COEFVAR 30	COEFVAR 40	EXPHIT	EXPHIT 20	EXPHIT 30
COEFVAR20	0.333						
COEFVAR30	0.290	0.214					
COEFVAR40	0.463	0.134	0.214				
EXPHIT	0.736	0.330	0.327	0.464			
EXPHIT20	0.612	0.368	0.139	0.213	0.669		
EXPHIT30	0.278	0.089	0.332	0.181	0.510	0.021	
EXPHIT40	0.312	0.062	0.129	0.399	0.523	–0.039	0.049

Distribution of EV measures by AIME quintile

AIME quintile	COEFVAR	EXPHIT
1	2.294	0.403
2	1.112	0.178
3	0.774	0.128
4	0.620	0.099
5	0.623	0.075

Variable definitions:

Average lifetime earnings:	average annual earnings over the lifetime (1992 dollars)
AIME:	Average indexed monthly earnings over the lifetime (1992 dollars)
COEFVAR:	Coefficient of variation ages 20–50
COEFVAR#:	Coefficient of variation by decade of life
EXPHIT:	(Probability of wage loss * average size of loss)/(own lifetime average earnings)
EXPHIT#:	(Probability of wage loss * average size of loss)/(own lifetime average earnings) by decade of life

Source: Authors' calculations using the Health and Retirement Survey.

six EV measures developed, which shows higher correlation between the lifetime measures than the decade-specific measures. The decadal EXPHIT measures are less correlated among themselves than are the symmetric COEFVAR measures. We also show that both EV measures vary by lifetime earnings levels, as proxied by AIME quintiles. In both the symmetric and asymmetric

Table 5.2 Factors associated with lifetime and decadal earnings variability (weighted data)

	COEFVAR	COEFVAR 20	COEFVAR 30	COEFVAR 40	EXPHIT	EXPHIT 20	EXPHIT 30	EXPHIT 40
AIME1000	-0.622**	-0.246**	-0.324**	-0.473**	-0.129**	-0.179**	-0.106**	-0.101**
	(0.013)	(0.015)	(0.015)	(0.013)	(0.003)	(0.007)	(.005)	(0.006)
Female	-0.100**	0.284**	0.152**	-0.352**	-0.056**	0.022	-0.084**	-0.104**
	(0.025)	(0.028)	(0.028)	(0.025)	(0.006)	(0.013)	(0.010)	(0.011)
Age	0.031**	0.020**	0.013**	0.022**	0.002**	0.006**	-0.004**	0.005**
	(0.003)	(0.003)	(0.003)	(0.003)	(0.001)	(0.001)	(0.001)	(0.001)
Black	-0.228**	-0.054	-0.074*	-0.181**	-0.053**	-0.111**	-0.004	-0.051**
	(0.034)	(0.038)	(0.038)	(0.033)	(0.008)	(0.018)	(0.013)	(0.015)
Hispanic	0.021	-0.242**	-0.023	0.022	-0.033**	-0.096**	-0.025	0.023
	(0.043)	(0.047)	(0.047)	(0.042)	(0.010)	(0.022)	(0.016)	(0.019)
LTHS	-0.007	0.019	-0.096**	-0.044	0.011	-0.046**	0.030**	0.045**
	(0.025)	(0.028)	(0.028)	(0.025)	(0.006)	(0.013)	(0.010)	(0.011)
BAplus	0.212**	0.184**	0.124**	0.156**	0.018**	0.011	0.004	0.036**
	(0.020)	(0.022)	(0.022)	(0.020)	(0.005)	(0.010)	(0.008)	(0.009)
Evdivorce	-0.142**	-0.046*	0.017	0.018	-0.003	-0.057**	0.033**	0.017*
	(0.019)	(0.021)	(0.021)	(0.019)	(0.004)	(0.010)	(0.007)	(0.008)
Evwidow	-0.099**	-0.069	-0.049	0.033	-0.01	-0.058**	0.025*	0
	(0.032)	(0.036)	(0.036)	(0.032)	(0.008)	(0.010)	(0.013)	(0.014)
ADLany	0.015	0.013	-0.02	0.029	0.039**	0.032	0.050**	0.038*
	(0.038)	(0.042)	(0.042)	(0.037)	(0.008)	(0.020)	(0.015)	(0.017)
Constant	0.309	0.034	0.339	0.191	0.248**	0.147	0.535**	0.087
	(0.158)	(0.175)	(0.175)	(0.155)	(0.035)	(0.081)	(0.061)	(0.069)

Note: * significant at 5%; ** significant at 1%.
Standard errors in parentheses.

Variable definitions:

AIME1000:	Respondent AIME/1000
Female:	Respondent female (=1), male (=0)
Age:	Respondent's age in 1992
Black:	Respondent black (=1), not black (=0)
Hispanic:	Respondent Hispanic (=1), not Hispanic (=0)
LTHS:	Respondent with less than a high school degree (=1), greater than high school (=0)
BAplus:	Respondent with a college degree of greater (=1), less than a college degree (=0)
Evdivorced:	Respondent was ever divorced
Evwidow:	Respondent was ever widowed
ADLany:	Respondent has difficulty performing any activities of daily living (ADL)

Source: Authors' calculations using the Health and Retirement Survey.

measures, it is clear that earnings volatility is highest for people in lower life-time earnings quintiles. In the analysis of retirement wealth, below, we explore separately how both lifetime EV and age-specific EV influence outcomes.

Further descriptive information on earnings variability appears in Table 5.2, where we regress lifetime and decadal EV measures on a vector of controls including the respondent's lifetime earnings level (AIME), sex, education, race/ethnic status and marital status. In addition, a health variable is included to assess whether the respondent was unable to carry out activities of daily living; this is clearly a noisy measure of lifetime health problems, but it still can provide insight into functional limitations. The estimates confirm our earlier conclusion that workers with higher lifetime earnings levels are also those with lower earnings variability, and the conclusion is strengthened after holding other factors constant. This trend is relevant for both lifetime and decadal EV measures, though the negative age relationship becomes stronger in the case of the symmetric measure, COEFVAR, but not for the asymmetric measure, EXPHIT. Evidently, the two EV concepts behave differently over the worklife. Table 5.2 also indicates that several demographic factors are significantly associated with EV patterns, even after controlling for lifetime earnings (via AIME). Surprisingly, both EV measures are lower for blacks than whites and for women than men. There is no systematic relationship for the Hispanic variable. Respondents with greater educational attainment are more likely to have higher COEFVAR late in life, but for EXPHIT the educational relationship is weak. Differences by sex emerge by decade of age, since women appear to have higher symmetric variability early in life and lower symmetric and asymmetric variability late in life as compared to men. Being divorced is associated with lower earnings variability early in life, while being widowed is associated with higher earnings hits later in life. The health limitation variable is positively associated with the asymmetric EV measure over the lifetime and later in life.

EARNINGS VARIABILITY AND RETIREMENT WEALTH

Before turning to the evidence tying EV measures to retirement wealth, a few comments are in order about anticipated results.

Hypotheses

First, we test whether EV influences wealth differently, depending on the type of retirement wealth under consideration. In the USA, for instance, the social security benefit formula is a redistributive function of average lifetime earnings, and thus it provides higher replacement rates to lifetime low-earners. By contrast, private pension benefit rules are less redistributive, mainly because they usually focus on final earnings replacement. Consequently, it is reasonable to expect that pension wealth levels would be far more sensitive to earnings variability than social security wealth, particularly for nonmarried individuals. The case for married couples is less clear, since a nonworking spouse is entitled to social security benefits based on his or her working spouse's lifetime earnings; this may make the household's total social security wealth more sensitive to an earner's pay fluctuations than in the case of a single person. Hence we have:

Hypothesis 1: Social security wealth levels are less sensitive to earnings variability than pension and financial wealth levels.

Second, we hypothesize that any given earnings fluctuation would have a larger effect on nonmarried workers' wealth than on married household wealth levels. This is because lifetime pay fluctuations would be expected to have a direct impact on retirement wealth for single individuals. By contrast, married households have opportunities for risk-sharing which could mitigate this link. For example, the wife might boost her labor market work when her husband experiences a negative earnings shock (this is the long-discussed 'added worker' effect in the labor economics literature).[7] There is even the possibility that, through assortative mating, individuals would seek marital partners who have human capital risk characteristics orthogonal to their own, so as to more effectively manage risk within marriage. In any event, smaller sensitivity of retirement wealth to EV measures might be expected for married couples than for single individuals. Hence we have:

Hypothesis 2: Retirement wealth for nonmarried workers will be more sensitive to EV measures than for married households.

Third, we hypothesize that financial wealth may be the form of wealth most sensitive to pay variability, of all the types of wealth we examine. This is because, as mentioned above, social security and pensions tend to be formulaically related to earnings. Housing wealth is also less likely to be influenced by lifetime earnings fluctuations, by virtue of the fact that mortgages must be paid on a regular basis. By contrast, financial wealth buildups have more of a discretionary character, requiring the individual to save rather than spend liquid income. Recent studies on how hard workers find it to exhibit self-control when it comes to saving (Madrian and Shea, 2001) therefore would imply that automatic savings mechanisms are better able to build up retirement assets than less automatic means. We would also anticipate that changes in other wealth could be most easily offset by changing financial assets, which again implies that this type of wealth would be treated as a buffer stock sort of holding. This might be less true of housing wealth, as compared to nonhousing financial assets. Hence we have:

Hypothesis 3: Financial wealth will be more sensitive to pay fluctuations than other forms of wealth, including housing, pension and social security.

Fourth, we hypothesize that earnings variability early in life would be expected to have only a negligible effect on retirement wealth, since shocks would have a longer period to be smoothed by changes in consumption and/or saving. Conversely, earnings shocks closer to retirement would be expected to have a larger impact on retirement wealth, since fewer years remain to offset unexpected changes in earnings.

Hypothesis 4: Earnings variability early in life would be anticipated to have a smaller effect on retirement wealth than later in life.

In what follows, we evaluate the empirical data for evidence on each of these hypotheses.

Findings for Earnings Variability

Our empirical goal is to determine whether and how EV measures are linked to retirement wealth, controlling for socioeconomic, health and preference factors of respondents. In this section, we use multivariate analysis to explore whether fluctuations in earnings over the life cycle are associated with greater or lesser levels of pension, social security, housing and other financial wealth. Summary statistics for the key wealth measures appear in Table 5.3. Since wealth has a highly skewed distribution, mean household wealth for a 62-year-old HRS respondent was around $633 000 in our data, while median total household wealth was approximately $495 000 (all in 1992 dollars).[8] Total retirement wealth according to our formulation is made up of four components: employer pensions, social security, net housing wealth, and other financial wealth (stocks, bonds, etc.). For our sample, medians amounted to about $139 000 for pension wealth, around $138 000 in social security wealth, about $67 000 in housing equity and $151 000 in financial wealth.

To evaluate how retirement wealth is associated with earnings variability among the older population, we regress retirement wealth measures on the key EV measures of interest, along with a range of important control variables.[9] Results for social security, pension, financial and housing wealth appear in Table 5.4, where separate equations are given for nonmarried and married households.

Turning first to social security wealth, we had posited that variation in life-

Table 5.3   *Total retirement wealth and components for HRS respondents (1992 dollars, weighted data)*

	μ	σ	Median 10% of AIME
Social security wealth	151 197	55 529	137 942
Pension welath	186 158	285 312	139 408
Financial wealth	217 804	630 648	150 791
Net housing wealth	78 265	84 929	66 813
Total wealth	633 425	750 497	494 957

Note: Retirement wealth measures are contingent on retirement at age 62.

Variable definitions:

Social security wealth:	Total household social security wealth
Pension wealth:	Total household pension wealth from all pensions
Financial wealth:	Total household financial wealth
Net housing wealth:	Total household nonfinancial wealth
Total wealth:	Total household wealth = pension wealth + social security wealth + financial wealth + net housing wealth

Source: Authors' calculations using the Health and Retirement Survey.

time earnings would have relatively little impact since the benefit rules use smooth earnings in calculating benefits. It is interesting, therefore, that for nonmarried households, coefficients on both lifetime EV measures are negative and statistically significant in the social security wealth regressions. This suggests that earnings fluctuations in fact do have a detrimental impact on social security benefits, which could be the result of the fact that periods of joblessness can affect workers' later insured status for social security benefits, including people who are jobless for parts of their lives or work in uncovered jobs (Levine et al., 2000). In other words, attachment to 'good jobs' early in one's career can make retirement wealth much more secure. This is a reasonable explanation for the nonmarried sample, since we find that early-life pay variability does not hurt social security wealth, but negative pay fluctuations in later middle age have a strong negative effect for singles (Hypotheses 1 and 4). For married workers, social security wealth has a rather different impact, since all EV lifetime measures are positive when statistically significant. A possible explanation for this is that, according to the benefits formula, nonworking spouses receive social security benefits that are a multiple of workers' retiree benefits, and since the formula is redistributive, negative earnings fluctuations are not directly translated into lower household benefits.

Table 5.4 *Effects of earnings variation on (ln) retirement wealth (weighted data)*

Nonmarried households

Variable name	Social security wealth		Pension wealth		Housing wealth		Financial wealth	
	COEFVAR	EXPHIT	COEFVAR	EXPHIT	COEFVAR	EXPHIT	COEFVAR	EXPHIT
Lifetime earnings variance	-0.55**	-0.382**	-0.703*	-7.065**	0.303	-0.26	0.669**	1.195
	(0.013)	(0.061)	(0.274)	(1.251)	(0.282)	(1.304)	(0.167)	(0.775)
Earnings variance ages 20–29	0.022*	-0.061*	0.407	-1.900**	0.205	0.97	0.259*	0.899**
	(0.010)	(0.028)	(0.216)	(0.575)	(0.222)	(0.596)	(0.132)	(0.337)
Earnings variance ages 30–39	-0.017	-0.115**	-0.163	-1.997**	0.611**	-0.844	.038	-0.971*
	(0.011)	(0.033)	(0.219)	(0.682)	(0.224)	(0.707)	(0.134)	(0.453)
Earning variance ages 40–49	-0.67**	-0.197**	-0.49	-2.808**	-0.245	-0.75	0.168	0.681
	(0.014)	(0.037)	(0.278)	(0.752)	(0.286)	(0.780)	(0.171)	(0.462)

Table 5.4 *Continued*

Married households

Variable name	Social security wealth				Pension wealth			
	COEFVAR		EXPHIT		COEFVAR		EXPHIT	
	Respondent	Spouse	Respondent	Spouse	Respondent	Spouse	Respondent	Spouse
Lifetime earnings variance	0.041** (0.006)	0.005 (0.005)	0.124** (0.025)	0.006 (0.017)	-0.106 (0.159)	-0.336** (0.120)	-4.195** (0.703)	-2.249** (0.547)
Earnings variance ages 20–29	0.017** (0.005)	0.023** (0.004)	0.067** (0.09)	0.033** (0.009)	0.017 (0.145)	0.169 (0.135)	-0.636* (0.294)	-0.573* (0.232)
Earnings variance ages 30–39	0.005 (0.005)	-0.002 (0.005)	0.03 (0.016)	-0.025 (0.014)	0.042 (0.140)	-0.094 (0.133)	-1.568** (0.482)	-0.993** (0.362)
Earnings variance ages 40–49	0.004 (0.007)	-0.001 (0.007)	0.014 (0.015)	-0.009 (0.012)	-0.1 (0.160)	-0.277 (0.161)	-1.685** (0.367)	-1.736** (0.287)

Table 5.4 Continued

Married households

Variable name	Housing wealth				Financial wealth			
	COEFVAR		EXPHIT		COEFVAR		EXPHIT	
	Respondent	Spouse	Respondent	Spouse	Respondent	Spouse	Respondent	Spouse
Lifetime earnings variance	0.279** (0.094)	0.153* (0.077)	-0.033 (0.422)	-0.045 (0.390)	0.216** (0.059)	0.135** (0.47)	0.690** (0.252)	0.442* (0.177)
Earnings variance ages 20–29	-0.112 (0.100)	0.026 (0.088)	0.343* (0.164)	0.219 (0.167)	0.098 (0.052)	0.067 (0.050)	0.325** (0.099)	0.222** (0.081)
Earnings variance ages 30–39	0.003 (0.084)	0.024 (0.085)	-0.084 (0.265)	-0.22 (0.204)	0.067 (0.048)	-0.008 (0.051)	0.118 (0.173)	0.008 (0.134)
Earnings variance ages 40–49	0.093 (0.094)	0.061 (0.091)	-0.574* (0.235)	-0.029 (0.183)	0.089 (0.063)	0.166** (0.060)	0.104 (0.149)	0.079 (0.148)

Note: * significant at 5%; ** significant at 1%.
Standard errors in parentheses.
The models of lifetime earnings variance include only one EV measure. Remaining models include all three decadal measures.

Source: Authors' calculations using the Health and Retirement Study. Complete regressions results are available upon request.

Turning to the results for pension wealth, we find that, among nonmarried respondents, pension wealth is more sensitive to earnings losses than symmetric earnings EV measures, and in all cases this wealth measure is more sensitive than social security wealth. For both nonmarried and married respondents, the EXPHIT measure is large in magnitude, negative and statistically significant, particularly later in life. This makes sense given that DB pensions in particular tend to reward high final salaries with higher eventual benefits; the effect is similar but less signficiant for married respondents.

Table 5.4 also indicates how EV measures are associated with housing and financial wealth. Results for nonmarried persons again differ from those of marrieds. For singles, symmetric earnings fluctuations are associated with higher housing wealth and only for people in their thirties, but asymmetric shocks have no statistically significant impact. By contrast, for married couples, symmetric lifetime EV is associated with higher total housing wealth, perhaps indicating substitution between couples' work effort when pay levels fluctuate. Results for financial wealth also appear in Table 5.4, where we see that COEFVAR estimates for nonmarried respondents are significant and more positive than in the other equations (Hypothesis 3). Consequently, it appears that financial wealth rises when other forms of wealth decline in times of pay volatility, acting as a buffer asset in times of earnings variability. The lifetime EXPHIT coefficient is not significant for singles, but it is significant and positive during the earlier years. By contrast, among married couples, higher EV raises financial wealth just as in most of the other cases. Consequently, for couples, financial wealth does not appear to act as a buffer asset in times of earnings variability.[10]

For ease of interpretation, we next translate the coefficients reported in the previous tables into dollar figures. This was done by first predicting retirement wealth by type for each respondent in the sample using the models presented in Table 5.4; we then simulated how retirement wealth would change from a 10 per cent increase in each EV measure. We report the difference between predicted and simulated values as the marginal effect of a change in EV on retirement wealth. Means of the marginal effects for each wealth type by the EV measure are reported in Table 5.5.

One clear lesson is that the impact of EV measures on retirement wealth is fairly small compared to the mean wealth measures reported in Table 5.3. In the case of social security wealth, a 10 per cent increase in the symmetric lifetime EV measure (COEFVAR) is associated with $407 lower social security wealth for nonmarried respondents and $787 more for married couples. Having higher earnings hits (EXPHIT) has a similar effect for nonmarried respondents, but less of an effect for married households. Measured effects for pensions are more important, and the measures work in the direction of reducing pension wealth. Symmetric earnings variation appears to have a positive

Table 5.5   *Mean simulated effect of a 10% increase in EV on retirement wealth (weighted data)*

	10% increase in mean of:	
	COEFVAR	EXPHIT
Social security wealth:		
Nonmarried	−407	−448
Married	787	391
Pension wealth:		
Nonmarried	−1574	−1969
Married	−415	−2787
Financial wealth:		
Nonmarried	2405	622
Married	2527	1310
Housing wealth:		
Nonmarried	115	−15
Married	1371	−25

Note: Derived using the regressions results described in the text and reported in Table 5.4.

Source: Authors' calculations using the Health and Retirement Study.

effect on the financial wealth of both married and unmarried respondents (with a 10 per cent increase associated with more financial wealth of about $2405 and $2527, respectively). The effects of lifetime earnings drops on financial wealth appear to be larger for married couples than single respondents ($1310 compared to $622), but both effects are small compared to the positive effects for COEFVAR. Since the only EV coefficients with significance in Table 5.4 for net housing wealth are the COEFVAR measures for married couples ($1371), it is not surprising that the calculated marginal effects for the other cases are quite small, ranging from $15 to $115.

CONCLUSIONS

This research had two goals: first, to see how earnings variability (EV) differs in the population according to income levels and socioeconomic characteristics; and second, to examine whether and how pay variability over the lifetime is associated with retirement wealth levels. Our most interesting findings using HRS data matched with administrative records on lifetime earnings are as follows:

- Workers with higher lifetime earnings *levels* experience lower earnings *variability*. This conclusion is robust to controls for lifetime income levels and sociodemographic factors.
- The inverse relationship between lifetime pay and lifetime earnings variability grows statistically stronger with age in the case of the symmetric EV measure, COEFVAR, but weaker for the asymmetric measure, EXPHIT. Evidently, the two EV concepts behave differently over the worklife.

The second phase of our analysis used a multivariate model to relate the various EV measures to retirement wealth measures. Results point to several conclusions, holding other things constant:

- Retirement wealth is more sensitive to earnings variability for nonmarried individuals than for married households.
- Focusing on wealth components, we find that social security wealth is less responsive over the lifetime to earnings variability measures than other forms of wealth when results are statistically significant. For nonmarried workers, the effect is negative for asymmetric pay fluctuations early in life, but for couples the relationship is positive. These patterns, we argue, result from eligibility and benefit rules.
- Pension wealth accumulations are sensitive to negative earnings fluctuations, especially so for nonmarried persons later in life. This result may stem from the manner in which defined benefit pension plan formulas heavily rely on earnings near retirement.
- Other financial wealth does not act as a buffer asset for couples but does for singles, given earnings variability.

In sum, earnings variability appears to have interesting and powerful effects on retirement assets. The implication is that market volatility harms not only covered workers' short-term retirement saving, but it can also undermine longer-run retiree wellbeing. Analysts focusing on the retirement impact of scary markets must take due account of these far-reaching consequences.

DATA APPENDIX

Earnings Measures

The data used to compute earnings variability measures are derived from social security earnings histories provided under restricted access conditions. Social security taxable earnings are available for 1950–91 and for 1980–91, we also had access to W2 earnings, which indicate total earnings even if pay exceeds the taxable earnings ceiling in a given year. For the EV measures described in the text, we used the greater of W2 or social security taxable earnings for years from 1980 on. For years before 1980, we follow Engelhardt and Cunningham (2002) in using right-censored Tobit models to generate predicted values of year-specific real earnings, using a vector of explanatory variables including polynominals in age and education, controls for race and sex, marital status, longest occupation, interactions of the above, and parents' educational attainment. Predicted earnings were substituted for capped earnings if they were greater than the taxable maximum; in a handful of cases (0.5 per cent) earnings were predicted to be higher than $1 million and were set to $1 million for the analysis (this was necessary only once or twice by decade of age for individual workers).

Retirement Wealth

Retirement wealth was derived for all age-eligible respondents in the HRS data file surveyed in 1992, along with real values of retirement wealth expected if the head retired at 62.[11] The 1992 measures include expected present values of contingent future income (pensions, social security), along with financial assets and housing wealth (1992 dollars). To project retirement wealth to age 62, we forecasted (see Mitchell and Moore, 2000) financial wealth by projecting four types of household assets, with future growth rates depending on their past trajectories: (1) net financial wealth, which includes such assets as savings, investments, business assets, and non-residential real estate less outstanding debt not related to housing; (2) net housing wealth – the current market value of residential housing less outstanding mortgage debt; (3) pension wealth, or the present value of retirement benefits; and (4) present value of social security. For instance, housing wealth is projected using HRS responses on the purchase price of each participant's house, year of purchase, and mortgage payment amount and frequency. Interest rates are drawn from the average interest rate for households in the American Housing Survey with the same year of purchase. Given these interest rates, we then determine amortization schedules for mortgages and project reduction in housing debt over time. This in turn implies an increase in net housing wealth. Pension wealth is projected to retirement based on the plan provisions of employer-provided summary plan descriptions and HRS data on salary and tenure of service where appropriate. Individuals are assumed to remain with their current employer until retirement age and invest their pensions, if they have authority to do so, and returns assumed on defined contribution pensions are consistent with historical averages. Mortality follows actuarial tables obtained from the Social Security Administration. Social security wealth is derived from the earning and projected benefits file (EPBF) as described in Mitchell et al. (2000b).

NOTES

1. The researchers acknowledge support from the Social Security Administration via the Michigan Retirement Research Center at the University of Michigan, under subcontract to the University of Pennsylvania. Additional support was provided by the Pension Research Council at the Wharton School and the Huebner Foundation. Earlier versions of this chapter were presented at the Fifth Annual Joint Conference of the Retirement Research Consortium, May 2003, Washington, DC and the 11th Annual Colloquium of Superannuation Researchers, July 2003, Sydney, Australia. Comments and suggestions from Gary Engelhardt and Eytan Sheshinksi are appreciated. Opinions are solely those of the authors and not of the institutions with which the authors are affiliated. This research is part of the NBER programs on Aging and Labor Economics. ©2004 Mitchell, Phillips, Au and McCarthy. All rights reserved.
2. See, for example, Levine et al. (2000a and b, 2002); Mitchell and Moore (1998); Mitchell et al. (2000); and Moore and Mitchell (2000).
3. Related research by Venti and Wise (1998) also uses the HRS to examine the dispersion of retirement wealth, but it employed respondent pension descriptions instead of employer-provided data, and it also omits social security wealth which we have argued is a substantial element of the retiree portfolio. That analysis does include controls for lifetime earnings levels but it does not examine earnings variability, as we do here. Work by Engen et al. (1999) and Scholz et al. (2003) also uses HRS to analyze retirement saving adequacy. Their findings, using different techniques, suggests that undersaving does exist but that it is not as serious a problem as reported in other work. While these studies are careful to consider lifetime earnings, they do not specifically consider lifetime variation in earnings.
4. Hurd and Zissimopoulos (2003) analyze the impact of unexpected declines in earnings growth levels, whereas we focus on first-differences in earnings trajectories.
5. Because of the confidential nature of the administrative data, researchers may access them only under restricted conditions; see www.umich.edu/~hrswww for details. The data were obtained for a majority of HRS respondents and spouses providing permission to link their survey data with administrative records supplied by the Social Security Administration and also with pension plan descriptions provided by respondents' employers; see Mitchell et al. (2000), and Gustman et al. (1999). A match with SS earnings records was feasible for approximately 75 per cent of the respondents; in addition we dropped approximately 700 married respondents from the analysis due to missing data on spouse lifetime earnings. While omitting these nonmatched cases might bias the sample, if those with a matched file differ from those lacking a match, early analysis suggests little reason for any concern. The analysis also excludes respondents reporting zero social security earnings, but positive W2 earnings for at least three years during the period 1980–91. This subset of workers probably did not contribute to social security over the lifetime and, consequently, their reported earnings from 1950–80 are not accurate representations of actual earnings.
6. This approach (results not reported here) follows Engelhart and Cunningham (2002); see also the Data Appendix.
7. A caveat to this anticipated difference by marital status, of course, is that people who report themselves as nonmarried on the verge of retirement may well have been married earlier in life, which would mitigate observed marital status differences in the EV coefficients. The models also control for marital history (ever married and ever divorced) as well as for the number of children, for both married and currently nonmarried respondents.
8. In keeping with past practice, we report the median 10 per cent of the distribution. These figures are comparable to those reported by Moore and Mitchell (2000).
9. Controls include AIME, several health status measures, education measures, marital status

indicators, number of children, sex, age, race/ethnicity, risk aversion and planning horizon indicators, and whether the worker ever had a defined benefit or a defined contribution pension plan. Equations for married respondents include the relevant characteristics of their spouses, including spousal EV measures. For additional discussion see Mitchell et al. (2000).

10. Rather than reviewing all the results for other independent variables, we simply summarize here the other results available from the authors on request. In general, the results are sensible and conform to those reported in our earlier work. Not surprisingly, single as well as married workers with higher levels of AIMEs tend to have accumulated statistically significantly larger pension, social security, and financial assets, as well as housing wealth, across the board. Higher educational attainment is generally associated with higher retirement wealth levels. Larger families tend to have less wealth than smaller ones, perhaps reflecting constraints on saving. Hispanic sample members tend to have rather low wealth, but there is no significant relationship for Black respondents in equations that control for earnings variation. Health and preference controls also appear to be linked to retirement wealth in predictable ways. Those having difficulty with activities of daily living (ADLs), who are pessimistic about surviving to age 75, smokers, and those who have low cognitive scores, tend to have less wealth than their counterparts. Moderate drinking is associated with relatively higher wealth than not drinking at all. The models also control for a number of 'preference proxy' variables, including a measure of risk aversion that uses responses from a battery of questions on gambles to determine a respondent's taste for risk. Here we find that risk-averse respondents tend to hold more wealth than do their risk-taker counterparts. We also find, consistent with prior work, that those stating they have relatively long planning horizons hold more retirement wealth than do respondents with shorter horizons. Finally, we included a variable identifying which respondents contacted the Social Security Administration to learn about their benefit amounts. Probably not surprisingly, those who did contact SSA had less wealth than those who did not, overall.

11. This discussion follows Mitchell et al. (2000a).

REFERENCES

Dynarksi, Susan and Jon Gruber (1997), 'Can families smooth variable earnings?', *BPEA*, **1**: 229–303.

Engelhardt, Gary and Christopher R. Cunningham (2002), 'Federal tax policy, employer matching, and 401(k) saving: Evidence from HRS W-2 records', *National Tax Journal*, **55**(3): 617–45.

Engen, Eric M., William G. Gale and Cori E. Uccello (1999), 'The adequacy of household saving', *Brookings Papers on Economic Activity*, Washington, DC: Brookings Institution.

Gustman, Alan, Olivia S. Mitchell, Andrew A. Samwick and Thomas L. Steinmeier (1999), 'Pension and social security wealth in the health and retirement study', in Robert Willis (ed.), *Wealth, Work, and Health: Innovations in Survey Measurement in the Social Sciences*, Ann Arbor, MI: University of Michigan Press: 150–208.

Hurd, Michael and Julie Zissimopoulos (2003), 'Saving for retirement: Wage growth and unexpected events', RAND Working Paper, presented at the 5th RRC Conference, May, Washington, DC.

Levine, Phillip, Olivia S. Mitchell and James F. Moore (2000a), 'Women on the verge of retirement: Predictors of retiree well-being', in O.S. Mitchell, B. Hammond and A. Rappaport (eds), *Forecasting Retirement Needs and Retirement Wealth*, Philadelphia, PA: University of Pennsylvania Press: 167–207.

Levine, Phillip, Olivia S. Mitchell and John Phillips (2000b), 'A benefit of one's own: Older women and social security', *Social Security Bulletin*, **63**(3): 47–54.

Levine, Phillip, Olivia S. Mitchell and John Phillips (2002), 'Worklife determinants of retirement income differentials between men and women', in Z. Bodie, B. Hammond and O.S. Mitchell (eds), *Innovations in Retirement Financing*, Philadelphia, PA: University of Pennsylvania Press: 50–73.

Madrian, Brigitte and Dennis Shea (2001), 'The power of suggestion: Inertia in 401(k) participation and savings behavior', *Quarterly Journal of Economics*, **116**: 1149–87.

Mitchell, Olivia S. and James Moore (1998), 'Retirement wealth accumulation and decumulation: New developments and outstanding opportunities', *Journal of Risk and Insurance*, **65**(3): 371–400.

Mitchell, Olivia S., James Moore and John Phillips (2000a), 'Explaining retirement saving shortfalls', in O.S. Mitchell, B. Hammond and A. Rappaport (eds), *Forecasting Retirement Needs and Retirement Wealth*, Philadelphia, PA: University of Pennsylvania Press: 139–66.

Mitchell, Olivia S., Jan Olson and Thomas Steinmeier (2000b), 'Earnings and projected benefits', in O.S. Mitchell, B. Hammond and A. Rappaport (eds), *Forecasting Retirement Needs and Retirement Wealth*. Philadelphia, PA: University of Pennsylvania Press: 139–163.

Moore James and Olivia S. Mitchell (2000), 'Projected retirement wealth and saving adequacy', in O.S. Mitchell, B. Hammond and A. Rappaport (eds), *Forecasting Retirement Needs and Retirement Wealth*, Philadelphia, PA: University of Pennsylvania Press: 68–94.

Scholz, John Karl, Ananth Seshadri and Surachai Khitatrakun (2003), 'Are Americans saving "optimally" for retirement?' Working Paper, University of Wisconsin–Madison, WI (December).

Venti, Steven and David Wise (1998), 'The cause of wealth dispersion of retirement: Choice or chance?' *AER Papers and Proceedings*, **88**(2): 185–91.

6. How have older workers responded to scary markets?

Jonathan Gardner and Mike Orszag

INTRODUCTION

The large declines in equity markets observed in the UK and the USA in 2001 and 2002 had a significant impact on the retirement savings of many individuals approaching retirement. This decline in markets and savings offers a natural experiment from which we examine how individuals adjust their labour supply when markets move in the wrong direction. There is some limited macroeconomic evidence that the decline in equity markets did lead to a fall in the number of individuals retiring early. Eschtruth and Gemus (2002) report a significant increase in the labour market participation of older men in the USA and discuss the decline in the stock market as one reason for this decline. In the UK, the economic activity rate of men over 65 in March 2003 was at its highest level since 1992 and roughly 20 per cent higher than at the end of 2000. However, this must be treated with caution, both because of the level of aggregation of these data and also because there are many other factors at work influencing labour supply.

In order to study the response of individuals to bear markets, Watson Wyatt designed and commissioned a study of some 4000 individuals aged 50–64 in the UK, which went into the field in May 2003. We asked individuals how their savings had been affected by the changes in equity markets and how this had affected their retirement plans. We also asked them about their pension arrangements, income, educational background and various other characteristics.

We find that, as of May 2003, some 25 per cent of older working individuals had decided to postpone retirement past the date they had anticipated two years previously. There is a strong positive relationship between those delaying retirement and those most affected by the stock market decline. We also find that individuals who have more control over their retirement date were no more likely to have been more exposed to the equity market, which is in contrast to predictions about asset allocation in Bodie et al. (1992).

The remainder of the chapter is organized as follows. First we examine scary markets in the form of the decline in equity markets and the potential consequences. The next section presents a review of the literature on asset allocation and choice of retirement date and is followed by a review the design of the Watson Wyatt study. We then assess who was worst hit by scary markets and examine labour market responses to declines in asset markets. A final section concludes.

SCARY MARKETS

At the end of 1999 the FTSE All-Share Index stood at 3242. By the end of 2002 it had declined to 1894, a decline of 42 per cent. On a total returns basis (including dividends paid) the decline was 37 per cent, whereas it had increased by 75 per cent from the end of 1996 through to the end of 1999.[1] The S&P 500 decreased 38 per cent on a total returns basis whereas, on the back of the dot-com boom, it had risen 108 per cent from 1996 to 1999. In Europe, a rise of 86 per cent in markets from 1996 to 1999 was followed by a subsequent decline of 40 per cent over the next three years.

Nevertheless, the situation was by no means uniform throughout the world. In Australia, the ASX All-Ordinaries Index rose 6.3 per cent on a total returns basis from 1999 to 2002, while in New Zealand markets also increased. In both countries the late 1990s boom had been more moderate, with the market increasing by 43 per cent and 17 per cent respectively, between 1996 and 1999. Asian markets were, however, far from calm, with Hong Kong and Taiwan experiencing decreases in markets from the end of 1999 to the end of 2002 which were more dramatic than in the USA, the UK or continental Europe. (These figures are summarized in Figure 6.1.)

Such declines in stock markets are by no means unprecedented. For instance, the beginning of the 1970s exhibited bigger declines: in 1974 the FTSE All-Share Index declined by some 55.3 per cent.[2] However, unlike earlier stock market declines, in 2002 investors in the USA and the UK were relying to a greater extent than ever before on equity markets to finance their retirement. Defined contribution provision had grown significantly, in both the USA and the UK, over the 1990s, so the decline in markets was particularly painful for those individuals close to retirement who were heavily dependent on equity-based pensions for their retirement income.

Yet focusing on equity markets potentially understates the problems facing retirees. To secure a guaranteed income, retirees need to buy an annuity and annuity rates are closely tied to bond yields. Bond yields fell significantly in the UK from 1997 to the end of 2002. The fall in bond yields coupled with increased longevity led to falling annuity rates (see Figure 6.2). In December 1996, the best available 'level' annuity rate in the UK for a male aged 60 yielded about 10 per cent per annum.[3] By the end of 1999, this had fallen to

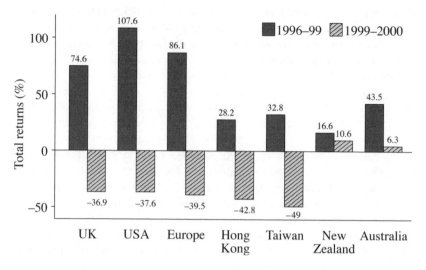

Source data: Global Financial Data Inc.

*Figure 6.1   Total returns on stock market indices: 1996–99 versus
                1999–2002*

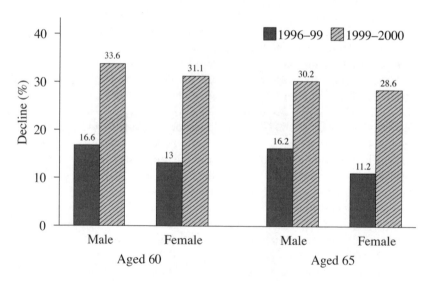

Source data: *Pensions World* (January editions 1997, 2000 and 2003).

Figure 6.2   Decline in annuity rates in the UK: 1996–99 versus 1999–2002

8 per cent and by 2002 it had fallen yet further to 6.7 per cent. When compounded with the collapse in the stock markets after 1999, those with money purchase pensions faced dramatically adverse movements in their prospective retirement income.

We now estimate the combined impact of declining annuity rates and falling equity values. To ensure that the annuity rates are internationally comparable and to account for differences in regulatory regime, competitiveness of annuity market or capital supply, we assume annuity rates equal the 10-year bond yield plus a mortality mark-up of 3.5 per cent. This approximation yields a notional annuity rate for a 65-year-old man of 11 per cent in the UK at the end of 1996, 8.7 per cent in 1999 and 7.9 per cent in 2002. These relate to quoted market rates of 11 per cent, 9.2 per cent and 7.7 per cent respectively.

Figure 6.3 shows the combined impact of changes in equity markets and notional annuity rates on retirement income from 1999 to 2002. It compares the income in retirement of a hypothetical individual who had invested entirely in equity, over the preceding three years, as opposed to the same individual three years earlier. Similarly, the figures were calculated for an individual who invested half their portfolio in ten-year government bonds, with the remainder invested in equities. Given the deteriorating position facing retirees, we represent these figures as percentage declines.

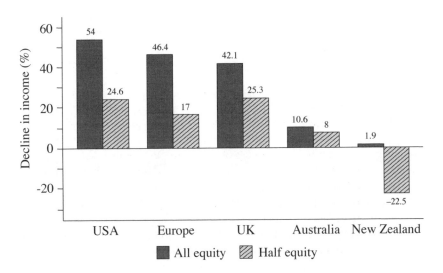

Source data: Global Financial Data Inc and *Pensions World*.

Figure 6.3   Hypothetical decline in retirement income for individuals from 1999 to 2002 (combined effect of equity and annuity markets)

Figure 6.3 indicates that the decline in purchasing power of retirement funds has been dramatic in the USA, the UK and Europe for those invested entirely in equity. For those who moved into bond investments, the decline in retirement income has been much less onerous. In the UK, investment of half the portfolio in bonds would have cut losses from 42 per cent to 25 per cent. But the late 1990s was an era where individuals were short on caution and the extent to which individuals did cut their losses through portfolio shifts was therefore limited.

OVERVIEW OF THE LITERATURE

Perhaps the first attempt to look at retirement decisions jointly with asset allocation decisions was Bodie et al. (1992) who add human capital and choice over leisure to earlier work by Merton (1969, 1971). The key result is that flexibility over labour supply leads to a higher degree of equity investment in an individual's portfolio. The optimal portfolio weight in equity is:

$$\theta = -\frac{V_A}{AV_{AA}}\left[\frac{\mu - r}{\sigma^2}\right] - \frac{V_{Aw}}{AV_{AA}}\sigma_w w \qquad (6.1)$$

where V is the value or utility function, A is the sum of human capital and financial wealth, μ is the rate of return on equity, σ^2 is the variance of equity returns, r is the interest rate, w is the wage and σ_w is the standard deviation of wage growth.

Individuals may be willing to invest more in equity if they have more labour supply flexibility because of the wealth effect. Indeed, *ceteris paribus*, those who have control over their labour supply have greater potential wealth and therefore are predicted to be more willing to take risks in equity markets. By contrast, an increase in the risk of future wage growth (measured as the standard deviation of wage growth) implies riskier human capital and leads to a reduction in the exposure to the risky asset.

The continuous time analysis in Bodie et al. (1992) has been expanded in a number of directions. Basak (1999) extends the analysis to a general equilibrium setting. Liu and Neis (2002), by contrast, build a retirement decision into the model. In their model, retirement decisions depend strongly on asset market performance, but an interesting result is that when wages are positively correlated with stock prices (as for instance in Cardinale, 2003), an increase in stock prices may cause workers to continue working instead of retiring. Kenc (2003a, b) uses a duality approach to solve the dynamic optimal control problem for optimal asset allocation and retirement behaviour. This approach allows consideration of more realistic wage profiles as well as being more amenable to numerical solution. Finally, Campbell and Viceira (2002) examine analytic approximations to models in which there is non-diversifiable labour income risk.

One of the key assumptions underlying much of this literature is that retirement is voluntary. Yet evidence on this point is mixed. The UK Cabinet Office (2000) found that at most one-third of early retirees, who retire between age 50 and the official state pension retirement age in the UK (65), retire voluntarily. Studies that, by contrast, point to the importance of labour demand (employer) factors in determining retirement dates are: Lee (2003), Herbertsson (2001), Downs (1995), and Gray (2002).

Furthermore, there is a large body of evidence that retirement is also driven by many non-economic factors, such as the retirement date of the spouse, health and the organization of work. Whilst non-optimizing models may also explain work past retirement when stock markets decline (one example is the loss aversion model of Kahneman and Tversky 1979, 1991).

Williamson and McNamara (2001) review the empirical evidence on work past retirement. In terms of the likely impact of the decline in the stock market on retirement behaviour, Gustman and Steinmeier (2002) estimate a structural model based on data from the US Health and Retirement Study. They find that during the late 1990s the effect of the asset market boom was to lower labour market participation of those in the study by 3 per cent. The net effect is a change in the average retirement age of three months. Similarly, the projected effect of the asset market bust is to increase labour market participation of older workers, with an anticipated short-term rise in the average retirement age of three months.

These effects appear small. The asset market boom in the USA involved returns of over 20 per cent per annum in the late 1990s. As we have noted above, the asset market bust involved a decline of up to a half in realized retirement income, of those with money purchase arrangements, from early 2000 to the end of 2002. Yet in the case of both the boom and the bust, the model projects little effect on the retirement age: to a large degree DB arrangements will mute the impact of equity markets.

To broadly summarize the main predictions from the literature:

- The proportion of assets invested in equities should increase with the level of non-financial (human) capital relative to financial capital.
- Individuals with flexible retirement dates should hold more assets in equity.
- A decline in financial wealth should induce more work.
- Spousal decisions should be important in influencing work behaviour.

DATA AND SURVEY

This study uses data from a special survey that was carried over a week during mid-May 2003. The fieldwork was conducted via a web-based survey for Watson Wyatt by the YouGov polling agency. The individuals surveyed were selected from a population of respondents numbering around 40 000. These included approximately 23 000 men and 17 000 women; 11 000 individuals aged 18–29, 15 000 individuals aged 30–44, 10 000 individuals aged 44–59, and 4000 individuals aged 60 or over. For all individuals, we observe data regarding individual's characteristics, demographic and economic status.

Our analysis specifically restricted attention to individuals aged between 50 and 64. A total of 4051 interviews was obtained from individuals in this age range. In studying the impact of declines in stock market values on retirement decisions we focused on individuals close to the margin, either nearing retirement or in the early stages of retirement, who were likely to be most affected by changes in asset values.

Of the survey participants, 57 per cent were currently working, 33 per cent were retired or semi-retired (where an individual is retired from their main employment but is now working part-time) and 10 per cent reported that they were not retired but were also not working. With regard to the exposure to equity risk, some 59 per cent had some equity-related investments – where this could be in the form of direct shareholdings or indirect holdings invested in equities (such as savings and pensions products).[4] With regard to pension provision, 19 per cent reported they had had no private pension, 45 per cent had one private pension, 23 per cent two private pensions, 9 per cent three, and 4 per cent four or more. Of those with a private pension, in 64 per cent of cases an employer-defined benefit (DB) scheme was likely to (or did) provide the main source of retirement income, in 12 per cent of cases an employed-defined contribution (DC) scheme and for 24 per cent personal pensions provided the major source of pension income.

The key questions for our study are those that characterize asset loss. In all cases we characterize asset loss as a relative effect, that is, the per centage loss in savings when comparing the survey date to three years before. We do not know the exact amounts invested, or the absolute decline in savings.[5] Nor do we know the split between pension and non-pension investments, or the division in asset allocations between equities and bonds, although we can infer that those with the greatest decline in savings are likely to have had the greatest exposure to equities. Nevertheless, this format has the advantage that it is relatively easy for people to understand and comprehend, facilitating more accurate responses and less question non-response.

The core question with regard to retirement plans is, almost by definition, subjective, and individuals may evaluate their response in different ways. So, for example, one person may report that they are considering postponing retirement only if this is a relatively definite decision, whereas another individual may report similarly on the basis of their current outlook. Nevertheless, such subjective responses will only bias estimates if individuals respond in systematically different ways, for unobserved reasons. Moreover, retirement decisions, where voluntary, are by their nature subjective, and such questions remain probably the best indicator of future behaviour.

There are, however, potential limitations to the survey. First, while 45 per cent of UK households now have Internet access in the home (Office for National Statistics 2003), we are sampling from a potentially self-selecting sample. Those who use the Internet tend to be more educated and more affluent (see Gardner and Oswald 2001). This may be especially true for the older age group we analyse, where Internet use is less prevalent. Second, web-based surveys make stronger assumptions regarding the literacy and technical proficiency of respondents. Yet recent evidence has also suggested that web-based surveys provide more accurate reports than a traditional telephone interview (Chang and Krosnick 2003.

To check for any potential sample bias, we examined our empirical results by socio-economic group. Estimates are found to be very similar across occupational class. Moreover, in all regression models we include as explanatory variables age, gender, education and occupational class – the variables most likely to correlate with selection into the sample.

WHICH INDIVIDUALS SUFFERED THE MOST?

Two forms of questions were used to try to quantify the losses in savings that resulted from the decline in equity markets. The first asked respondents to describe what had happened to the value of their savings in the last three years:

Thinking of all moneys you had set aside as savings before 2000 (such as pensions, bonds, ISAs, stocks and shares) have they increased or decreased in value over the last 3 years?

Responses were qualitative, with categories: 'increased a lot', 'increased a little', 'remained about the same', 'decreased a little', and 'decreased a lot'. Whilst we do not know the previous exposure to equities, it seems likely that those who have suffered the greatest declines in savings are also those who had greater investments in equity products. This question will reflect both the absolute decline in savings and subjective factors, which will influence how an individual reacts to a given savings loss. This subjectivity, nevertheless, has some advantages. First, workers' perceptions are likely to be an important determinant of behaviour. Second, the question may capture the *relative* impact of the decline in savings more effectively than attempting to compare an individual's savings to their other asset wealth – on which individuals are reticent. These subjective measures may then allow us to infer, albeit with some error, the relative declines in savings.

The responses to this question are shown in Figure 6.4. Some 48.6 per cent of individuals responded that their savings 'declined a lot', with 20.1 per cent reporting they 'declined a little'. A majority then saw their savings decline over the period in question. In 11.2 per cent of cases, the value of savings has remained largely flat, whilst for 18.8 per cent there has been a small increase in savings. Only 1.3 per cent saw a large increase in savings. For those whose savings increased in value, we can hypothesize that they were either largely invested in bonds or other guaranteed-return products, or they increased their savings rate, or they may even have received an inheritance. It is important to note that we capture the change in the stock of savings, which is the relevant issue for our analysis, not the decline in moneys invested in the stock market, though these may be closely related.

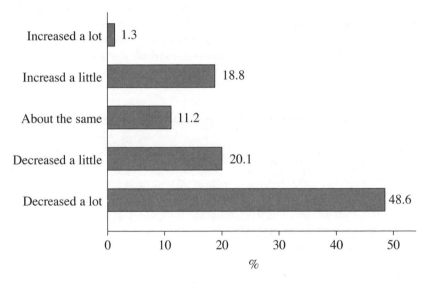

Source data: 2003 Watson Wyatt YouGov Scary Market Survey.

Figure 6.4   The change in the value of savings, 2000–2003

A second question, more quantitative in tone, was subsequently asked.[6] For those individuals who had responded that their savings had increased or decreased, we then asked:

By approximately how much have all the moneys you had set aside as savings before 2000 increased (decreased) in the last 3 years?

Response categories were: 'less than 5 per cent', 'between 5 and 10 per cent', 'between 11 and 25 per cent', 'between 26 and 50 per cent', and 'more than 50 per cent'. Sample responses are shown in Figure 6.5. Some 8.2 per cent report losses of greater than 50 per cent, 24.9 per cent a fall in savings between 26 per cent and 50 per cent, and 20.7 per cent losses of between 11 and 25 per cent. Around a quarter (25.7 per cent) report their savings have changed by less than 5 per cent, only 2.3 per cent respond that their savings have increased by more than 10 per cent.[7]

Using responses from these banded categories we can estimate the mean decline in savings for individuals with different characteristics, using the interval regression technique. Assuming the change in savings is normally distributed, this technique maps the true change in savings on to the ordered bands described above. Estimation then maximizes the probability of observing a response within a band given the characteristics of the individual and the band cut-points.

Table 6.1 reports the estimated mean change in savings for different sub-samples of individuals. In all cases the mean change is negative. The average change in the value of savings, in the sample, is estimated to be −17.0 per cent.

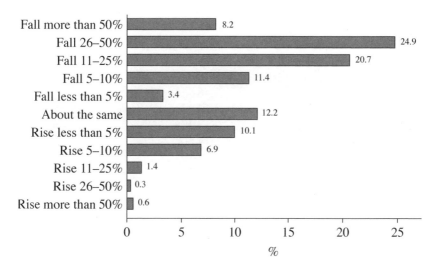

Source data: 2003 Watson Wyatt YouGov Scary Market Survey.

Figure 6.5   The proportionate decline in savings, 2000–2003 (%)

This figure is slightly higher for men than for women, but not statistically significantly different. To be clear, this does not imply that there is no difference in the amounts lost, but rather that their proportionate decline is no different. Those with less education report losing less as a proportion of their income, and as they are, on average, likely to have lower absolute amounts of savings, we can infer that absolute losses are also lower. Those in the private sector lost more than those in the public sector, and professionals lost more than non-professionals. Those who are retired reported losing more than those currently working, though this may be explained by the fact that those employed were still in the accumulation phase – and so offset losses with further contributions. In all cases the differences are statistically significant.

Those with personal pensions lost more than those with occupational pensions, both DB and DC, and this difference is statistically robust. It may be

Table 6.1   Summary statistics: proportionate change in savings

Sub-sample	Mean	Standard deviation
All	−17.04	(20.94)
Male	−17.24	(20.91)
Female	−16.47	(20.99)
Low education[a]	−13.54	(19.69)
Medium education[b]	−16.12	(21.12)
High education[c]	−19.10	(21.11)
Main pension: employer DB	−16.60	(21.22)
Main pension: employer DC	−15.77	(19.01)
Main pension: personal pension	−18.52	(20.61)
Private sector	−18.71	(21.63)
Public sector	−14.87	(19.35)
Professional occupation[d]	−18.30	(21.18)
Non-professional[e]	−14.60	(20.26)
Currently retired	−18.19	(20.65)
Currently working	−15.79	(20.61)
Self-employed	−19.82	(21.40)
Flexible retirement date	−16.59	(20.56)
Fixed retirement date	−14.52	(20.62)

Notes:
[a] 'Low education' denotes no formal or lower vocational qualifications.
[b] 'Medium education' denotes intermediate educational qualifications.
[c] 'High education' denotes degree-level or professional qualifications.
[d] 'Professional occupation' denotes a manager or a professional in current or last occupation.
[e] Non-professional includes the remaining occupations.

that those who have chosen personal pensions, or work in occupations where they are the norm, are less risk averse, or more wealthy, or have greater flexibility with their retirement planning. In any case, they appear to have been more exposed to equities.

Therefore, in accordance with Bodie et al. (1992), those with more human capital, here taken to be those with greater education or in managerial or professional occupations, are found to have been more exposed to equities. However, one of the interesting features in Table 6.1 is that individuals who have flexibility over their retirement plans appear to have lost no more, and hence be no more likely to hold equity, than those without flexibility. In Bodie et al. (1992), individuals with flexible retirement dates should be willing to risk greater losses in their retirement savings – as they have the option to make up losses through working longer. In contrast, we see no statistically significant difference in the change in savings between those with fixed and those with flexible retirement dates.

In Table 6.2 we examine whether the differences in sample means discussed above are robust to the addition of explanatory variables and report multivariate regression results. We model the proportionate decline in savings as a function of retirement flexibility, age, education, income and other characteristics. Again we see that flexibility over retirement date has little impact on the savings loss, whilst education remains a strong predictor of equity exposure. By contrast, the effects of occupation and income are not statistically robust.

HOW HAVE SCARY MARKETS AFFECTED RETIREMENT PLANS?

To assess whether individuals had revised their retirement plans in response to declining equity markets, we asked employed respondents whether they had changed the age at which they planned to retire, compared to their plans two years previously. Individuals could state they had not changed their plans, that they now planned to retire earlier, or that they planned to retire later.

The majority, some 66.0 per cent, report that they have not revised their retirement date, with 8.9 per cent responding they plan to retire earlier and 25.1 per cent that they plan to retire later. However, these figures must be treated with caution as other factors may be driving retirement decisions. Individuals may be too optimistic at earlier ages, in which case we may observe a larger proportion planning to retire later simply from revising expectations as they get older (over the two-year period). Early retirement is also often induced by changes in health (Leonesio et al. 2000; Mein et al. 2000; Marshall et al. 2001; Baker 2002) or retirement of the spouse (Blau 1997;

Table 6.2   Flexible retirement and savings loss (dependent variable: the percentage change in savings)

Regressor	(1)	(2)	(3)
Flexible retirement date	−0.977 (1.229)	0.487 (1.320)	−0.577 (1.369)
Self-employed		−4.303 (1.552)*	−3.954 (1.646)*
Log household income			−0.041 (1.204)
Age	−0.207 (0.161)	−0.175 (0.162)	−0.214 (0.169)
Intermediate qualification	−0.547 (1.658)	−0.405 (1.655)	−0.441 (1.709)
Degree or professional qualification	−4.847 (1.765)*	−4.527 (1.764)*	−5.718 (1.851)*
Female	−0.074 (1.372)	−0.386 (1.370)	−1.019 (1.469)
Married	1.298 (1.603)	1.033 (1.595)	0.843 (1.688)
Own house with mortgage	−0.061 (1.210)	−0.060 (1.208)	−0.583 (1.279)
Renter	5.201 (2.033)*	5.372 (2.014)*	5.971 (1.997)*
Managerial	−0.239 (1.486)	−0.671 (1.495)	−1.340 (1.565)
Clerical	2.697 (2.025)	2.097 (2.034)	0.692 (2.199)
Blue-collar	2.463 (1.842)	2.251 (1.841)	1.624 (1.986)
Public sector	3.714 (1.291)*	3.290 (1.298)*	3.234 (1.345)*
Observations	1376	1376	1230

Notes:
The sample includes only those currently in employment.
The coefficients on education are with respect to the omitted base of a lower qualification. Housing tenure dummies are relative to owning a house outright. The default occupational category is that of a professional worker. All regressions also include controls for region.
Equations are estimated by interval regression (Stewart 1983). Negative coefficients indicate a greater savings loss.
Standard errors are in parentheses and are robust to arbitrary heteroscedasticity. *denotes coefficients that are statistically significantly different from zero at the 5 per cent confidence level.

Baker 2002). We then turn to how retirement expectations are correlated with declines in savings.

Figure 6.6 examines whether individuals had revised their retirement plans by different types of private pension. Those for whom a DB pension will be the main source of private pension income are most likely to be planning to retire earlier, with 11.6 per cent planning to do so. For those with DC or personal pensions the figures are 6.8 per cent and 5.6 per cent respectively. Similarly, retirement plans are more likely to have remained unchanged than for those with DB pensions. By implication, those with money purchase pensions are more likely to plan to retire later. Of those with a personal pension, 32.9 per cent suggest they are planning to retire later. For those with a DC pension the figure is 30.6 per cent, whilst for those with a DB pension it is only 19.3 per cent.

It is well documented that DB pensions, in practice, provide strong incentives to retire earlier (see Clark and Schieber 2002; Lazear 1983; Mulvey 2003). Hence it may not be that we are capturing an effect of reduced lifetime wealth, rather a symptom of the plan design. Figure 6.7 then shows how retirement planning varies by the fall in the savings (for exposition we restrict attention to the percentage planning to postpone retirement).

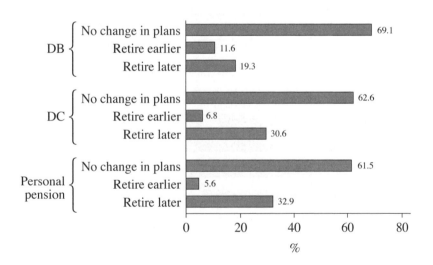

Source data: 2003 Watson Wyatt YouGov Scary Market Survey.

Figure 6.6   Changes to the expected retirement age by main source of private pension income

Among those who savings fell by half, 34.1 per cent report that they are planning to postpone retirement. For those with reductions in savings of between a quarter and a half, the figure is 34.5 per cent. Where savings have fallen by 11–25 per cent, we observe that 29.9 per cent plan to retire later. Thereafter, the proportion reporting they are planning to postpone retirement monotonically declines with improved savings performance, with the only exception being the small group of individuals whose savings increased by more than 11 per cent.

We now turn to regression analysis to examine how robust these patterns are to the addition of control variables. Given that the response categories are unordered, mutually exclusive and conceivably non-nested, we model whether individuals have revised their retirement plans by the multinomial logit model. Coefficient estimates are reported in Table 6.3 and are relative to the omitted category (no change in plans). Hence a positive coefficient on retiring later indicates that the individual is likely to plan to retire later. Interpretation is analogous for the retiring earlier option.

Consistent with Figure 6.7, as the relative decline in savings increases we observe a greater propensity for individuals to respond that they are planning to postpone retirement. Moreover, these effects are statistically well determined, even with a wide range of other control variables. We can calculate the

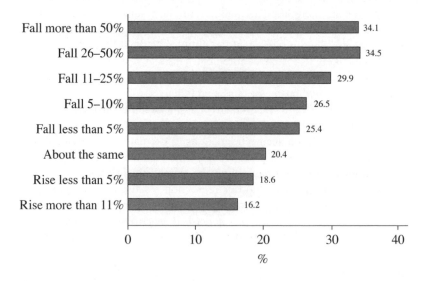

Source data: 2003 Watson Wyatt YouGov Scary Market Survey.

Figure 6.7   Changes to the expected retirement age by change in the value of savings (%)

marginal effects corresponding to these coefficients, which are the increased probability of reporting a response. An individual whose savings have fallen by more than 50 per cent is 20.4 per cent more likely (than a respondent whose savings have not declined) to plan now to retire later. For those with savings losses of between 26 and 50 per cent, the figure is approximately 16 per cent. Those with savings losses of between 11 and 25 per cent are 11 per cent more likely to retire later and 3 per cent more likely to retire earlier. For all other variables capturing the decline in savings, there is very little relationship with the likelihood of retiring early.

One potential constraint on whether an individual can postpone retirement is whether their employer allows them to work beyond any set retirement date. In columns three and four of Table 6.3, we control for whether the individual can work past the normal age of retirement, and indeed find that results are substantially the same. Furthermore, we also found that results were robust within sub-samples of individuals by pension type (DB or DC) and when we examined only those respondents with retirement flexibility.[8] Those who reported that they had the ability to work past the normal age of retirement were 5.2 per cent less likely to plan to retire earlier and 6.1 per cent more likely to retire later, in addition to any impact of savings declines.

With the exception of age and being self-employed, no other covariates are found to have a statistically significant association with retirement plans. The self-employed are more likely to plan to retire later, and this partially reflects the fact that they have the flexibility to do so. However, a large effect remains even after controlling for retirement flexibility, with the self-employed some 8 per cent more likely to postpone retirement. This may reflect a greater absolute size of losses or, alternatively, that, coinciding with the fall in stock markets, the valuation on small businesses has also fallen.

Age may itself reflect a selection effect. For a fixed planned retirement age, those who are observed to be working at older ages are more likely to have revised upwards their planned retirement age. Alternatively, individuals may only review their retirement plans as they approach their planned retirement date, or younger workers may simply be unrealistic in their expectations. Nevertheless, omitting age from our regression results did not significantly alter coefficient estimates on the savings decline measures.

A supplementary question was later asked, regarding the importance of savings decline on the retirement decision:

Thinking of all the moneys you had set aside as savings before 2000 how important has the change in the value of these savings been to your decision to change the age at which you plan to retire?

Responses were ordered: very important (1), fairly important (2), fairly

Retirement provision in scary markets

Table 6.3   The decline in savings and the retirement decision (dependent variable: changes to the planned retirement date)

Regressor	Retire earlier (1)	Retire later (2)	Retire earlier (3)	Retire later (4)
Decline in savings: 50% or more	0.253 (0.444)	1.045 (0.256)*	0.314 (0.482)	1.070 (0.271)*
Decline in savings: 26–50%	0.041 (0.302)	0.831 (0.184)*	0.175 (0.324)	0.865 (0.196)*
Decline in savings: 11–25%	0.559 (0.272)*	0.650 (0.193)*	0.738 (0.293)*	0.687 (0.206)*
Decline in savings: 5–10%	−0.074 (0.355)	0.412 (0.231)	0.014 (0.381)	0.306 (0.247)
Decline in savings: Less than 5%	0.093 (0.585)	0.652 (0.350)	0.075 (0.682)	0.587 (0.361)
Log household income	0.152 (0.217)	−0.147 (0.122)	0.085 (0.248)	−0.168 (0.129)
Flexible retirement date			−0.677 (0.254)*	0.247 (0.169)
Age	0.022 (0.028)	0.107 (0.019)*	0.038 (0.030)	0.093 (0.020)*
Intermediate qualification	−0.007 (0.299)	0.347 (0.198)	−0.112 (0.320)	0.366 (0.209
Degree or professional qualification	−0.305 (0.339)	0.248 (0.206)	−0.294 (0.358)	0.275 (0.218)
Female	0.105 (0.257)	0.342 (0.161)*	0.280 (0.288)	0.335 (0.172)
Married	0.299 (0.346)	0.141 (0.188)	0.569 (0.383)	0.188 (0.201)
Public sector	0.229 (0.221)	−0.334 (0.159)*	0.099 (0.240)	−0.259 (0.168)
Self-employed	−0.468 (0.355)	0.437 (0.162)*	−0.084 (0.399)	0.376 (0.182)*
Observations	1325	1325	1195	1195
Log-L	−1055.9		−940.8	
Pseudo R^2	0.070		0.076	

Notes:

The sample includes only those currently in employment.

The coefficients on the decline in savings are with respect to the omitted categories, no decline in savings or a savings increase. The coefficients with respect to education are with respect to the omitted base of a lower qualification. Other controls (not reported) include housing tenure, occupation and region dummies.

Positive coefficients with respect to retiring early (late) indicate a greater likelihood of retiring early (late) relative to stating no change in retirement plans.

Standard errors are in parentheses and are robust to arbitrary heteroscedasticity. *denotes coefficients that are statistically significantly different from zero at the 5 per cent confidence level.

unimportant (3) and very unimportant (4). Equations were then estimated using the ordered logit technique (reported in Table 6.4). Given the scaling, positive coefficients indicate cases where the change in savings plays less of a role in the retirement decision. Again, in discussing results we talk in terms of the more interpretable marginal effects.

Confirming the intuition of previous results, those with DC pensions are more likely to claim that the change in savings is an important factor in their retirement decision. Those respondents whose main pension income is from a personal pension are 12.6 per cent more likely, than those with DB pensions, to feel that the change in savings is a very important factor in their retirement decision. For those with a DC pension the comparable figure is 7.5 per cent. In both cases, the coefficients are statistically significantly different from zero.[9]

In column two of Table 6.4, we see that, as would be expected, those who suffered large losses are more likely to report that these losses were an important factor in their retirement decision. Where the relative decline in savings is 50 per cent or more, respondents are 20.6 per cent more likely, than those who had no losses, to feel that the change in savings is a very important factor in their retirement decision. The remaining savings loss coefficients then monotonically decline with the proportionate loss. Hence the results pass this somewhat tautological reasonableness test.

The estimates also show that those with larger household incomes are less likely to feel, for a given proportionate decline in savings, that the fall in their savings has contributed to their decision. This may be because those with greater household income also have greater alternative wealth to fall back on. Or it may reflect that a certain minimum standard of living is still available to those with greater assets.

We now turn to those who are currently retired and examine whether those who had suffered larger declines in their savings were more likely to consider a return to work. If they were considering a return to work, we also asked them for how long. Figure 6.8 shows the breakdown in responses by the fall in savings. There does not appear to be a clear discernible pattern in responses by the decline in savings, and we cannot reject the null hypothesis that there is no significant difference in response rates by the change in savings, for all conventional significance levels. These results remain in regression analysis, when we control for the same set of variables as used in previous tables.[10]

The lack of correlation between the change in savings and the desire to return to work (in contrast to the tenor of results for those currently employed) suggests a high degree of irreversibility in the retirement decision, although it is not clear whether this reflects some psychological aversion to returning to work or alternatively some biases in the labour market against older workers. Some workers may also be prevented from returning by ill-health. In any case,

Table 6.4   *Importance of decrease in savings on retirement decision*
              (dependent variable: important of change in savings on changing
              retirement date)

Regressor	(1)	(2)
Main private pension: employer DC	−0.504	
	(0.175)*	
Main private pension: personal pension	−0.778	
	(0.132)*	
Decline in savings: 50% or more		−1.239
		(0.226)*
Decline in savings: 26–50%		−1.068
		(0.154)*
Decline in savings: 11–25%		−0.857
		(0.143)*
Decline in savings: 5–10%		−0.422
		(0.156)*
Decline in savings: less than 5%		−0.268
		(0.308)
Log household income	0.162	0.281
	(0.100)	(0.101)*
Age	−0.022	−0.022
	(0.015)	(0.015)
Intermediate qualification	−0.101	−0.109
	(0.152)	(0.157)
Degree or professional qualification	0.191	0.260
	(0.158)	(0.161)
Female	0.024	−0.042
	(0.123)	(0.125)
Married	−0.050	−0.136
	(0.156)	(0.165)
Public sector	0.378	0.529
	(0.124)*	(0.123)*
Self-employed	−0.199	−0.371
	(0.142)	(0.133)*
Observations	1330	1274
Log-L	−1762.0	−1674.9
Pseudo R^2	0.034	0.046

Notes:
The sample includes only those currently in employment.
The coefficients on the pension variables are with respect to the omitted group, those with DB pensions. The coefficients on the decline in savings are with respect to no decline in savings or a savings increase. Other controls (not reported) include housing tenure, occupation and region dummies.
Negative coefficients indicate the change in savings is more important in determining the retirement decision.
Standard errors are in parentheses and are robust to arbitrary heteroscedasticity. *denotes coefficients that are statistically significantly different from zero at the 5 per cent confidence level.

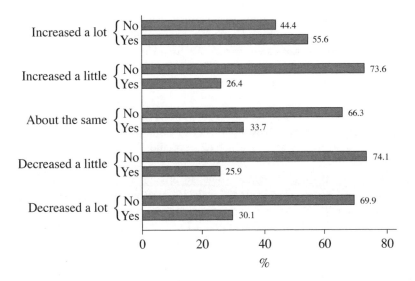

Source data: 2003 Watson Wyatt YouGov Scary Market Survey.

Figure 6.8   *The proportion considering a return to work by the change in savings (%)*

this provides some potential support for a real options approach to retirement decisions (Stock and Wise 1990) and is also consistent with the empirical work on early retirement in Gruber and Wise (2003).

CONCLUSIONS

In this chapter, we have examined the response of older workers in the UK to declines in equity markets. The bear market from the end of 1999 to the end of 2002 is the first time in which significant volumes of retirement savings were at risk in equity markets. The euphoria of the late 1990s was such that this decline, at least in its scale, was probably unanticipated by most investors. The experience of the past few years is hence a natural experiment to examine the response of older workers to changes in their private retirement wealth.

We reviewed results from a survey of over 4000 individuals in the UK aged 50 to 64. Some 48.6 per cent of individuals said their savings had 'declined a lot' and some 20.1 per cent that they had 'declined a little'. These declines were broad-based, with only a few correlates predicting the scale of loss. Indeed, in contrast to the predictions about asset allocation in Bodie et al.

(1992), we find that individuals who have more control over their retirement date were no more likely to have been more exposed to the equity market.

We then examined retirement plans. We found that 25 per cent of older workers were planning to retire later than they had planned two years previously. We also found a strong positive relationship between those delaying retirement and those most affected by the stock market decline. On the other hand, for those individuals who had already retired, there appeared little correlation between the degree of loss and the likelihood of returning to work, providing support for theories in which the retirement decision is modelled as irreversible.

Overall, our analysis provides some surprising support for continued research into the issues raised in Bodie et al. (1992). Roughly 25 per cent of the older population planned to delay retirement in response to changes in the stock market – and this is in the UK, where defined contribution pensions are not the dominant form of private pension provision. On the other hand, the degree to which individuals do not have choice over their retirement age means that the model is not fully applicable to large sections of the population. That individuals without flexible retirement ages seem to have been more exposed to the stock market is also a result which seems at odds with the predictions in Bodie et al. (1992). That individuals do not appear willing to return to the labour market, once retired, also provides support for the idea that retirement is a largely irreversible decision, as in models such as Stock and Wise (1990).

NOTES

1. Using indices produced by Global Financial Data Inc. (Taylor 2003).
2. Total returns indices of Global Financial Data Inc.
3. Annuity rates quoted in this chapter are from the January edition of the 1997, 2000 and 2003 issues of *Pensions World*. The 1997 issue covers rates as of December 1996, which are payable monthly in advance and are guaranteed for five years. The January 2000 issue quotes rates from December 1999, which are payable monthly in arrears without a guarantee. The January 2003 issue covers annuity rates in the compulsory purchase market in December 2002, which are payable monthly in arrears without guarantee.
4. This percentage of equity investment is broadly similar to that found for the US HRS in Gustman and Steinmeier (2002)
5. Previous experience suggested that non-response and mis-reporting for such questions would be high.
6. Both this question and the last are only asked of those with private pensions.
7. Due to the small number of responses in the last three categories, increases in savings of more than 10 per cent are grouped when used as an explanatory variable.
8. Results are available upon request.
9. Restricting attention to only those individuals who had changed their retirement plans or who planned to retire later, we found qualitatively similar, though substantively larger, estimated effects.
10. In results not reported, though available upon request, we found those who had been retired longer were less willing to consider returning to work, holding constant their current age.

REFERENCES

Baker, M. (2002), 'Retirement behaviour of married couples: evidence from the spouse's allowance', *Journal of Human Resources*, **37**(1): 1–34.

Basak, S. (1999), 'On the fluctuations in consumption and market returns in the presence of labour and human capital: an equilibrium analysis', *Journal of Economic Dynamics and Control*, **23**: 1029–64.

Blau, D.H. (1997), 'Social Security and the labour supply of older married couples', *Labour Economics*, **4**: 373–418.

Bodie, Z., R.C. Merton and P. Samuelson (1992), 'Labour supply flexibility and portfolio choice in a life cycle model', *Journal of Economic Dynamics and Control*, **16**: 427–49.

Campbell, J.Y. and L.M. Viceira (2002), *Strategic Asset Allocation*, Cambridge: Cambridge University Press.

Cardinale, M. (2003), *Cointegration and the Relationship Between Pension Liabilities and Asset Prices*, Working Paper 2003–RU01 Watson Wyatt, UK.

Chang, L.C. and J.A. Krosnick (2003). *National Surveys Via Random Digit Dialling Telephone Interviewing vs. the Internet: Comparing Sample Representativeness and Response Quality*, Ohio State University.

Clark, R. and S. Schieber (2002), 'An empirical analysis of the transition to hybrid pension plans', in J.B. Shoven and M. WSarshawsky (eds), *Public Policies and Private Pensions*, Washington DC: The Brookings Institution, 11–42.

Downs, A. (1995) *Cruelest Cut: Laying Off Older Workers. Corporate executions: the ugly truth about layoffs – how corporate greed is shattering lives, companies and communities*, New York: Amacom: 127–38.

Eschtruth, A. and J. Gemus (2002), 'Are older workers responding to the bear market?', Center for Retirement Research, Boston College.

Gardner, J. and A. Oswald (2001), 'Internet use: the digital divide', in A. Park, J. Curtice, K. Thomson et al. (eds); Thousand Oaks, CA: Sage, Vol. 18. *British Social Attitudes: Public Policy, Social Ties*, 159–73.

Gray, D. (2002), 'Early retirement programs and wage restraint: empirical evidence from France', *Industrial and Labour Relations Review*, **55**(3): 512–32.

Gruber, J. and D. Wise (2003), *Social Security and Retirement Programs around the World: Micro Estimation*, Cambridge MA: National Bureau of Economic Research.

Gustman, A.L. and T.L. Steinmeier (2002), *Retirement and the Stock Market Bubble*, Cambridge MA: National Bureau of Economic Research.

Herbertsson, T.T. (2001), *Why the Icelanders do not Retire Early*, Stockholm: Pensionsforum.

Kahneman, D. and A. Tversky (1979), 'Prospect theory: An analysis of decision under risk', *Econometrica*, **37**: 263–91.

Kahneman, D. and A. Tversky (1991), 'Loss aversion in riskless choice: A reference dependent model', *Quarterly Journal of Economics*, **106**(4): 1039–61.

Kenc, T. (2003a), *Dynamic Portfolio Effects of Labour Income*, Imperial College, London.

Kenc, T. (2003b), *Retirement Decisions Under Uncertainty*, Imperical College Management School, London.

Lazear, E.P. (1983), 'Pensions as severance pay', in Z. Bodie and J.B. Shoven (eds), *Financial Aspects of the United States Pension System*, Chicago, IL: University of Chicago Press, 57–90.

Lee, C. (2003), *Labour Market Status of Older Males in the United States, 1880–1940*, Cambridge MA: National Bureau of Economic Research.

Leonesio, M., D. Vaughan et al. (2000), 'Early retirees under Social Security: health status and economic resources', *Social Security Bulletin*, **63**: 1–16.

Liu, J. and E. Neis (2002), *Endogenous Retirement and Portfolio Choice*, UCLA.

Marshall, V., P. Clarke et al. (2001), 'Instability in the retirement transition: effects on health and well-being in a Canadian study', *Research on Ageing*, **23**(4): 379–409.

Mein, G., P. Martikainen et al. (2000), 'Predictors of early retirement in British civil servants', *Age and Ageing*, **29**(6): 529–36.

Merton, R.C. (1969), 'Lifetime portfolio selection under uncertainty: the continuous-time case', *Review of Economics and Statistics*, **51**: 247–57.

Merton, R.C. (1971), 'Optimum consumption and portfolio rules in a continuous time model', *Journal of Economic Theory*, **3**: 373–413.

Mulvey, J. (2003), 'Retirement behaviour and retirement plan designs: Strategies to retain an ageing workforce', *Benefits Quarterly 2003*, **19**(4): 25–35.

Office for National Statistics (2003), *Internet Access First Release – Households and Individuals*, ONS.

Stock, J. and D. Wise (1990), 'Pensions, the option value of work and retirement', *Econometrica*, **58**(5): 1151–80.

Taylor, B. (2003), *Encyclopedia of Global Financial Markets*, Global Financial Data, Inc., http://www.globalfinancialdata.com.

Tversky, A. and D. Kahneman (1991), 'Loss aversion and riskless choice: A reference dependent model', *Quarterly Journal of Economics*, **57**: 1039–61.

UK Cabinet Office (2000), *Winning the Generation Game*, London: UK Cabinet Office Performance and Innovation Unit.

Williamson, J. and T. McNamara (2001), *Why Some Workers Remain in the Labour Force Beyond the Typical Age of Retirement*, Center for Retirement Research, Boston College.

7. Financial engineering for Australian annuitants[1]

Susan Thorp, Geoffrey Kingston and Hazel Bateman

Where now remains a sweet reversion.
We may boldly spend, upon the hope of what
Is to come in.
A comfort of retirement lives in this.
William Shakespeare, *Henry IV* Part I, Act 4, Scene 1

INTRODUCTION

After a decade of focus on accumulation under the Superannuation Guarantee, attention is now shifting to decumulation as workers with mandated superannuation retire and 'boldly spend, upon the hope of what is to come in'. Decisions about investment portfolios, risk management and regulation are no less critical in retirement (when labour income no longer acts as a safety valve for financial pressures) than during working life. Designing efficient retirement income streams is a key to enhancing welfare later in life.

Policy-based analysis of retirement income streams is frequently centred on a desired subsistence consumption path or replacement rate, but the conventional tool of theoretical analysis, the constant relative risk aversion (CRRA) utility function, implicitly sets this consumption floor to zero. Results derived from CRRA models tend to oversimplify attitudes to risk, and analysis can consequently overlook important aspects of portfolio management. Our approach is to readdress a number of retirement income issues using a utility formulation drawn from the habit persistence paradigm, one that is better adapted to a non-zero consumption floor, thus creating a critical link between policy and theory. To do this, we engage some of the tools of financial engineering.

Financial engineering can be defined as the application of dynamic hedging theory to the management of assets and liabilities. It tends to control risk by constructing floors under the range of adverse outcomes rather than minimizing the volatility of returns. So we focus on maintaining a consumption floor (similar to a minimum replacement rate) while allowing for exposure to volatile returns once that consumption floor is insured. Such a set-up seems well suited to the special problems and uncertainties of the drawdown phase.

Using simulations and other calibrated numerical experiments, we offer new perspectives on income stream choices for Australian annuitants. In particular we demonstrate that to ensure a constant subsistence rate of consumption over a plausibly long retirement, annuitants need more conservative portfolio strategies than are commonly advised. Even those with large accumulations have little scope for risky asset exposure if they plan to provide for a long horizon without the help of risk pooling, making a *prima facie* case for longevity insurance.

Analysis begins by describing the pensions and annuities now used for retirement payouts. Next we sketch the theoretical framework needed to build retirement income streams with consumption floors. We then put the theory to work by simulating the optimal consumption and portfolio choices of our representative agent over a variety of time horizons and risk tolerances, and finally explore the pros and cons of delaying lifetime annuity purchase for the same agent.

RETIREMENT INCOME STREAMS: A REVIEW

Australian retirees can choose from an extensive range of income stream products.[2] These can be grouped into three categories: lifetime annuities; term certain annuities; and allocated annuities or pensions (hereafter 'allocated pensions'). Lifetime annuities guarantee an agreed income stream for the life of the beneficiary whereas term certain annuities end after a fixed period. Allocated pensions, really a phased withdrawal product, create a variable income stream from an investment account. Australian retirees prefer allocated income streams, which offer ongoing control over capital and payout pattern, to the income certainty and longevity insurance offered by life annuities.

Fixed Income Streams: Lifetime and Term Annuities

Fixed income streams are available as *lifetime* or *term* annuities. By guaranteeing a preset (escalating or indexed) income stream for the life of the beneficiary in exchange for forfeiting control over capital, lifetime annuities give protection against longevity and poor returns. Despite the fact that lifetime annuities convey desirable tax and social security concessions, they remain relatively unpopular with retirees, and sales of lifetime contracts are a small part of the total market. Their small market share could be partly due to pricing issues. Underlying market fluctuations can make timing a purchase critical; and empirical analyses point to high administrative loadings partly owing to adverse selection (Doyle et al. 2002).

By contrast, term annuities are more popular. Terms can range from 1 to 25 years (including life expectancy). A special subset of term annuities are life expectancy annuities with no residual capital value (RCV), which convey the same social security and tax advantages as lifetime annuities. Regulatory incentives notwithstanding, term annuities with positive RCV have been the most popular among fixed income stream choices, frequently used to house accumulations between preservation age and actual retirement (Doyle et al. 2002, p 6).

Variable Income Streams: Allocated Pensions

Allocated pensions have been the foremost product among income streams in Australia. Their main advantages are a flexible drawdown of income, access to capital, and choice among a wide variety of investment portfolios, but they carry the disadvantages of an array of risks borne by the pensioner.

Allocated pensions offer flexible income streams but there are limits to the amount and timing of withdrawals. Each income stream is fixed annually but payments are usually made more often, most commonly each month. Whatever the frequency, annual income payments must fall between legislated upper and lower limits, which change with the age of the pensioner. The maximum drawdown is designed to exhaust the account balance around the age of 80 years, while the minimum extends payments out past 100 years of age. Following either the upper or lower limits makes a hump-shaped income stream which declines rapidly as the account balance approaches zero.

Figure 7.1 shows the income streams drawn from a $500 000 account balance (beginning at age 65), accumulating at 5 per cent per annum, and assuming that withdrawals follow the boundaries set by the minimum and maximum pension valuation factors. The minimum withdrawal stream provides a modest but smooth income path for about 20 years before tapering towards zero, whereas the maximum withdrawal produces 15 years of steep slide, ending precipitously around age 80. In reality, most allocated pension holders choose conservative drawdowns well below the legislated maximum, possibly protecting themselves against unexpectedly long lives or unusually bad investment returns. Limited payouts are also consistent with the international evidence for surprisingly strong saving during retirement (Hurd 1990).

Regardless of their drawdown rate, investment risk is a real concern to retirees holding allocated pensions. Average portfolio mix is given in Figure 7.2,

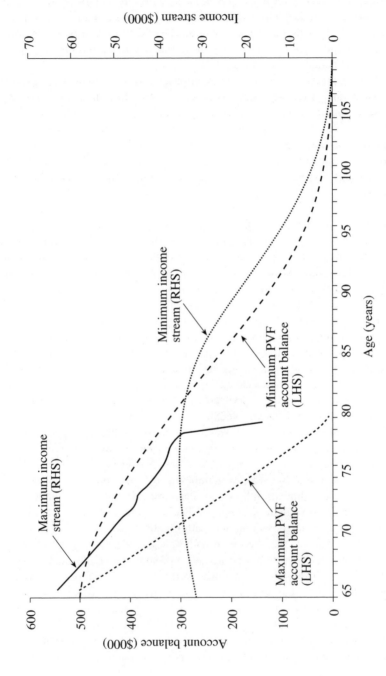

Figure 7.1 Allocated pension minimum and maximum drawdown streams

which aggregates allocated accounts by asset class. More than 45 per cent of funds are invested in equity, the remainder mainly in fixed interest and cash, with about 10 per cent in Australian property. We can infer that Australian retirees drawing pensions experience proportionate volatility in their account balances, with negative returns a real possibility.

Finally, unlike lifetime annuities, allocated pensions make capital accessible. Account balances can be wholly or partly withdrawn, though partial withdrawals are often restricted by frequency or size.

Sales of Income Streams

Since the early 1990s, sales of allocated pensions have dwarfed other annuity categories. Figure 7.3 charts sales of allocated pensions and fixed annuities since 1989. Allocated pensions dominate sales. Term annuities with RCV are a very much weaker second. Sales of lifetime products continue to decline in favour of term annuities. By December 2003, IFSA (2002) reported that allocated pensions amounted to 89 per cent of the eligible termination payment (ETP)[3] funds under management, with all types of fixed income products accounting for the remaining 11 per cent.

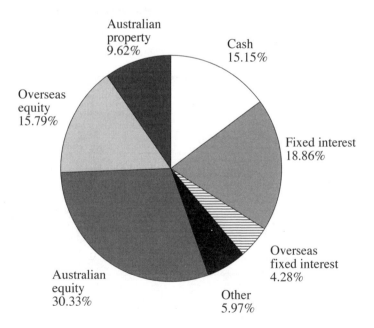

Source: Plan for Life Actuaries and Researchers.

Figure 7.2   Allocation of pension funds by asset class, 2002

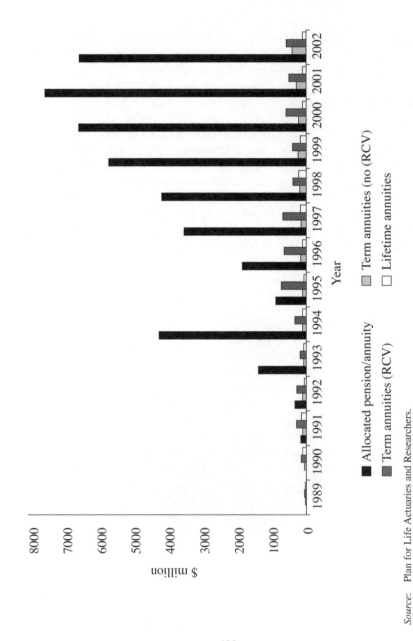

Source: Plan for Life Actuaries and Researchers.

Figure 7.3   Pensions and annuities eligible termination payment sales, 1989–2002

Australian retirees can choose from allocated streams which provide for potentially higher investment returns, but offer no longevity insurance, and may be subject to investment risk; fixed income streams with more or less inflation and longevity insurance, but less investment uncertainty; and the means-tested age pension. Social security and taxation regulations interact with retirement income streams in complex ways, but the key features of the system are the more generous tests for pensioners who sacrifice access to their capital over the duration of their life expectancy, income test relief to capital drawdowns, and quite general tax rebates. The popularity of allocated products (and unpopularity of lifetime annuities) suggests that flexibility and investment choice remain important decision variables into retirement.

Now we have sketched the income streams market, our next focus is to find the balance between a certain income stream and exposure to risky assets which will maximize the welfare of retirees. The next section sets up the theoretical foundations of optimal portfolio allocations for an agent who aims to keep consumption above a pre-specified level over his or her remaining lifetime.

THEORETICAL FOUNDATIONS

Predictions from life-cycle theories depend on assumptions about agents' preferences for consumption and risk. The conventional constant relative risk aversion (CRRA) model, for example, assumes that agents derive satisfaction from the absolute level of their consumption. An alternative view is that utility from consumption is better measured relative to some reference level (Rubinstein 1976). In other words, utility increases only as consumption rises above a floor or subsistence.[4] Generalizing the CRRA model to include a (constant or time-varying) consumption floor can permit a richer description of risk tolerance.

Assumptions about risk tolerance are crucial to portfolio selection. Whereas CRRA investors selecting portfolio weights for an unchanging investment opportunity set will choose a constant exposure to the risky asset over all levels of wealth, investors who care about relative consumption will increase their weighting in the risky asset (albeit from a lower starting exposure) as consumption increases away from its subsistence floor. To the extent that consumption is positively correlated with the business cycle, these investors will exhibit pro-cyclical risk tolerance.

This generalized utility (HARA – hyperbolic absolute risk aversion)[5] model also meshes more naturally with the superannuation policy debate. The most common metric for the adequacy of an accumulation is the long-term income stream (or replacement rate) which it can generate. Superannuation calculators (such as the 'Are you on track' calculator at the AMP website) frame retirement provision in terms of 'required gross income in today's dollars' in order to identify the minimum consumption stream on which a person can adequately subsist. To describe such a preference for subsistence consumption one needs a non-zero consumption floor in the utility function.

Correspondingly, a simplified version of a habit persistence model is useful for modelling retirement income streams. The model outlined here includes a fixed consumption floor designed to mimic a well-established habit.

Optimal Allocation and Consumption Paths

Consider the lifetime consumption stream and portfolio allocation for an investor with any concave utility function.[6] Assume the date of death, T, is known with certainty and the investor receives no labour income, consuming only out of wealth and investment returns. The agent can choose between one risk-free and one risky asset. In the final period all remaining wealth is consumed, leaving no bequest.

The investor's problem is to maximize utility over retirement by choosing a consumption stream and allocating wealth between the assets.

$$\max E[\hat{U}(C_0, C_1, \ldots C_{T-1}, W_T)] = \max E \left[\sum_{t-0}^{T} U(C, t) \right] \qquad (7.1)$$

The investor knows:

$P_i(t)$ = the price of security $i, i = 0,1$;
$W(t)$ = current wealth;

and can choose:

$C(t)$ = current consumption;
$N_i(t)$ = number of shares of each asset.

The wealth constraint is given by

$$W(t) - C(t) \equiv I(t) = \sum_{0}^{1} N_i(t) P_i(t) \qquad (7.2)$$

so all wealth not consumed in a given period is allocated between the risky and risk-free assets.

Define the share of wealth allocated to security i as:

$$w_i(t) \equiv \frac{N_i(t) P_i(t)}{I(t)} \qquad (7.3)$$

$$w_0 + w_1 = 1$$

and define next period's gross return to asset 1, a random variable:

$$\tilde{z}(t) \equiv \frac{\tilde{P}_1(t+1)}{P_1(t)} \tag{7.4}$$

The agent's portfolio return is the weighted sum of returns over both assets in the portfolio, defined by:

$$\tilde{Z}(t) \equiv w_1(t)[\tilde{z}(t) - R] + R \tag{7.5}$$

Using R as the gross return to the risk-free asset, w_0 as the portfolio weight allocated to the risk-free asset, and the full investment condition, the value of wealth available for consumption in period $t+1$ is:

$$w(t+1) = [W(t) - C(t)]\{w_1(t)[\tilde{z}(t) - R] + R\} \tag{7.6}$$

The derived utility of wealth function for period t can be written as:

$$J[W(t),t] = \max_{c,w} E_t \left[\sum_{s=t}^{T} U(C,S) \right]$$

$$J[W(T),T] = U(W_T,T) \tag{7.7}$$

If the agent's preferences are described by $U(C,t) = (\delta^t C^\gamma)/\gamma$, as for the conventional constant relative risk aversion (CRRA) investor (here denoted by superscript P), the derived utility of wealth function, by backward induction, is

$$J(W,t) = \frac{\delta^t a_t^{\gamma-1} W_t^\gamma}{\gamma}$$

$$\tag{7.8}$$

$$a_t \equiv \left[1 + (\delta E_t[\tilde{Z}^{P\gamma} a_{t+1}^{\gamma-1}])^{\frac{1}{1-\gamma}} \right]^{-1}$$

optimal consumption is

$$C_t^P = \alpha_t W_t \tag{7.9}$$

and the optimal portfolio is

$$E_t[(\alpha_{t+1}\tilde{Z}^P)^{\gamma-1}(\tilde{z} - R)] = 0. \tag{7.10}$$

If returns are independently and identically distributed, so that $\tilde{Z}^P$ and a_{t+1} are uncorrelated, then the investor looks only to the next period in decision making. If the investment set is changing stochastically over time (so that the moments of the risky asset returns distribution or the interest rate are not constant), then the portfolio held by a multiperiod investor takes into account the future beyond the next period as well.

Making a transition to a positive consumption floor produces analogous results. Choosing a utility function with a subsistence consumption, $\hat{C}$,

$$U(C,t) = \frac{\delta^t (C - \hat{C})^\gamma}{\gamma}, \gamma < 1 \tag{7.11}$$

yields a derived utility of wealth function

$$J(W,t) = \frac{\delta^t a_t^{\gamma-1}(W - \hat{W}_t)^\gamma}{\gamma} \tag{7.12}$$

where

$$\hat{W}_t = \hat{C}_t \sum_{s=t}^{T} R^{t-s} \tag{7.13}$$

and a_t is defined as in (7.8). It can be shown that the optimal consumption path (with HARA denoted by superscript H) is given by

$$C^H = \hat{C} + \frac{(W - \hat{W}_t)}{W_t} \alpha_t W_t \tag{7.14}$$

$$= \hat{C} + \frac{(W - \hat{W}_t)}{W_t} C_t^P$$

The HARA agent always consumes their subsistence amount $\hat{C}$, then consumes proportionately to the CRRA agent, after allowing for the wealth set aside 'in escrow' to provide future periods' subsistence, $\hat{W}_t$.

A similar relationship can be set out for allocations between the risky and risk-free assets:

$$w_{0t}^H = \frac{\hat{W}_{t+1}}{(W - C^H)R} + \frac{W - C^H - \hat{W}_{t+1}/R}{W - C^H} \, w_{0t}^P$$ (7.15)

$$w_{1t}^H = \frac{W - C^H - \hat{W}_{t+1}/R}{W - C^H} \, w_{1t}^P$$

Again the intuition is straightforward: the HARA investor needs to ensure future subsistence by putting the net present value of all future $\hat{C}$s into the risk-free asset. The remainder of his or her wealth is then allocated in the same proportions as for the CRRA investor. Given a value for the curvature parameter, γ, the greater the 'cushion' between current wealth and $\hat{W}_t$, the more exposure to risk is optimal.

Here one can see the relationship between utility maximization with a consumption floor and portfolio insurance strategies. In its simplest form portfolio insurance uses actual or synthetic put options to enable an equity investor to avoid losses, but capture gains, at the cost of a fixed premium (Leland 1980). The distinguishing feature of portfolio insurance, according to Perold and Sharpe (1988), is that not only does the agent have a floor level of wealth such as that defined by $\hat{W}_t$, but the curvature of the utility function is sufficiently low that the investor responds to rising stock prices by buying more stocks. However, they observe that only 'buy-and-hold' strategies can be followed by all investors so, in this sense, portfolio insurance has to be a minority taste.

The constant w_1^P in (7.15) is analogous to the m of Black and Perold's (1992) constant proportion portfolio insurance (CPPI). Their CPPI decision rule sets exposure to the risky asset at a constant multiple of the cushion between current and floor wealth, $W - \hat{W}_t$. The optimal level of this m for HARA investors is w_1^P, a point made implicitly in Merton (1971) and explicitly in Kingston (1989). CPPI investors shift money from the worse-performing to the better-performing asset, buying into rising markets and selling into falling markets, a strategy that protects $\hat{C}$ while capturing risky payoffs.

The following section presents simulations of these optimal paths to map out a pattern of insured consumption, loosely calibrated to Australian conditions.

SIMULATION OF CONSUMPTION AND WEALTH STREAMS

Having derived the conditions for optimal consumption and portfolio allocation in discrete time, we can gain some insight by simulating a range of consumption and investment paths for a representative agent. For the time being, the analysis will abstract from interaction with the social security and taxation systems.

Profile of Representative Agent

Mortality

The representative agent is assumed to be 65 years old at retirement and male, with mortality described by the 1995–97 Australian Life Tables. Having survived to age 65, he could expect to live another 16 years, to 81 years; the probability of living to 91 is 12 per cent; and to 100 is 1 per cent, giving an indication of the potential value of longevity insurance. Simulation paths are worked over certain lifetimes of three lengths: life expectancy (81 years), 25 years (to age 90) and 40 years.

Accumulation

The simulations start with an endowment of $500 000 at age 65.

Consumption floor

While the original goal of the Superannuation Guarantee was to achieve a replacement rate of 40 per cent of final income, no specific benchmark has since been set by the government (Commonwealth of Australia 2002, p. 13, para. 2.21). Policy discussion flags an amount of $25 000–$30 000 per year for an individual who owns their home, providing a replacement rate close to 60–65 per cent of 2002 average weekly earnings. Further, empirical studies of the habit model suggest that whatever the relative merits of alternative time paths, it is clear that the difference between consumption and its habit-level floor should probably be small (Chen and Ludvigson 2003).

Given that the age pension is not counted here as a part of wealth and that the assumed habit level is fixed, the consumption floor is set at $20 000 per year. This level is lower than conventional replacement rates but not far below base-line measures of adequacy. While $20 000 may seem low, recall that optimal paths can never fall below this value and will be above it in almost every period.

Attitude to risk

Sensitivity analysis is conducted over three different levels of risk tolerances, setting the curvature parameter, γ, to -1, 0 and 0.5. The case $\gamma = 0$, in conjunction with assumed capital market parameters, turns out to approximate the central buy-and-hold case. Hence, the $\gamma = -1$ case describes 'buy low, sell high' behaviour while $\gamma = 0.5$ considers portfolio insurance.

Asset returns

The annuitant is offered a portfolio of one risky and one risk-free asset providing real returns. These approximate a well-diversified portfolio of equities and a portfolio of inflation-indexed bonds.

Real risky asset prices are described by conventional geometric Brownian motion

$$dP_1(t) = \alpha P_1(t) + \sigma P_1(t)dz \qquad (7.16)$$

where dz is a standard Wiener process; thus the log of one-period gross returns is normally distributed.

Values for α and σ are set by reference to long-term forecasts of the real equity premium and observed sample values of the standard deviation of the market index for equities, setting $\alpha = 0.06$ and $\sigma = 0.17$ and generating data as drawn from a normal distribution.

The risk-free asset is assumed to follow:

$$dB(t) = rB(t)dt \qquad (7.17)$$

with $r = 0.03$.

The discrete time analogue to this process gives a one-period gross return to the risky asset of 1.0618 with a standard deviation of 0.18, and a gross return to the risk-free asset of 1.03.

Simulation Results

Simulations compare the consumption and portfolio choices of an individual who cares about absolute levels of consumption with one who derives satisfaction from consumption relative to a \$20 000 floor. Practically, this means comparing the HARA with CRRA or 'power' paths for the same level of endowed wealth and curvature parameter, γ. The agent begins with a \$500 000 endowment and uses the rules described by equations (7.14) and (7.15) to optimally consume in the current year and save into the next. Each period the agent is subject to a random draw from the risky asset returns, which feeds into next period's choices.

Average consumption and wealth paths

As an example of simulation results, consider Figure 7.4, which shows consumption and wealth paths for individuals whose horizon is 81 years, or life expectancy, and whose curvature parameter is $\gamma = 0$. For the sake of illustration, the risky asset return in this example is set equal to its mean each period, so consumption and wealth paths appear smooth over the whole of retirement. The HARA agent consumes between \$37 000 and \$50 000 each year, as compared with the CRRA agent who, benefiting more from the artificially fixed equity

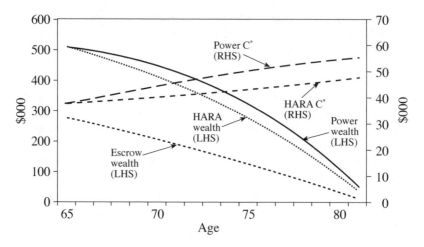

Figure 7.4   Consumption and wealth paths to age 81

return, achieves a much steeper consumption path. Wealth declines gradually for both types, but is always lower for the HARA agent, whose best allocation is more weighted towards the indexed bond.

As the time horizon expands, the policy of consumption insurance becomes more important to the portfolio choices of the individuals. For comparison, consider Figure 7.5, which conducts the same experiment as in Figure 7.4, but with lifetime expanded to 105 years. The escrow constraint annexes almost the

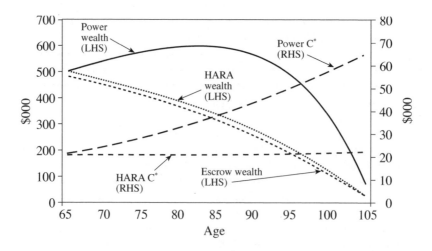

Figure 7.5   Consumption and wealth paths to age 105

whole of wealth over this horizon, and the consumption path barely deviates from the $20 000 floor. Even with an endowment of $500 000 the agent has only just enough to cover base-line consumption out to age 105.

Average portfolio allocations

Portfolio allocations for each risk tolerance over three different time horizons are shown in Table 7.1. Two features deserve comment: first, for given values of γ, the HARA utility investor is prepared to give the risky asset only about half as much weight as the CRRA investor. At $\gamma = 0.5$, the HARA investor is prepared to short the risk-free asset later in life to gain more exposure to higher returns, but for $\gamma = 0$, exposure is 46–57 per cent of wealth, and for $\gamma = -1$, is closer to 25 per cent, and almost constant. Second, because of the decreasing demands of future consumption floors and the moderate level of impatience, risky exposure increases over the remaining lifetime. This is illustrated dramatically at the 40-year horizon, where the most risk tolerant of the HARA investors gradually increases exposure to the risky asset from 7 to 75 per cent of wealth as he gets closer to the terminal date and $\hat{W}_t$ shrinks. (By comparison, the related CRRA investor is willing to borrow almost their whole wealth again in the bond market to double their exposure to the risky asset.)

Not surprisingly, a combination of conservatism and a long life strains the resources of the representative agent. As the curvature parameter falls and the time horizon lengthens, optimal exposure to the risky asset drops away dramatically. For $\gamma = 0$, the range is from 4 to 10 per cent, but for $\gamma = -1$ risky asset allocation barely rises from 2 to 3 per cent of overall portfolio. Almost the whole of wealth passes into the risk-free asset to insure against long life, and investment risk and allocation patterns are optimally conservative.

Simulations with random risky asset draws

Once random draws from the risky asset distribution are allowed, consumption and wealth paths become jagged, and consequently so do the portfolio weights of the HARA investor, whose allocations adjust period by period to

Table 7.1 Range of risky asset exposure as percentage of wealth

	CRRA	HARA		
	All	81 years	90 years	105 years
$\gamma = 0.5$	191	88–134	51–128	7–75
$\gamma = 0$	100	46–57	27–43	4–11
$\gamma = -1$	51	23–26	13–17	2–3

Note: Allocations involving borrowing could be implemented via derivatives such as warrants.

Table 7.2   Simulated probability of consumption <$20 000 in at least one year (%)

	81 years	90 years	105 years
$\gamma = 0.5$	52	100	100
$\gamma = 0$	21	48	78
$\gamma = -1$	3	25	67

protect future subsistence levels. In fact, consumption paths for the uninsured CRRA agent are quite likely to drop below the $20 000 floor at least once over the course of a retirement. Repeated simulations of the power utility path were conducted to gain an estimate of the likelihood that any consumption path calculated using random draws from the risky asset falls below $20 000 in at least one year. Table 7.2 records the results of those simulations. While the most conservative power investor has only a 3 per cent chance of a bad year to age 81, the chance increases to one in four by age 90, and living to a very old age (105) makes a year of below-subsistence consumption more likely than not. Of course, the more risk-tolerant investors face much higher probabilities, and the likelihood of $C < $20 000$ in at least one year approaches certainty as γ and the time horizon increase. Breaching the consumption floor is a real and increasing risk (to agents who do not actively protect it), as wealth is stretched over a longer life.

Simulations for age pension recipients
On the one hand there is a high likelihood of at least one very lean year for those not insuring the consumption floor, but on the other hand, the simulations so far have not accounted for the insurance value of the age pension. In the Australian context the age pension might act as a safety net for many, if not most, retirees in years of low returns, so it is interesting to consider how much this additional floor could affect the agent's willingness to bear risk.

Table 7.3   Risky asset exposure with full age pension

	81 years		90 years		105 years	
	$9000	$20 000	$9000	$20 000	$9000	$20 000
$\gamma = 0.5$	145–172	88–134	127–175	51–128	109–183	7–75
$\gamma = 0$	76–84	46–57	68–81	27–43	57–82	4–11
$\gamma = -1$	39–40	23–26	34–37	13–17	29–35	2–3

As a preliminary foray into this question, the optimal portfolio allocations can be recalculated assuming the agent receives \$11 000 of his preferred \$20 000 floor through the full age pension. The results are summarized in Table 7.3, illustrating the increasing exposure to risky assets that a universal age pension could potentially allow. Exposures almost double over the life expectancy horizon, more than double over a 25-year horizon and increase by about ten times for the 40-year timespan. A small publicly provided lifetime annuity can substantially increase optimal risky asset weights.

Even an endowment of \$500 000 has not given the representative agent much freedom to invest outside the bond market because of the demands of guarding the consumption floor. By comparison, recall that the average exposure to risky assets of an allocated pension account is around 50–55 per cent. Observed investment patterns in allocated pension accounts suggest that many retirees either rely on the age pension safety net, have 'safe assets' stored in other places (e.g. bank accounts), display some myopia, or are persuaded by advisers to hold more aggressive portfolios than may be in their best interest.

Since protecting oneself from longevity and investment risk places such stringent restrictions on portfolio allocations and consumption paths, these simulations could be used to make a *prima facie* case for annuitization. However, a developing area of research on the best time to annuitize (Milevsky and Young 2002, 2003) has demonstrated that immediate full annuitization is not always an optimal strategy. We re-evaluate the Milevsky–Young analysis for the HARA case.

OPTIONS TO DELAY ANNUITIZATION

As noted above, and contrary to the predictions of economic theory, Australians (along with the rest of the world) show a marked reluctance to buy life annuities (IFSA 2002). The list of possible explanations for this, apart from the adverse selection already noted, includes the wish to make bequests to heirs, alternative support from family members or from life income streams provided by the government, the wish to self-insure against the contingencies of expensive health care or nursing home care, high life-office margins arising from incompleteness in either the maturity structure or the contingency structure of government bonds on issue, and inadequate consumer education (Mitchell and McCarthy 2002). As comprehensive as this list is, it does not seem completely convincing.

Milevsky and Young's (2002, 2003) new explanation of this reluctance to annuitize begins with the observation that renegotiable annuity contracts are not available in general, so that the decision to purchase longevity insurance is irreversible. The literature on real options demonstrates that in an uncertain environment it often pays to delay investments that cannot easily be reversed. Using a Merton (1969) continuous time model with constant relative risk aversion, Milevsky and Young show that, for retirees constrained to make a complete and irreversible switch into a life annuity, the best age to annuitize may be well into retirement.

Advantages to delaying annuitization in their model arise from the possibility that higher returns in future periods will improve the budget constraint of the retiree, providing an enhanced stream of income after annuitization. Moreover, by explicitly modeling the annuitant's *subjective* knowledge of their own mortality as against the annuity provider's *objective* assessment, Milevsky and Young are able to show that people who expect to live either longer or shorter lives than implied by the objective standard will have cause to delay annuitization. Annuitants who anticipate longer lives will build up their wealth in the risky environment and take advantage of the progressive falls in the price of life annuities as they age. Annuitants who anticipate shorter lives find the objectively priced annuities expensive, and avoid them for longer. These results appear to be both surprising and general.

Annuitization with a Consumption Floor

In the event that the potential annuitant and the annuity provider agree about the prospects of survival, the date of annuitization for a CRRA (zero-floor) agent is determined by comparing the returns to the risky asset (the Sharpe ratio) with the benefits of the certain income stream offered under the annuity. The investor's tolerance for risk, survival prospects and expectations of asset returns are all factors in the decision.

If the agent prefers to insure a floor level of consumption, the advantages to delaying annuitization are weakened. The full analysis of the HARA case is set out in Kingston and Thorp (2004), but the intuition can be summarized in Figure 7.6. For brevity, attention is restricted to the case where utility is defined as the log of the difference between actual consumption and floor consumption, corresponding to Milevsky and Young (2002), Appendix D and analogous to the $\gamma = 0$ case in our simulation model. The Sharpe ratio of 0.18 corresponds to the assumptions made earlier in the text.

As the agent ages, the probability of dying (symbolized here as λ) rises. This increasing force of mortality makes annuity prices more favourable over time. It is not until λ is sufficiently high that the agent will finally and irreversibly close out the prospect of increasing wealth via the risky asset, and make the switch into annuities. By contrast, the HARA retiree is already protecting all future subsistence consumption in escrow wealth, and thus holds a smaller proportion of total wealth in the equity portfolio than the agent with a zero floor. Lower exposure to the potentially high-yielding risky asset

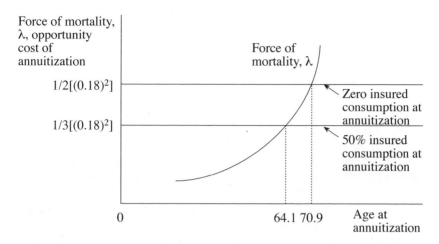

Figure 7.6   Optimal age at annuitization with and without a consumption floor

reduces the option value of delaying annuitization proportionately.

In this way, introducing a positive consumption floor has a similar effect to raising relative risk aversion. In addition, the agent recognizes that it costs less to store escrow wealth in an annuity rather than a bond portfolio over an infinite horizon, thus creating another incentive to switch into complete annuitization at an earlier date.

Table 7.4 shows the optimal time to annuitize with and without insured consumption. (At 50 per cent insured consumption, the HARA agent displays relative risk aversion of two; at zero insured consumption, the RRA is one.)

There are two key observations to make here. First, the combination of a conservative forward-looking Sharpe ratio and a 50 per cent consumption

Table 7.4   Optimal age at annuitization, male (female)

Sharpe ratio	Zero insured consumption		50% insured consumption
	RRA=1	RRA=2	RRA=2
0.18	70.9 (76.1)	64.1 (70.3)	64.1 (70.3)
0.30	80.9 (84.6)	74.1 (78.8)	74.1 (78.8)

Notes: The Sharpe ratio of 0.18 obtains for the main capital-market parameter values assumed earlier in this chapter, namely, $\alpha = 0.06$, $r = 0.03$, and $\sigma = 0.17$. The Sharpe ratio of 0.30 obtains for the capital-market parameters assumed by Milevsky and Young (2002), namely, $\alpha = 12$, $r = 0.06$, and $\sigma = 0.20$. Modal and scale parameters of the Gompertz distribution were, for males (females) $b = 9.78$ (8.35) and $m = 88.95$ (92.76).

floor causes any advantage in delayed annuitization to vanish for males and to shrink to about five years for females. Not so, however, if choices are guided by an optimistic 'historical' assumption for the Sharpe ratio, linked to the high returns to equity that were recorded during the twentieth century in the USA, Australia, and a handful of other countries (Jorion and Goetzmann 1999). Following Milevsky and Young,[7] and using the higher Sharpe ratio, raises the optimal delays to almost ten years for men and 14 years for women. Second, optimistic estimates of survival probability will also delay annuitization.

Actual immediate annuity prices in Australia match up reasonably well to the calculations in Table 7.4. Quotes for a $100 000, consumer-price-indexed immediate life annuity for a 65-year-old female (with a ten-year guarantee) offer initial income of $4892.[8] Assuming a risk-free real interest rate of 3 per cent, this quote implies (from the purchaser's perspective) an average life expectancy for female annuitants of around 97 years, representing a discounting of population mortality estimates in the order of 55–60 per cent. This is consistent with the parameters underlying Table 7.4.

CONCLUSIONS

In this chapter we have sketched the current market for retirement income stream products in Australia and constructed some numerical experiments which shed light on optimal investment and annuitization strategies, considering these questions within a HARA framework. One advantage of this approach is that it focuses on the protection of a floor level of consumption rather than a general distaste for risk, and thus meshes well with practitioner and policy-based measures of welfare in retirement.

Out of the array of immediate annuity and allocated pension products currently available, Australian retirees have preferred the allocated pension, a product which gives the retiree the most flexibility and the least insurance against investment and longevity risk. Recent survey data indicate that, on the one hand, allocated pensioners manage their accounts conservatively, drawing down balances quite slowly, while on the other hand choosing a 50–55 per cent average exposure to risky assets.

This degree of risk exposure may be at odds with securing a sufficiently long minimum consumption rate, since simulation experiments outlined here suggest that conservative portfolio allocations are necessary to guarantee an income stream as low as $20 000 past life expectancy. The insurance role of the age pension is one possible explanation for annuitants' portfolio choices. More optimistic views on prospective returns and risks to shares are another. Both candidate explanations deserve attention in future research.

These issues raise the well-documented but puzzling reluctance of annuitants to take up life annuities. We extend recent work by Milevsky and Young (2002, 2003) by investigating whether the optimal time to annuitize is brought forward or delayed for agents who want to protect a positive consumption floor. The extra burden of annuitizing the consumption floor brings forward the switch to a life annuity.

NOTES

1. The authors would like to acknowledge the helpful comments of Henry Jin, Robert Kohn, Sachi Purcal, Tony Richards and Mike Sherris.
2. A proportion of the Australian workforce receives occupational pensions in retirement under the terms of defined benefit superannuation schemes. Most of the discussion to follow focuses on members of defined contribution schemes for whom annuitization is voluntary.
3. ETPs are specific categories of lump-sum payments made at termination of employment or from superannuation funds or retirement savings accounts, which receive special tax treatment.
4. More recently, the habit formation literature has generalized the idea of relative utility by allowing the consumption floor to vary over time according to an internal or external reference path. See Constantinides (1990) or Campbell and Cochrane (1999) for examples.
5. The hyperbolic absolute risk aversion model, with a fixed consumption floor, is a time-separable special case of the habit persistence models. Merton (1971 and 1990) describes the portfolio allocation properties of this model in continuous time.
6. See Ingersoll (1987) and Campbell and Viceira (2002) for similar analysis.
7. The Milevsky–Young Sharpe ratio is based on Ibbotson Associates data, and their estimate of the Gompertz parameters were fit to Annuity Mortality table IAM2000 with projection scale G (see Milevsky and Young 2002, Table 1a, p. 23).
8. As quoted for AMP Life, *Personal Investor*, August 2003, p. 104.

REFERENCES

Black, F. and A.F. Perold (1992), 'Theory of constant proportion portfolio insurance', *Economic Dynamics and Control*, **16**, 403–26.

Campbell, J.Y. and J.H. Cochrane (1999), 'By force of habit: a consumption-based explanation of aggregate stock market behaviour', *Journal of Political Economy*, **107**(2), 205–51.

Campbell, J.Y. and L.M. Viceira (2002), *Strategic Asset Allocation: Portfolio Choice for Long Term Investors*. Oxford: Oxford University Press.

Chen, X. and S.C. Ludvigson (2003), 'Land of addicts? An empirical investigation of habit-based asset pricing models', unpublished manuscript, New York: New York University.

Commonwealth of Australia (2002), 'Superannuation and standards of living in retirement', Senate Select Committee on Superannuation, December. URL: http://www.aph.gov.au/senate_super.

Constantinides, G. (1990), 'Habit formation: a resolution of the equity premium puzzle', *Journal of Political Economy*, **98**(3), 519–43.

Doyle, S., O.S. Mitchell and J. Piggott (2002), 'Annuity values in defined contribution retirement systems: the case of Singapore and Australia', UNSW Centre for Pension and Superannuation Discussion Paper no. 02/02, Sydney: University of New South Wales.

Hurd, M. (1990), 'Research on the elderly: economic status, retirement, and consumption and saving', *Journal of Economic Literature*, **28**(2), 565–7.

Ingersoll, J.E. (1987), *Theory of Financial Decision Making*, Totowa, NJ: Rowman & Littlefield.

Investment and Financial Services Association (2002), Retirement Income Streams Report, December.

Jorion, P. and W. Goetzmann (1999), 'Global stock markets in the twentieth century', *Journal of Finance*, **54**, 953–80.

Kingston, G. (1989), 'Theoretical foundations of constant proportion portfolio insurance', *Economics Letters*, **29**, 345–7.

Kingston, G. and S. Thorp (2004), 'Asset allocation and annuitisation with HARA utility', unpublished manuscript, School of Economics, University of New South Wales, Sydney.

Leland, H.E. (1980), 'Who should buy portfolio insurance?', *Journal of Finance*, **35**(2), 581–94.

Merton, R.C. (1969), 'Lifetime portfolio selection under uncertainty: the continuous time case', *Review of Economics and Statistics*, **51**, 239–46.

Merton, R.C. (1971), 'Optimum consumption and portfolio rules in a continuous time model', *Journal of Economic Theory*, **3**, 373–413.

Merton, R.C. (1990), *Continuous Time Finance*, Oxford: Blackwell.

Milevsky, M.A. and V.R. Young (2002), 'Optimal asset allocation and the real option to delay annuitisation: It's not now or never', Discussion Paper PI-0211, The Pensions Institute, Birkbeck College, University of London.

Milevsky, M.A. and V.R. Young (2003), 'Annuitization and asset allocation', *Management Science*, forthcoming.

Mitchell, O.S. and D. McCarthy (2002), 'Annuities for an aging world', NBER Working Paper no. 9092, National Bureau of Economic Research, Cambridge, Massachusetts, August.

Perold, A.F. and W.F. Sharpe (1988), 'Dynamic strategies for asset allocation', *Financial Analysts Journal*, January–February, 16–27.

Plan For Life (2003) *The Pension and Annuity Market Research Report*, Issue 39, May, Plan For Life Actuaries and Researchers, Mt Waverly.

Rubinstein, M. (1976), 'The strong case for the Generalized Logarithmic Utility Model as the premier model of financial markets', *Journal of Finance*, **31**, 551–71.

8. Smoothing investment returns

Anthony Asher

INTRODUCTION

Pensioners want smoothed incomes in retirement, but it is doubtful whether they can or should be given an absolute guarantee. Defined benefit schemes, which do smooth income, are open to manipulation and may not be financially viable. Defined contribution schemes can produce reasonably smooth incomes if assets are diversified and investment results are smoothed. This chapter describes smoothing algorithms that efficiently switch to safer investments before retirement. The algorithms provide a better alternative to traditional smoothing mechanisms because they are not subject to arbitrary discretion or to anti-selection.

Other things being equal, we expect people to want a predictable and smooth income stream in retirement. This would enable them to fund regular consumption and to budget for less regular expenses. In spite of this, both private and public superannuation schemes have been changed, over the past 20 years particularly, from defined benefit (DB) to defined contribution (DC). Investment risk is thereby transferred from the sponsor (employer or state) to the members. The benefits paid are therefore not necessarily predictable or smooth. The issue has been discussed, *inter alia*, by Knox (1993), Khorasanee (1995) and Blake (2000).

This chapter addresses the question of how DC funds can provide smoother investment returns. In the next section, we look at the difference between long- and short-term investment risks and the problems faced by DB funds in coping with changes to the social and economic environment. This inflexibility, and their opaqueness, can be seen as causes of their current unpopularity. The rest of the chapter then describes the smoothing algorithms.

THE MANAGEMENT OF RISK

Longer-term Risks

The transfer of risk from sponsors to fund members can be seen to have a long-term and a short-term component. This is perhaps best illustrated in the context of mortality risk, which is also transferred from DB scheme sponsors to DC members. It applies to the costs of the death benefits payable to members' dependants, and to the risks of longevity. The relatively short-term risks of fluctuations in experience can be absorbed by insurance contracts and life annuities. These can be purchased from life insurance companies or self-insured by the fund. Longer-term fluctuations require changes to premium rates. The distinction between the long- and short-term risks effectively depends on the financial capability of sponsors and insurance companies to provide guarantees. They can do so for short-term risks, but not for the long term.

The issue of financial capability is also relevant to long- and short-term investment risks. The risks are, however, much larger. Estimates of the long-term net real rate of return vary from about 1 per cent to 5 per cent annually. The lower return is that available from indexed-linked stocks – after inflation, taxes and expenses. The upper end of the range arises from the estimates of Dimson et al. (2004) of the likely equity premium. The equity premium arises from a number of sources: the inherent risk and the costs of investing are probably the most important. Dimson's estimate of 3.5 per cent for the equity premium is lower than that reported by Welch (2000) in a survey of economists, but probably more realistic. With typical contributions and expenses, the difference between 1 and 5 per cent would translate into a DC pension of between 35 and 130 per cent of average income when spread over a 60-year span. This compares with a variability of perhaps 10 per cent each way in the value of a life annuity as a result of unexpected changes to mortality over the life of a typical pensioner.

If long-term investment returns are lower than expected, members of DC funds will have to contribute more during their working lives, accept lower pensions or work for longer. The last strategy can be very effective: each year of additional contributions will increase a pension by some 10 per cent. The major role for investment smoothing is to provide members with more time to adjust their plans for retirement in line with variations in long-term investment returns.

Cross-subsidies and Inequities in DB Funds

The DB design does not provide a model for such smoothing, not least because it is impossible to guarantee investment returns forever. In a DB fund, the long-term variability in investment returns will produce differences to contribution rates of the same order as differences in DC benefit levels. Lower investment returns will lead to higher contributions by sponsors (either the employer or the state) over a period that is likely to extend beyond the working life of the members.

In employer-sponsored schemes, there would be no inequity if the salary packages of new employees reflected the *ex ante* fair value of the promised benefits, and the employer absorbed the profits and losses arising from deviations in investment returns from those expected. Neither condition is usually met. The first condition would require salary packages to be adjusted for the value of the pension benefits accruing. It is, however, practically impossible to distinguish between groups of members, such as different generations of recruits. This creates cross-subsidies between the groups, the value of which is seldom, if ever, determined.

The failure to calculate the value of the cross-subsidies between different groups of employees also means that the second condition cannot be met. Little attempt is usually made to determine whether the employer is bearing a fair share of costs. This opaqueness and imprecision in the allocation of costs open the way for strong opportunistic parties to benefit at the expense of others, either by manipulating changes to benefit levels, or by frustrating equitable changes. The beneficiaries are likely to be shareholders, but could also be senior management or union officials. This insurable moral hazard is explored in more detail in Asher (2000).

These issues are writ large in a state-sponsored scheme. Even if the relationship between contributions and benefits is determined initially in such a way as to be fair, economic and demographic changes will soon create unintended, and frequently implicit, cross-subsidies between different groups of contributors. Making changes is politically fraught, as the acrimony of current debate on the issue bears witness.

If the rules of DB funds were never changed, they would give rolling guarantees that extended for the lifetime of every cohort of new members: an infinite guarantee. This is clearly unreasonable, but there is no simple way of setting the rules to ensure that no interested group will wrest an unfair advantage for itself.

Modern finance and accounting, with their increased focus on market values, have begun to identify the cross-subsidies that arise in DB funds, and the unacceptable risk that they can bring to the finances of the sponsor. It is perhaps not surprising that growing numbers are being converted into DC funds, which have four clear advantages over DB designs:

- Members' entitlements are clearly set out and not subject to management discretion or political manoeuvring.
- The relationship between contributions and benefits is clearly fair, and free of significant but implicit cross-subsidies.
- The risks to the sponsor are not inherent in the benefit design, and any guarantees can be explicitly managed.
- Members are free to participate in the equity premium, so possibly reducing contributions or increasing benefits.

Managing Risks in Retirement

In the long run, the equity premium means that investments in equities produce lower pension costs. The price is significant short-term volatility: falls of 30 per cent and more within a year have been commonly experienced.

Once they have retired, it is likely to be difficult for fund members to re-enter the employment market to make up for investment losses. Members therefore need protection against such significant falls in income after retirement. This protection should probably begin before the retirement date, as plans for retirement presumably take some time to implement. Superannuation funds therefore need investment instruments that offer protection against investment fluctuations over this relatively long, but finite, period.

The strategy employed by most DC funds and their members is to use a combination of investments in order to give an optimum mix of security, inflation protection and participation in the equity premium. To the extent that the equity premium arises from the correlation of share prices with the universe of consumption, it may be possible to develop other assets that share this risk without the short-term volatility. One possibility would be to develop investments that provide a cash flow that could match pensions, and was linked to a wage index. This is the approach taken by the new Swedish notional DC national scheme. Asher (1994) suggests a method for utilizing housing finance.

In the absence of these instruments, the next section describes how volatile investment returns can be smoothed to produce a more acceptable income flow, and provides a family of algorithms to do this fairly and efficiently.

CURRENT METHODS OF SMOOTHING

Lifestyle Switching to Guaranteed Assets

For the reasons discussed above, many DC arrangements, even if they are largely invested in equities before retirement, arrange for members' investments to be switched to fixed, or inflation-protected, annuities at retirement. A common variation on this approach, called 'lifestyle investing', is described by Booth and Yakoubov (2000). The switch to more stable investments is phased in over a few years, rather than made at a single date. As they find, however, the success of such a strategy depends on the availability of suitable long-term indexed-linked instruments, and foregoes some of the equity premium. It does, however, reduce the volatility of the final benefits.

Cairns et al. (2003) describe a further theoretical development that they call 'stochastic lifestyling', which dynamically matches retirement income to the member's final salary. Given that final salary can be distorted by recent promotions, or a reduction in working hours related to ill health or impending retirement, it is not clear, however, that this is an appropriate benchmark.

Delaying Action

One approach to smoothing investment returns is to delay the decision to change crediting rates until the end of some time period. This is not as alarming as it first appears. Unit trusts will normally delay transacting until the end of a day. Many unit-linked DC funds will allocate units at the end of a month, while non-linked funds will apply the same crediting rate for a year at a time. In almost every case, however, they will reserve the right to calculate unit prices, or change the crediting rate, at some intermediate time if market conditions change and some participants may otherwise be disadvantaged. This could happen, for instance, if market values dropped dramatically. In this case, failing to recalculate unit prices will mean that departing members are given more than a fair share of the assets – to the detriment of remaining members. The inequity may be aggravated, and the solvency of the fund perhaps threatened, if some members are able to elect to leave in order to take advantage of the artificially high unit price. This risk of some members making elections that harm others is called anti-selection in the actuarial literature. Delaying action should, however, be seen more as an administrative convenience than a method to address market fluctuations.

Smoothed Bonuses

Many DB and DC funds historically operated through policies with life insurance companies. The companies declared smooth bonuses on these policies to distribute investment and other profits. DC funds often declare their own smoothed bonus or crediting rates.

One actuarial method of determining the bonus is to begin with a calculation of a smoothed value of assets. Head et al. (2000) provide a description of their development and justification in the context of DB funds. One common approach is for the value of shares to be determined by discounting future dividends at the actuarial valuation rate. An alternative is to assume that share prices will (immediately) return to a level that reflects some long-term average dividend yield. Other approaches to smoothing involve some averaging of the market value of assets.

To the extent that these actuarial values for the assets differ from their market values, they are, arguably, unrealistic. Actuaries who use the method respond that their smooth actuarial value represents a more realistic estimate of the long-term value of assets than the market price. Market prices may well be overly influenced by the needs or views of those who happen to be transacting at that time.

Even if this were true, three major problems arise. The first is the possibility of anti-selection. Incoming policyholders or members benefit if the difference between market and actuarial value is positive; maturing policyholders and exiting members gain when it is negative. They thus have the incentive to make decisions that disadvantage other members.

The second is that when market values are below actuarial values, the fund is exposed to the risk that a combination of further falls in market values and an outflow of funds may lead to an unacceptable drop in the benefits available to the remaining members, or even to insolvency if the fund is entirely exhausted. This problem may be further aggravated by anti-selection. Fund trustees and company managers are therefore understandably reluctant to allow a shortfall of assets to become significant. This reduces their ability to cushion falls in benefit payments – which is the original reason for smoothing.

The third problem is more subtle. As a result of the reluctance to pay benefits in excess of the market value of the underlying assets, most smoothing involves limiting the increase in the crediting rate when market values rise rapidly. This creates a tendency for smoothing reserves to build up with no obvious methodology of release. In the absence of protection for policyholders or members, the resulting surplus is open to expropriation by stronger and opportunistic parties. Asher (1991) discusses one such incident, where an 'orphan estate', built up from the contributions of previous generations of policyholders, was expropriated by a new shareholder.

Clay et al. (2001) discuss UK with-profit policies and make various recommendations as to disclosure and the protection of vulnerable parties. They believe, however, that smoothing necessarily requires discretion on the part of the fund's governing body, in order to ensure equity and solvency. The discussion of their paper reflected widespread doubt as to whether the three problems discussed above can be resolved without using an objective algorithm for smoothing.

Alternative Algorithms

Thomson (1997) suggests an algorithm that optimizes measures of smoothness and solvency in order to produce both an investment policy and a crediting rate for a DC fund. The results appear to avoid negative bonuses (which are not easily understood by members), but produce more volatile bonus rates than would be common practice.

Khorasanee and Ng (2000) propose an arrangement where the contributions made by, or on behalf of, active members are explicitly reallocated to retiring members in order to allow for smoother returns. As pointed out in the discussion by Sze (2001), this approach does not appear to be fair, particularly if investment returns are poor and the fund is declining.

Blake et al. (2003) investigate the benefits of a smoothing algorithm that truncates higher and lower returns so that bonuses lie within a limited range. Blake et al. do not, however, provide a justification for the method. All three methods are vulnerable to anti-selection.

A NEW ALGORITHM

Here we propose algorithms that smooth using a set of forward contracts of different durations.

A Series of Forward Contracts

We can take an investment policy issued by a life insurance company as an example. The benefits of a member of a DC fund are identical from an investment perspective. The maturity payout of a unit-linked policy depends on the market price of the units attached. The payout would be smoothed if the maturing policyholder were to enter into a series of forward or future contracts,[1] each for some of the units attached to the policy, in each of the months before maturity. For purposes of illustration, assume the smoothing will take place over 60 months.

The remaining policyholders in the life fund would be the obvious counterparties to forward contracts. When the payouts on policies maturing, or likely to claim, in the next five years is small relative to the size of the fund, then the fund as a whole could be the counterparty. Alternatively, policyholders wishing to increase their exposure to volatile investment markets could be specifically allocated as counterparties.

Younger policyholders may be liquidity constrained – unable to borrow – and may want greater exposure to higher-yielding equities. Such greater exposure seems appropriate, as found, for instance, by Cairns et al. (2003). An important caveat is that such findings depend critically on assumptions as to borrowing rates and the size of the long-term equity premium. Long forward positions gear up exposure to equity markets, and a significant fall in market values would reduce surrender values considerably. If one assumes that equity values will recover, however – as is normally the case – young policyholders in the accumulation phase would be compensated by being able to accumulate new units at a low price. But it would be necessary to make this patently clear to them in advance, in order to avoid unhappiness at unexpectedly low shorter-term returns.

The allocation of the long position would depend on the surrender values of the policies being sufficiently large to serve as margins. Given the illiquid nature of the forwards, the margin required would be significantly higher than that required on futures contracts regularly marked to market. Determining the size of the margins required is a problem not addressed here. The objective nature of the algorithm nevertheless allows for it to be addressed explicitly, unlike the implicit algorithms of discretionary smoothing.

The payouts on policies maturing (or likely to claim) in the next five years may become large relative to the size of the fund for a particularly aged work-force. In such a case, it may be necessary to enter into future contracts in a suitable futures market, reduce the fund's equity exposure or reduce the smoothing. Contract design may be dominated by tax considerations, which may also lead to participation in the forward contracts by the insurance company's shareholders.

Pricing Forwards and Futures

Determining forward prices is relatively simple. Entering into a contract to buy an asset at a particular price at a future date is equivalent to borrowing money to buy the asset now, and repaying the loan at that date. Similarly, the counterparty could sell the asset now and put the money on deposit. The forward price of the asset should therefore be the current market price plus interest for the period.

The rate of interest to use will depend on market conditions, the bargaining power of the participants, tax, expenses and credit risks. The terms on similar listed future contracts will provide a first estimate for the interest rates to use. Because the market in long-term future contracts (over a year or two) is relatively thin, short-term rates will have to be used to give an indication of the important considerations. The starting point in determining a fair rate would normally be the rate of return on riskless government stock – the standard assumption of financial economics. Those who take the short position in future contracts are able to participate in the market at this rate, so should be given a higher rate for participating in these illiquid forward contracts. They are also taking some counterparty risk, suggesting that a further margin should be added.

Policyholders taking the long position would probably be subject to borrowing rates significantly higher than the risk-free-rate – even though their position would be secured by the surrender values of their policies. This would suggest that the pre-tax interest rates should perhaps be somewhat higher than those for good-quality corporate debt. The rate on home loans might be considered as a retail analogy for a secured loan, and thus function as a ceiling.

Smoothed Maturity Value

The smoothed payout at maturity of those units committed to forward contracts would be determined by the following formula

$$\text{Maturity value} = \sum_{t=1}^{n} U_{-t} P_{-t} (1 + i_{-t})^t \qquad (8.1)$$

where:

maturity takes place at $t = 0$
n is the smoothing term
U_{-t} is the number of units committed to forward contracts at time $-t$
P_{-t} is the market price of the units at time $-t$, which includes reinvested dividends.
i_{-t} is the spot rate of interest of term t at time $-t$.

Insurers, or the policyholders, could choose an appropriate value for the smoothing term n, and formula for U_{-t}. An obvious formula would be

$$U_{-t} = 1/(t + 1)* \left[TU_{-k} - \sum_{t=k}^{n} U_{-t} \right] \qquad (8.2)$$

where:

TU_k is the total number of units allocated to the policy at time k.

For policies with no premiums during the smoothing term, this would provide for an equal number of units to be committed to future contracts in each of the n periods. Where premiums are still being paid during the smoothing term, this formula would produce an increase in the number of units as the policies near maturity. If a more equal weighting over the period were wanted in such cases, an appropriate adjustment to Equation (8.2) would need to be made for the units that were expected to be bought by the unpaid premiums.

Anti-selection

The approach described here allows for the determination of fair, market-consistent, surrender values without the anti-selection risk that some policy-holders will be able to trade their units on terms disadvantageous to others. This is because the forward prices can be worked backwards to determine their current market value for purposes of surrender. The surrender value at time k before maturity will be

$$SV_k = \sum_{t=k}^{n} U_{-t} P_{-t} (1 + i_{-t})^t / (1 + i_{-k})^k + \left[TU_{-k} - \sum_{t=k}^{n} U_{-t} \right] * P_k \qquad (8.3)$$

where:

SV_k is the surrender value at time k.
Time 0 would still be the planned maturity date, $0 < k < n$

Another type of anti-selection problem arises if new policyholders wish to take out a policy with a term of less than n, the smoothing term. A similar problem exists if an existing policyholder wishes to pay an additional premium in the last n years of the policy's term. These cases are analogous to a reverse surrender, and Equation (8.3) would then form the basis for the number of units to allocate to the policy. The additional premium would be equivalent to the surrender value. There would be any number of ways of determining U_{-t}, the number of units that would be committed to forward contracts at the time the additional premium was paid. One approach would be for no immediate allocation, that is $U_{-t} = 0$ for all values of t less than k. An alternative would be for a proportionate allocation; that is $U_{-t} = TU_{-k}/n$ for all values of t less than k. TU_{-k} has to be determined as it is the number of new units to allocate in respect of the additional premium.

Effects on Investment Returns

It can be seen that the smoothed return is equivalent to that obtained by 'lifestyle' disinvesting from equities, and buying zero-coupon fixed interest assets as maturity approaches. As discussed above, this foregoes the equity premium as retirement approaches. The difference is that this algorithm provides for gearing in the initial years of the policy that allows for the recapture of the equity premium that will be foregone later. It is unlikely that the two will exactly counterbalance each other, but they should be of broadly the same value *ex ante*.

The proposed algorithm has other advantages over the lifestyle approach because most of the transactions should be internal (between generations of policyholders). This reduces the administration and its costs, saves the costs of brokerage on dealing, and saves the difference between the interest rates on borrowing and investments.

CREATING ALTERNATIVE INSTRUMENTS

This model can also be used to create new investment instruments.

Inflation Linked Assets

Inflation-linked instruments of appropriate term can be created by the formula

$$\text{Maturity value} = \sum_{t=1}^{n} U_{-t} P_{-t} (1 + r_{-t})^t (CPI_0/CPI_{-t}) \qquad (8.4)$$

where:

CPI_t is the consumer price index at time t
r_{-t} is the spot real rate for term t at time $-t$.

This means that the internal lifestyle investments obtain an inflation-linked return, and that the policyholders acting as counterparties borrow at an inflation-linked rate. The former is not a new instrument; the latter is. This removes the risk to both parties of unexpected changes to the rate of inflation.

Other Linkages

There is no reason to stop there. Inflation could be replaced by a wage index, GDP per capita, or any other suitable index that allowed pensioners to participate in a country's overall prosperity. In each case, the rate of interest would need to be suitably adjusted to take into account perceptions of the relative risk and expected growth of the index.

The expected rate of interest used would be higher because of the systemic risk involved. Younger policyholders might be prepared to pay the higher rates because they would be hedging their exposure to the volatility of the growth in wages or GDP per capita.

Dividend Links

Another method would be to use an index of dividend growth and the dividend yield. This yields the formula

$$\text{Maturity value} = \sum_{t=1}^{n} U_{-t} P_{-t} (1 + dy_{-t})^t (D\ index_0/D\ index_{-t}) \qquad (8.5)$$

where:

dy_{-t} is the dividend yield on a share index, and
$D\ index_t$ measures the rate of growth in dividends on those shares.

This method gives a rate of return somewhat higher than the dividend yield plus the rate of growth of the dividend index. This method is suggested, not so much for its smoothing benefits, but because it can be reconciled with the traditional actuarial approach to dividend smoothing discussed earlier. The units used in this chapter first need to be redefined so that the dividends are no longer reinvested in the units. This allows us to formulate a new price related to the dividend index:

$$P_t^1 * dy_t = D \ index_{-t}$$

Equation (8.5) can then be reformulated as follows:

$$\text{Maturity value} = \sum_{t=1}^{n} U_{-t} P_{-t} \ (D \ index_0 / D \ index_{-t}) + \text{accumulated dividends}$$

The middle term can then be developed as follows:

$$\sum_{t=1}^{n} U_{-t} P_{-t} \ (D \ index_0 / D \ index_{-t}) = \sum_{t=1}^{n} U_{-t} \ (D \ index_0 / dy_{-t})$$

$$= P_0^1 * dy_0 * \sum_{t=1}^{n} U_{-t} / dy_{-t}$$

$$\leq P_0^1 * dy_0 / (\text{Average } dy)$$

$$\approx P_0^1 * dy_0 / (\text{Long-term } dy) = \text{actuarial value} \qquad (8.6)$$

The conclusion to be drawn from this development is that the actuarial value is an approximation to an average of forward contracts. The inequality in (8.6) is greater if the dividend yields vary significantly. The traditional approach effectively removes the benefits of dollar cost averaging, but is otherwise not necessarily unfair.

AN ILLUSTRATION

Figures 8.1 and 8.2 illustrate the effects of applying this algorithm in South Africa over the past three decades.

Smoothing Achieved

Given relatively high and volatile rates of inflation, nominal spot rates were inappropriate, so Equation (8.4) was used. Real rates of interest were not available over the period, so dividend yields were used instead. A value of $n = 60$ months was used.

The results are encouraging. Figure 8.1 shows payouts at six-monthly intervals of an investment of one per month for ten years. The large payouts in the 1980s especially reflect two decades of inflation in excess of 15 per cent p.a.

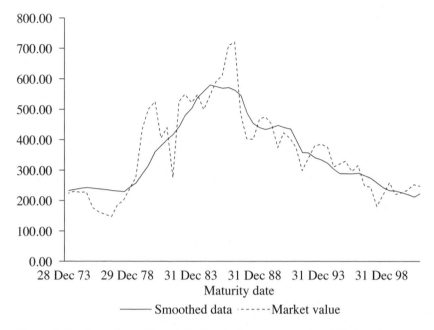

Figure 8.1   Smoothing d/y *+ inflation in ten-year monthly JSE investment*

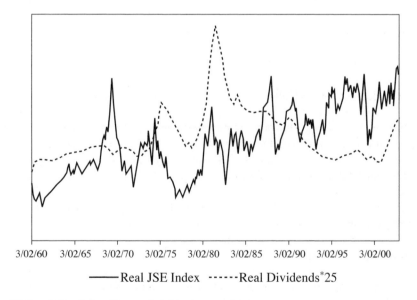

Figure 8.2   Smoothing using d/y *+ growth*

Maturing smoothed policyholders would have received much smoother returns than linked policyholders. They would have been protected from much of the share market slump of the 1970s, and the sharper stock market cracks of 1982, 1987, 1992 and 1998. They would not, however, have benefited from all the higher prices of the late 1970s and mid-1980s. The results do not appear to be particularly sensitive to adjustments in the smoothing term, real yields or formula.

This smoothing was to be expected. If we were using a single premium policy and the forward contracts were spread equally over 60 months, the monthly variance in payout (ignoring the effect of interest rate changes) would be reduced to $1/\sqrt{60}$ or about 13 per cent of that of an unsmoothed return.

A Problem with Actuarial Values

The actuarial values based on inequality seemed a reasonable approximation to this smoothing algorithm. Figure 8.2 shows the real values of the JSE All Share index, and the actuarial value of the assets if the assets are valued by treating the real dividend index as perpetuity at 4 per cent. The actuarial value may be made more or less consistent with forward pricing. Smooth it is not because the dividend index is far from smooth. It may be smoother in more diversified markets, and there may be ways of *ad hoc* adjustment, but it does not appear suitable for smoothing in South Africa.

OTHER ISSUES

Guarantees

Traditional with-profit policies offer an underlying and increasing guarantee as well as smoothing investment returns. The discussion of Clay et al. again raised long-standing debates as to the value to policyholders of these guarantees, and the common failure to explicitly cost them. This algorithm will significantly reduce the cost of investment guarantees. The exact reduction in costs must be left to further research, but the reduction in variance makes it clear that it will be substantial. Of course, the smoothing is relatively short term – five years in the illustration. Guaranteeing longer-term rates is not really possible.

Application to Retirement Funds

This algorithm can obviously be applied to DC retirement funds, life office annuities and pensions. The method of determining a surrender value would apply to withdrawals and early retirements. The method can be applied to the smoothing of lump sum payments and (with greater administrative complexity) to the smoothing of pension payments. Monthly smoothing of pensions would perhaps find little favour, but an annual smoothing (where amounts were disinvested annually and spread over the year) could well provide an acceptably smooth income.

There seems no point in applying it to DB funds, however, as the employer would effectively be on both sides of the forward contracts.

Investment Choice

The method can be applied to policies or funds that offer investment choice. The choice of fund will be the prerogative of the policyholders holding the long position in the forwards, as the maturing policyholders have locked in their returns for the period. The relative risk of the investments chosen might then affect their margin requirements and perhaps limit their ability to change their investment elections. Keeping track of such elections would add another, but not insuperable, layer of complexity to the administration of the funds.

CONCLUSION

Smoothing is recognized as a useful element in managing the risks of investing for retirement. The main mechanisms used in the past have been DB pension funds and smoothed bonus policies. They both suffer from being unclear as to the effects of their operation, and open to abuse.

Smoothing with the forward algorithms suggested here provides an objective and fair manner of smoothing that efficiently mimics lifestyle investment strategies. The contracts can be marked to market so they are not vulnerable to anti-selection, and do not lock members into long-term contracts. It also allows for the creation of a number of alternative linkages that can be used to smooth income in retirement.

When developing alternative smoothing algorithms, both theoreticians and practitioners could use the formula developed here to check on fairness and resistance to anti-selection.

NOTE

1. A future contract is listed, a forward is not. They are otherwise substantially the same.

REFERENCES

Asher, A. (1991), 'Actuarial implications of the Liberty/Prudential merger', *Transactions of the Actuarial Society of South Africa*, **IX**(I), 241–67.

Asher, A. (1994), 'Managing the financial costs of housing', *Journal of Actuarial Practice*, **2**(1), 125–44.

Asher, A. (2000), 'Fiduciary duties and good faith in the management of retirement fund surpluses', *The South African Actuarial Journal*, **1**, 1–33.

Blake, D. (2000), 'Does it matter what type of pension scheme you have?', *Economic Journal*, **110**(F), 46–81.

Blake, D., A.J.G. Cairns and K. Dowd (2003), 'Pensionmetrics 2: stochastic pension plan design during the distribution phase', *Insurance: Mathematics & Economics*, **33**(1), 29–48.

Booth, P. and Y. Yakoubov (2000), 'Investment policy for defined-contribution pension members close to retirement: an analysis of the "lifestyle" concept', *North American Actuarial Journal*, **4**, 1–19.

Cairns, A.J.G., D. Blake and K. Dowd (2003), 'Stochastic lifestyling: optimal dynamic asset allocation for defined contribution pension plans', *Discussion Paper PI-0003*, The Pensions Institute, Birkbeck College, University of London.

Clay, G.D., R. Frankland, A.D. Horn, J.F. Hylands, C.M. Johnson, R.A. Kerry, J.R. Lister, and L.R. Loseby (2001), 'Transparent with-profits: freedom with publicity', *British Actuarial Journal*, **7**, 365–465.

Dimson, E., P. Marsh and M. Staunton (2004), 'Irrational optimism', *Financial Analysts Journal*, **60**(1), 15–25.

Head, S.J., D.R. Adkins, A.J.G. Cairns, A.J. Corvesor, D.O. Cule, C.J. Exley, I.S. Johnson, J.G. Spain and A.J. Wise (2000), 'Pension fund valuations and market values', *British Actuarial Journal*, **6**, 55–141.

Khorasanee, M.Z. (1995), 'Simulation of the investment returns for a money purchase fund', *Journal of Actuarial Practice*, **3**(1), 93–116.

Khorasanee, M.Z. and H.K. Ng (2000), 'A retirement plan based on fixed accumulation and variable accrual', *North American Actuarial Journal*, **4**, 63–79.

Knox, D.M. (1993), 'A critique of defined contribution plans using a simulation approach', *Journal of Actuarial Practice*, **1**(2), 49–70.

Sze, M. (2001), 'Stochastic simulation of the financial status of the security trust fund in the next 75 years', Report of the 1994–1996 Advisory Council on Social Security.

Thomson, R.J. (1997), 'Strategies for the management of a defined contribution fund', *Transactions of the Actuarial Society of South Africa*, **XI**, 309–43.

Welch, I. (2000), 'Views of financial economists on the equity premium and on professional controversies', *Journal of Business*, **73**(4), 501–37.

9. Ansett's superannuation fund: a case study in insolvency

Shauna Ferris

INTRODUCTION

In the early 1990s, Ansett was the largest domestic airline in Australia. But in September 2001, after several years of declining profitability, the company finally collapsed and was placed under administration. Over the next few months, more than 15 000 people lost their jobs.

The Ansett employees all belonged to employer-sponsored superannuation funds. There were five different Ansett funds, each covering a different category of employees, including one fund for pilots, one for flight attendants, one for engineers, and so on. Most of the employees belonged to a defined benefit fund called the Ground Staff Superannuation Plan, which promised generous benefits in the event of retrenchment. But did the fund have enough money to pay these benefits?

According to the June 2001 annual report to members, the fund had assets of about $580 million. The members were told that according to the most recent actuarial report, the fund was in a 'sound financial position' and 'members' current benefit entitlements were covered by the plan's assets'. At that time, the fund assets exceeded the legal minimum solvency requirements by a considerable margin. Nevertheless, just a few months later, after the collapse of Ansett, the trustees were forced to report a shortfall of more than $100 million.

The trustees sought additional funds from the Ansett administrators, to cover the benefit liabilities. But the administrators denied the liability, and fought to avoid making any payment to the fund. Unfortunately, the law was not at all clear – so the courtroom battles dragged on for more than two years, with legal costs exceeding $6 million. Finally, in November 2003, the trustees and the Ansett administrators reached a negotiated settlement. The fund received nothing, and the members were left with a shortfall which had grown to almost $150 million. On average, members would get less than 80 per cent of their benefit entitlements from the fund; the average loss per member was about $17 800 – and of course for some members it was much more.

How could this problem arise? Shouldn't solvency legislation protect superannuation fund members from such losses? Was Ansett an isolated incident, or could the same problems affect other funds? Should the legislation be amended to provide better protection? And if so, how could this be accomplished?

Many other countries have already introduced solvency legislation for defined benefit funds. In the wake of the Ansett story, the key issues are:

- What level of benefits should be protected by minimum funding standards?
- What action should be taken when assets fall below the minimum funding requirement?
- Should the fund be a priority creditor when an employer becomes solvent?
- Should there be a guarantee fund to cover the shortfall when the employer becomes insolvent?

The Ansett case was the first major test of the Australian solvency legislation, and it clearly reveals a number of deficiencies in the legislation. This chapter tells the Ansett story, and in doing so highlights how superannuation funds are vulnerable not only to scary economic, financial and labour markets, but to corporate collapse and regulatory deficiencies as well. The chapter begins with a description of the legislative background in relation to the solvency of Australian superannuation funds followed by a description of Ansett's superannuation arrangements. We then tell the story of the collapse of Ansett and its impact on the superannuation fund. This leads to a discussion of the legal arguments which arose, the judicial findings and their implications. A final section concludes with international comparisons and suggestions for reform.

AUSTRALIAN SUPERANNUATION LEGISLATION AND FUND SOLVENCY

History

Before 1993, there were no statutory minimum funding standards for Australian defined benefit superannuation schemes. Each scheme was set up under its own trust deed. The trust deed would usually require an actuarial review every three or five years. The actuary would recommend a contribution rate, determined in accordance with professional standards.

The actuary would usually aim to ensure that assets should cover vested benefits. The vested benefit is the amount payable when a member voluntarily leaves the fund. For younger members, the vested benefit is simply the resignation benefit; for older members, the vested benefit is the early retirement benefit (which is usually more generous than the resignation benefit).

However, everything changed in 1992, when the Australian government introduced compulsory superannuation (called the Superannuation Guarantee or SG). Under this legislation, employers were required to pay contributions into a superannuation fund for their employees.[1] Initially, the compulsory contribution rate was set at 3 per cent of salary and wages (for small employers) or 4 per cent (for large employers). The rate was gradually increased, year by year, to a final compulsory rate of 9 per cent per annum.

Shortly after the introduction of the SG, the government decided to strengthen the solvency regulations. After all, if people are compelled by law to put their money into superannuation funds, then they have a right to some protection. Hence the government passed the Superannuation Industry (Supervision) Act 1993, commonly known as SIS.

Minimum Funding Standards under SIS

The SIS legislation has a multi-level solvency approach.[2] The assets are compared to: (1) minimum requisite benefits; (2) vested benefits; and (3) retrenchment benefits; and there are different consequences for breaching each standard.

Test 1: minimum requisite benefits and technical solvency

Under the SIS Regulations, a fund is considered to be technically solvent if the value of the assets available to pay members' benefits[3] exceeds the total value of the minimum requisite benefits (MRBs), plus any payments due to former members. In a defined contribution fund, this minimum benefit is equal to the member's own contributions plus the employer's compulsory SG contributions, accumulated with interest, less tax, insurance costs and administration charges.

In a defined benefit fund, the calculation of the minimum benefit is slightly more complicated. For a member who joined after the SG was introduced, the minimum benefit should be approximately equal to the minimum benefit for an accumulation fund (as defined above).[4] However, there is some flexibility in the method of calculation – actuaries may use an alternative approach to determine the minimum benefit, as long as this gives roughly the same benefits.[5] This flexible approach made it much easier for defined benefit funds which were established before 1992 to adapt their existing rules to meet SG requirements. A defined benefit fund is technically solvent if the assets exceed the MRBs. At present, this is a very weak minimum funding standard. The MRB only covers the benefits arising from member contributions and compulsory employer contributions. It does *not* cover benefits arising from voluntary employer contributions.

Traditionally, many employers (including Ansett) have provided benefits which exceed the minimum required under the SG legislation. The vested benefits specified in the fund's trust deed were often considerably higher than the minimum benefits required under the SG legislation. This discrepancy results from the phased-in introduction of the SG. The SG system only started in 1992, and the compulsory contributions were phased in over ten years. The minimum requisite benefits also started at a low level, and are gradually increasing. In some funds (including the Ansett fund), the MRB is only about 60 per cent of the vested benefit defined in the trust deed. This is, to some extent, a transitional problem. The SG minimum contribution is now 9 per cent, and will remain at this level. So the MRBs will gradually increase over time. Hence the difference between the MRB and the vested benefit should gradually reduce. In the meantime, a fund may be technically solvent (according to the SIS legislation), even though its assets are well below the level of vested benefits. This provides a poor level of security for fund members.

Test 2: vested benefits and an unsatisfactory financial condition

Ideally, of course, a higher level of solvency is desirable: assets should at least cover vested benefits. The SIS legislation does recognize this, and a fund is considered to be in an 'unsatisfactory financial condition' whenever assets are less than vested benefits. If an actuary or auditor discovers that a fund is in an unsatisfactory financial condition, then he/she must inform the trustees in writing (S130 of SIS).[6, 7] The trustees must provide a written report to the actuary, describing the action that the trustee intends to take to deal with the matter. If the trustee does not respond, or the actuary or auditor is not satisfied with the trustee's response, then the actuary or auditor must report the matter to the Australian Prudential Regulation Authority (APRA).

This gives considerable discretion to the actuary to determine what action is satisfactory under the circumstances. The Institute of Actuaries of Australia has published a Guidance Note (IAAust GN 460) to help actuaries interpret this requirement. The Guidance Note states:

> Provided that the trustees have acknowledged the actuary's advice in the specified period, the lack of any other action by the trustees does not necessarily mean that the actuary must report the matter to the Commissioner. There may be circumstances, left to the actuary's professional judgement, where the absence of any action by the trustees, other than acknowledging the actuary's advice, is acceptable. For example, the legislation does not specify a period over which a satisfactory financial position must be achieved. In any case, a program to return the fund to a satisfactory financial position over an acceptable period may be already in place. (Para. 9.4)

However, while the legislation and this Guidance Note do not require action to be taken to return the fund to a 'satisfactory financial position' (as defined) over a particular period of time, in usual circumstances the actuary would take action to improve the financial position over a period of time reasonable to the fund's and, where appropriate, the employer's circumstances. (Para. 9.5)

Different actuaries have different views on what is 'reasonable'. Some may strongly encourage the employer–sponsor to make additional contributions in order to cover the deficiency as quickly as possible. Others may be more lenient and allow a longer period – say three years or five years or even longer – to make up any shortfall.

The situation is exacerbated if the employer is in financial difficulties. On the one hand, if the actuary is lenient, and allows the shortfall to continue for several years, this increases the risk to the employees: if the employer becomes insolvent, and the employees lose their jobs, it is quite likely that the notional shortfall will be crystallized. On the other hand, if the employer is forced to make additional contributions, then it may put the company under increased financial pressure, and may even precipitate insolvency. Of course, this might not be in the best interests of the members, who would lose their jobs. The regulator, APRA, has been encouraging actuaries to take a tougher line with employers.

However, the actuary cannot compel the employer to make any contributions: he/she merely recommends. If the employer chooses to ignore the advice, the actuary can 'blow the whistle' and report the matter to APRA. Unfortunately, even if the actuary reports the fund to APRA, it is not clear what action (if any) APRA can take to rectify the matter. APRA can (and does) encourage employers to make additional contributions where necessary – but APRA cannot require employers to make additional contributions. Under the current legislation, APRA is a toothless tiger.

In recent years, many employers have chosen to reduce funding levels, so that assets are only just above the vested benefits, with no 'buffer' for adverse experience. Hence a downturn in the market will have a deleterious effect on the security of members' benefits. Unfortunately, during the years 2001 and 2002, investment returns were poor. As a result, many funds fell into an unsatisfactory financial position. A survey by Deloitte Touche Tomatsu revealed that about 20 per cent of funds surveyed had assets below the level of vested benefits (Deloitte Touche Tomatsu and Institute of Chartered Accountants of Australia 2002). Some funds had assets which were only about 60 per cent of the vested benefits. APRA's own survey confirmed that many defined benefits funds were in an unsatisfactory financial position at this time.

Is the current situation acceptable? For most companies, the fact that the fund is in an 'unsatisfactory financial position' may never cause a problem. As long as the company remains in business, and as long as the employees keep their jobs, the notional shortfall does not crystallize. Over the next few years, investment returns may improve, and employers may make additional contributions – the shortfalls may well disappear. But if the company becomes insolvent while the fund is in an unsatisfactory financial position, then the losses will indeed crystallize. This is exactly what happened to Ansett: the share market collapsed, and the employer–sponsor collapsed, at the same time.

Test 3: retrenchment benefits and the 'last man out' problem

Some Australian superannuation funds provide additional benefits for retrenched members. That is, the retrenchment benefit might be higher than the vested benefit. Under the current legislation, there is no requirement for funds to maintain assets sufficient to cover retrenchment benefits for all members. If there are only a few retrenchments from time to time, then the cost can be covered by relatively small additional contributions from the employer. But if the fund assets do not cover retrenchment benefits, then any large-scale retrenchment programme is likely to lead to the insolvency of the fund. If the employer is retrenching a large proportion of the workforce, it probably will not have resources available to make large top-up contributions to the superannuation fund. Under these circumstances, the members are unlikely to receive their full benefits from the fund.

Of course, many of the fund members may be quite unaware of this problem. Under professional standards, actuaries calculate the difference between assets and retrenchment benefits. The trustees are informed, but there is no requirement to tell the fund members. This may lead to unrealistic expectations, such as the members assuming that the full retrenchment benefits will be paid as promised in the fund rules – when in practice this is unlikely. Following the June 2000 review of the Ansett Ground Staff Superannuation Fund, the actuary noted that the assets were about $84 million less than the total of the retrenchment benefits. It is doubtful whether the members were aware of this at the time.

The 'last man out' problem may arise whenever assets do not cover retrenchment benefits. Suppose that retrenchments occur slowly, over an extended period. If we pay the full retrenchment benefit to those who are retrenched first, then this will erode the solvency of the fund. Indeed, there might be nothing left for the members who remain – the last few people to be sacked will get nothing at all.

Suppose that the fund starts with $530 million in assets, but the total retrenchment benefits for all members would be $670 million. Suppose that x per cent of members are retrenched and they receive their full benefits from the fund, and that soon afterwards, the fund is wound up and the remaining assets divided equitably among the remaining members. Table 9.1 shows the

Table 9.1 The impact of retrenchment on remaining members

Initial assets ($m)	Percentage retrenched (x%)	Retrenchment payments ($m)	Remaining assets ($m)	Payment to remaining members x% of $670m
530	0	–	530	79
530	30	201	329	70
530	40	268	262	65
530	50	335	195	58
530	70	469	61	30
530	80	536	–6	–4

impact on the remaining members – the last column shows their payments as a per centage of their entitlements.

If 80 per cent of the members are retrenched, and they receive their full benefits, then the remaining members will get nothing when the fund is wound up. Clearly this is inequitable. For a fund in this situation, the most equitable solution is to wind up the fund immediately, and distribute the assets equitably – so that each member gets just 79 per cent of their full benefits. However, this is not always possible or even practical – particularly when the situation is clouded by uncertainty. As we shall see, the Ansett trustees were faced with a number of legal obstacles which affected their ability to deal with the 'last man out' problem.

Dealing with Insolvent Funds

The SIS legislation does set out certain methods for dealing with insolvent funds. The solvency of each fund is monitored by regular actuarial reviews. Each defined benefit fund must obtain a funding and solvency certificate (FSC) from an actuary. The actuary certifies that the fund is technically solvent at the valuation date, and specifies the minimum rate of employer contributions that are 'expected by the actuary to be required to secure the solvency of the fund on the expiry date of the certificate'. The expiry date is chosen by the actuary, and may be anywhere from one year to five years from the valuation date.

The actuary will also specify certain 'notifiable events' which might endanger the solvency of the fund (a fall in asset values of more than 10 per cent might be a 'notifiable event'). If any of these events occurs, the trustees must notify the actuary. The actuary will then conduct an immediate review of the fund's solvency. If necessary, the actuary will recommend additional employer contributions.

What are the consequences if a fund becomes technically insolvent? If the situation is considered hopeless, then the fund will be wound up. But as an alternative, the fund might be put under actuarial management. The actuary will become responsible for the fund, and devise a plan to return the fund to solvency within five years. The actuary will issue special FSCs on an annual basis, setting out minimum employer contributions required to return to solvency. If this recovery plan fails, then the fund will be wound up and the assets distributed in accordance with priorities set out in the regulations.

The Ansett fund was the first real test of the SIS legislation – the first fund to be placed under actuarial management, and the first to be wound up under the insolvency regulations. As we shall see, this process revealed a number of deficiencies in the law.

THE ANSETT GROUND STAFF SUPERANNUATION PLAN

Ansett set up five different superannuation plans for its employees. There were separate funds for pilots, flight attendants, engineers and ground staff. This case study deals only with the Ground Staff Superannuation Plan (although there were certainly problems in some of the other funds as well). For most members, the Plan provided defined benefits.[8] The fund provided benefits on retirement, resignation, death, disability, or retrenchment. The details of the rules are rather complicated, resulting from transitional provisions designed to allow for transfers in from an earlier scheme which existed before 1987. For the purposes of this case study, the details of the benefits are not important. We simply note that: the MRBs were low, only about 60 per cent of the vested benefits; the retrenchment benefits were higher, about 117 per cent of the vested benefits; and the benefits were to be funded by both employer and employee contributions.

The members paid contributions at the rate of 5 per cent of salary.[9] Under the trust deed, Ansett was required to pay the contributions in accordance with the recommendations of the actuary. Under clause 4.4 of the trust deed, 'Contributions by the Employer . . . will not be less than is required by the solvency requirements under the Act'. When new employees joined the fund, they were given a copy of the member booklet, which set out the fund rules in plain English. There were various versions of these rules, but they all contained assurances to the members. For example, the 1995 version of the booklet said:

> The Plan is a joint commitment between you and Ansett. Each year you pay the five

per cent we mentioned earlier and Ansett pays whatever amount is necessary to ensure that you receive the benefit promised to you.

These booklets became very important later on, when deciding the extent of Ansett's obligation to cover any deficiencies in the superannuation fund. Ansett made a lot of promises in these booklets – the question was later raised: did the company have any legal obligation to keep the promises made in these booklets?

WHAT HAPPENED AT ANSETT?

In the Plan, actuarial reviews were conducted every two years. Over the 1990s, the ratio of assets to vested benefits had fluctuated around 100 per cent, as indicated in Table 9.2.

The most recent actuarial review (before the collapse) was conducted as at 30 June 2000. At that time the fund had 8829 members, and the employer was contributing at 9 per cent of salaries. The actuary sent his report to the trustees on 3 April 2001.[10] He noted that the fund was both technically solvent and in a satisfactory financial condition (as per the SIS definitions). Assets were $599 million, vested benefits totalled $584 million and the ratio of assets to vested benefits was 103 per cent. The fund had about 70 per cent invested in growth assets (shares and property), which tend to be more volatile in value. The actuary noted that there was about a 20 per cent chance that assets would fall below 95 per cent of vested benefits over the next three years – but if this occurred, the employer contribution rate could be increased to compensate for the losses.

> An Index less than 100 per cent need not necessarily be viewed as an item of major concern, unless the value is well below 100 per cent or there is some doubt about the employer's ability and willingness to continue its support for the Plan.

Table 9.2   Assets to vested benefits

Year ending 30 June	Ratio of assets to vested benefits (%)
1990	106
1992	98
1994	101
1996	96
1998	106
2000	103

The actuary noted that the fund's assets were much lower than the total value of retrenchment benefits for all members, and the actuary's covering letter for the report stated that the fund was in a 'sound financial condition'.

At about this time, there were increasing concerns about Ansett's financial performance. As a result of the deregulation of the airline industry, the company was struggling in a very competitive market. Ansett was reporting major losses. In April 2001, some of the company's planes were grounded because of concerns about poor maintenance and inadequate compliance with safety standards. Many customers were seriously inconvenienced, and the groundings attracted a great deal of adverse publicity. Shortly afterwards, on 23 April 2001, the actuary wrote to the trustees, pointing out that the fund assets were insufficient to cover the total retrenchment benefits – the shortfall was about $84 million.

> The total liability in respect of retrenchment benefits is, based on data supplied to me, $683.33M. This exceeds the amount of assets by $84.44M. This position is not unexpected, and need not be a matter of concern unless there is a reasonable prospect of the contingency arising where a significant retrenchment program will occur and the employer is unwilling or unable to finance the additional benefit liability. I suggest that the trustee seek assurance from the employer, whenever a retrenchment program is initiated, that additional contributions will be made to cover the difference between (say) retrenchment benefits and vested withdrawal benefits for the affected members, unless actuarial advice indicates that such additional financing is not required.

By June 2001, the press was reporting that Ansett was facing formidable difficulties. There were warnings that Ansett might collapse, unless the company could raise additional capital (Boyle et al., 2001). However, the Ansett management continued to deny the severity of the problem (Easdown and Wilms, 2002, p. 129). The members were given the following information about solvency in the fund's annual report to members as at 30 June 2001.

> The plan actuary carries out a review every two years to check the financial position of the plan. At the last review (1 July 2000), the actuary reported that the plan was in a sound financial position and that members' current benefit entitlements were covered by the plan's assets. The next review is due effective 1 July 2002.

The annual report to members did not mention that the fund assets were about $84 million below the total value of retrenchment benefits. Under the SIS regulations, the members would have been entitled to request a full copy of the actuary's report, along with any subsequent written advice by the actuary which would be relevant to the overall financial condition of the fund (SIS Regulation 2.41 (1)). However, such requests are not very common and not many members make any attempt to read actuarial reports.

Ansett's financial position continued to deteriorate, and reached a crisis in early September. The administrators took over the airline on 12 September 2001. In the early hours of 12 September, Australians heard the news about the terrorist attack on the Twin Towers in New York. Overnight, the task of the administrators became much more difficult – the international airline industry was hard hit, and therefore the resale value of Ansett's assets plunged sharply.

Initially, the Ansett administrators wanted to go into liquidation. But the Ansett employees wanted to fight to try to save the airline. Within a few days, their union went to court and asked for a new administrator to be appointed – the court agreed. The new administrators decided against liquidation. They decided to keep the planes in the air, and look for business partners who might be willing to bail out the company. This was an expensive option – it cost about $6 million per week to maintain operations. But they thought the business would be worth more as a 'going concern'.

On 16 September 2001 the trustees of the superannuation fund wrote to the administrators to inform them of the potential shortfall, estimated at $84 million. Following the actuary's suggestion, the trustees asked for additional funding to cover any retrenchments. On 18 September 2001 the actuary wrote to the trustees to explain the situation more fully.

> Recommended contributions [in the 30 June 2000 actuarial report] did not include any allowance for funding of any shortfall against the plan's retrenchment benefits. Had there been any basis, at the time that the 2000 valuation was undertaken, to expect that retrenchment benefits were going to become payable for the absolute majority of the plan's members, then the contributions recommended would have been higher to the degree required to cover an expected excess of benefit payments over normal resignation/retirement benefits.

He then updated the estimates of assets and liabilities. The news was not good. During the months of July, August and September 2001, the market value of the fund's assets had fallen by about 10 per cent. The value of assets was now just $516 million. The total retrenchment benefits were estimated at $633 million, giving a shortfall of $117 million. Since employer contributions are taxed at 15 per cent, this means that the employer would have to contribute about $137 million to cover the shortfall. This calculation was based on the assumption that all employees would be retrenched. The shortfall was exacerbated because Ansett had not paid the usual employer contributions for the months of August and September 2001. The trustees wrote to the administrators to request urgent payment.

The members of the fund were naturally concerned about the security of their benefits. Their union was helpful in providing what little information was available. The National Union of Workers issued a special report for Ansett members on 20 September 2001, which stated:

> The ACTU has been informed that the defined benefit funds are fully funded to pay retirement and resignation benefits, which means that members should receive these benefits on exiting the fund. In the case of the Ground Staff Superannuation Plan, there is a retrenchment benefit which is higher than the resignation benefit. The plan is not funded for payment of the retrenchment benefit for all members at the one time as it was not expected that all plan members would be retrenched at once.

The actuary wrote to the trustees again on 20 September 2001, raising a question about the wording of the trust deed. Under the trust deed, 'retrenchment' was defined as 'a reduction of staff declared by the employer for the purposes of these rules'. The actuary noted that the retrenchment benefits would not be payable unless the employer made a 'declaration of retrenchment'. If a person was retrenched, but the administrators refrained from making such a declaration, perhaps the member's entitlement would be restricted to the much lower resignation benefit.

On 27 September 2001, this issue was raised at a meeting between the trustees and representatives of the administrators. The representatives of the administrators would not comment, other than to say that they were seeking legal advice. Shortly afterwards, the administrators made an offer of voluntary redundancy to most members of the ground staff. This did not specify the superannuation benefits that would be payable – instead it suggested that employees should ask the trustees of the Plan to provide information about benefits that would become payable. Thousands of members accepted the offer and were subsequently made redundant.

Soon afterwards, on 17 October 2001, the trustee's solicitors wrote to the administrators, asking them to confirm that anyone who accepted an offer of redundancy would be eligible for the retrenchment benefit under the superannuation rules. The administrators did not reply. The administrators subsequently gave evidence in court, stating that they had decided (on legal advice) not to make any declaration of retrenchment. One of the administrators stated:

> [he] believed that to make a declaration would be contrary to the interests of Ansett and to the interests of its creditors as a whole because of the risk that such a declaration might increase the liabilities of Ansett in circumstances where it was already insolvent.

On 18 October 2001 the trustees issued a newsletter to members. The newsletter included the following information:

> Based on advice received to date, the trustees have decided to make your retrenchment benefit available in two stages. The first stage will be made within the next week and will be for an amount equivalent to your ordinary resignation benefit or early retirement benefit. All payments are subject to the usual preservation requirements.

The second stage involves the consideration of any available balance. This may involve the trustee seeking directions from the Court as to appropriate amounts payable.

The main reason for this course of action is to determine the proper level of bene-fits that members will be entitled to should the plan be wound up. In this case, Defined Benefit plan members should be aware if large scale redundancies/retrenchments occur that fall within the definition of 'retrenchment' for the Defined Benefit Fund Rules, then the plan may have a large shortfall of assets in order to meet full retrenchment benefits.

The trustees reported that they were consulting with APRA and other regu-latory authorities to work out all the ramifications of the situation. Unfortunately, the legal position was not at all clear.

On 23 October 2001, the actuary wrote to the trustees advising that the recent poor investment performance of the fund meant that the previous FSC (effective 1 July 2001) would cease to have effect. The actuary would have to re-examine the solvency of the fund and then issue a new FSC. The actuary began a new investigation of the fund. Soon afterwards, the trustees froze all payments from the fund (Wood and Paxinos, 2001).

During November 2001, the trustees managed to obtain some money from the administrators. The administrators agreed that Ansett was legally obliged to make payments of 9 per cent of salary for the period up to the date when the company was put under administration; this amount was paid on 12 November 2001. The actuary completed his review of the fund's solvency, and reported back on 3 December 2001. Once again, the news was not good. The actuary advised that assets were now well below the vested benefits – the amount of the shortfall was estimated at $76 million.

By mid-December 2001, the trustees had decided to lift the 'hold' on payment of benefits – many retrenched workers were facing financial diffi-culties and desperately needed some money. But by this stage, the fund assets were less than the total vested benefits – it would not be possible to pay the full resignation benefits. The trustees decided to pay a reduced amount as a 'stage one' payment. Based on the actuary's advice, retrenched members would receive a maximum of 70 per cent of their resignation benefit or early retirement benefit (December 2001 trustee newsletter).

On 23 January 2002, the actuary issued a new FSC. He stated that the fund was technically solvent at present – even though the assets were much less than the vested benefits, they still covered the MRBs. He noted that payment of retrenchment benefits would jeopardize the security of benefits for contin-uing members, unless the employer paid additional contributions. The actuary recommended a two-tier contribution rate. For members still in employment, Ansett should pay 9 per cent. But for each retrenched member, the employer contribution should be a lump sum equal to the amount of the member's retrenchment benefit less the amount of the resignation benefit (increased to allow for tax on contributions).

At this stage, the actuary was in a difficult situation. If the retrenched members were entitled to a retrenchment benefit, then the fund would soon be insolvent. But legally, the situation was quite uncertain – if the administrators refused to make a 'declaration of retrenchment', then the fund might have a reduced liability. Perhaps the fund would remain technically solvent.

During this period, the Ansett administrators were desperately trying to put together a plan to rescue the airline. The airline had stopped flying in September, but the administrators had set up 'Ansett Mark II', flying a limited number of planes on the most important routes. In November 2001 they also entered into a tentative agreement to sell the airline – with luck, about 4000 Ansett employees would keep their jobs. But in late February 2002, these plans fell through. All flights ceased on 4 March 2002. By this time most employees had been retrenched, but some people were still working for the administrators.

By the end of the financial year, the situation had again deteriorated, due to poor investment returns. The returns for the financial year ended 30 June 2002 were –3.2 per cent. This was consistent with the poor returns earned by many other funds over the same period – in fact Ansett's performance was slightly better than average. The trustees decided to go to court to obtain additional money from the Ansett administrators, and the court case began on 16 July 2002.

The trustees realized that they could not represent all the members, because there was a conflict of interest between the retrenched members and the continuing members. If the retrenched members were given full benefits, this would reduce the amount available to pay benefits for those remaining in service. Therefore it was necessary to have separate legal representation for the two groups. The court case lasted several months – the judge's decision (described below) was not handed down until 20 December 2002.

LEGAL ISSUES

The trustees of the Ground Staff Superannuation Plan went to court. Initially, the matter was heard in the Supreme Court of Victoria (Ansett Australia Ground Staff Superannuation Plan Pty Ltd and Another v Ansett Australia Ltd and Others [2002], VSC 576). There were three issues to resolve :

1. Were the retrenched members of Ansett entitled to redundancy benefits under the trust deed?
2. If there was a shortfall in the fund, should Ansett be required to make additional contributions to fund these benefits?

3. If so, then what priority would the superannuation fund have, among the other creditors of the airline, under the Corporations Act 2001?

Issue 1: Were the Members Entitled to Retrenchment Benefits ?

Were the members of the fund entitled to retrenchment benefits under the rules of the trust deed? The trust deed gave a definition of retrenchment: 'a reduction of staff declared by the employer for the purposes of these rules'. The administrator argued that retrenched members did not have an automatic entitlement to the higher level of benefits. They argued that the trust deed gave the employer some discretion: the employer could decide whether or not to make a declaration. If the employer did not make a declaration, then the members were not entitled to the retrenchment benefits: they would receive the resignation benefits, which were significantly lower.

Members of the fund argued that this interpretation of the trust deed was incorrect. They said that the rules merely required the company to provide information to the trustees, so that they could determine whether or not the member had been retrenched. They argued that the trust deed did not give the company the right to any discretion over the payment of the benefit, once an employee had been retrenched. They pointed to the past practice of the company: in the past, all retrenched employees had been paid the retrenchment benefit, and there had never been any official company declaration especially for the purposes of the trust deed.

Which interpretation of the trust deed was preferred? In making her decision, the judge referred to a number of precedents for the interpretation of trust deeds. First, she noted that the basic approach should be 'practical and purposive', in that the rules of the scheme should be interpreted to give reasonable and practical effect to the scheme. Second, she noted that the interpretation of the trust deed should take into account the background facts and surrounding circumstances. All of the past practice suggested that the retrenched members were entitled to the retrenchment benefits without any special declaration. The member booklets suggested that retrenchment benefits would be paid to retrenched members. The members were never told that the benefit would depend on the discretion of the employer. In fact it seems that this issue was never raised by anyone until before the collapse of the airline.

After consideration of all the circumstances, the judge decided that members who had been made redundant by the administrators were entitled to the retrenchment benefits. As a result of this decision, the fund would be insolvent – unless the trustees could obtain additional funding from the Ansett administrators.

Issue 2: Was Ansett Obliged to Make Contributions to Cover the Cost of the Retrenchment Benefits?

Next, the judge had to consider Ansett's obligations under the SIS legislation and trust deed. The SIS Act requires employers to make contributions no less than the amount specified in the FSC. And the trust deed of the fund stated that the employer should make the contributions required to comply with the Act. So the judge concluded that Ansett did indeed have an obligation to make the additional contributions.

The judge also looked at Ansett's contractual obligations to the employees. After considering all the assurances which were given in the member booklets (as described above), the judge decided that Ansett had an obligation to pay contributions; she pointed out that this obligation arose from the contract between employer and employees.

> Given that membership of the plan was a condition of employment for those employees of Ansett eligible to join the plan, and that booklets were issued, with the obvious approval of Ansett, containing a description of the benefits available under the plan and promises by Ansett in relation to the provision of those benefits, the promises clearly formed part of the members' contract of employment with Ansett.

This decision was, in principle, good news for the fund members. But the fund trustees were simply added to the long list of Ansett's creditors. Based on the testimony of the administrators, Ansett certainly had nowhere near enough assets to pay all of its debts. Only the creditors with high priority would actually receive any money.

So this led to the third question to be decided by the court: did the superannuation fund have priority over the other creditors? If not, then the fund would probably be unable to obtain any money from Ansett.

Issue 3: Does the Superannuation Fund have Priority over Other Debtors, in Claiming Money from the Fund Administrators?

At this stage, the legal situation becomes even more complicated. Usually, when a company is liquidated, the priority of creditors is determined under section 556 of the Corporations Act. However, Ansett was not in liquidation – the company was under the control of administrators, and administrators are given a certain amount of flexibility in managing the company. Administrators can ask the creditors of a company to approve a Deed of Company Arrangement (DOCA). A DOCA can specify the order of priority of payment of creditors, and this priority might be different to the priority under the Corporations Act.

After paying the secured creditors, the Ansett administrators had just $620 million in assets to distribute. But the company owed $760 million to employees, for entitlements *other* than the superannuation fund liabilities. These liabilities included unused annual leave payments, long service leave payments, and non-superannuation redundancy payments. This money was owed to approximately 13 000 ex-employees, including 8400 members of the Ground Staff Superannuation Plan and 4700 members of other funds. Pilots, flight attendants and engineers were in separate funds.

If the superannuation fund had higher priority for payment (above the other employee entitlements), then the 8400 members of the ground staff fund would get their full superannuation benefit. But then the administrators would not have enough money to pay their *other* entitlements in full. Some of the ground staff fund members would be better off; but some would be worse off (the net effect varied depending on age and length of service). The other Ansett employees – those who were not members of ground staff fund – would all be worse off.

The union was representing the employees. The union leaders quickly realized that a win for some employees would be a loss for others. In fact, overall, about half of the employees would be better off if the trustees won priority; and about half the employees would be worse off.

The union made a pragmatic decision: they decided that 'money now is better than money later'. Under Australia's superannuation laws, most superannuation benefits must be preserved – that is, benefits cannot be paid in cash until the employee reaches retirement age. So if the superannuation fund won their case, the members would not be able to access all of their benefits until at least age 55. The average age of the members was 41, which implies a 14-year wait. Furthermore, many of the employees were unemployed and in desperate financial straits, and they needed the money to buy their groceries and pay their bills. The union leaders decided that it would be better to leave the deficit in the superannuation funds, and use the Ansett assets to pay the other employee entitlements (which are not subject to preservation rules). Therefore, in March 2002, the unions persuaded the administrators to put forward a DOCA which would give the superannuation fund the lowest priority.

The trustees of the superannuation fund were not happy about this – at the creditors' meeting called to approve the DOCA, they spoke out against these arrangements. But the unions, as representatives of the employee creditors, voted in favour of the DOCA at the creditors' meeting. The DOCA was passed by an overwhelming majority. However, the trustees were not willing to give up. They felt that they had a responsibility to act in the best interests of their own members – even if this meant overturning the DOCA.

In order to do this, they first had to show that the superannuation fund would have been a priority creditor under S556 of the Corporations Act. Then they would argue that it was unfair and inappropriate to create a DOCA which was contrary to the priorities in the Corporations Act. They would argue that the administrators had misled the creditors by failing to provide accurate information. If the DOCA was overturned, then the priorities of the Corporations Act could be reinstated. Unfortunately, S556 of the Corporations Act is not at all clear about the priority of unfunded superannuation fund liabilities. It seems that this problem was never considered when the law was framed.

Initially, the case was heard in the Supreme Court of Victoria, before Justice Warren. The judge was asked to determine whether the superannuation contributions should be included under S556(1)(a), S556(1)(dd), S 556(1)(e), or none of the above. S556(1)(a) gives priority to expenses incurred by the administrator in 'preserving, realising, or getting in the property of the company, or in carrying on the company's business'. S556(1)(dd) gives priority to 'any other expenses properly incurred by the administrator'.

Justice Warren considered this question: were the superannuation liabilities incurred by the administrators during their period of administration of the company? Or were the superannuation liabilities incurred by the Ansett company before the administrators took over?

This was clearly a tricky problem, legally. Justice Warren concluded that the liabilities were actually incurred by Ansett before the start of the administration. Ansett had a contingent liability; the amount of the liability would depend on the occurrence of certain events, such as retrenchments. Therefore, the liability was not 'incurred by the administrators' at all, it already existed when they took over the company. Consequently, the superannuation fund was not eligible for priority under S556(1)(a) or S556(1)(dd).

Next, the trustees argued that the superannuation shortfall contributions should fall under S556(1)(e). S556(1)(e) gives high priority to wages and superannuation contributions payable by the company in respect of services rendered to the company by employees before the date the administrators took over the company. Justice Warren decided that the shortfall contributions should not be given priority under S556(1)(e). The reasons for this decision were not made entirely clear in the judgment. As a result of this decision, the superannuation fund would *not* be a priority creditor at all – the fund would simply be an unsecured creditor. The administrators had already determined that the unsecured creditors would get nothing at all.

The trustees consulted their lawyers, who advised them that they would have a good chance of overturning Justice Warren's decision on appeal. So the trustees decided to appeal. Eventually (after a great of legal wrangling which need not concern us here), the case ended up in the Federal Court of Australia in November 2003.

The Federal Court judge observed that the situation was somewhat unusual. Employees in the Ground Staff Superannuation Plan were being represented on both sides of the dispute. On the one hand the administrators were representing the employees, and saying that their redundancy payments should get priority; on the other hand the trustees were representing the fund members, saying that their superannuation payments should get priority. In the meantime, the legal costs were mounting up into the millions of dollars, and the members were in limbo waiting for their payments. Indeed, many of the fund members were angry at the trustees for pursuing the matter – they regarded it as a waste of time and money.

Under the circumstances, the Federal Court judge ordered the trustees to attempt to negotiate a settlement with the Ansett administrators. Within a few days, a settlement was reached. The administrators would not pay any money to the fund; however, they would give some priority to the ground staff members in the allocation of the available assets.

Winding up

While these court cases were dragging on, the solvency status of the fund was in question. The actuary could not decide if the fund was solvent until he knew whether the fund was required to pay retrenchment benefits – although Ansett collapsed in September 2001, the issue of benefit entitlements was not settled until December 2002. Soon afterwards, the actuary declared that the fund was technically insolvent.

At this point, under the SIS legislation, the actuary might have decided to wind up the fund. However, throughout 2003, there was still a chance that the fund would be able to obtain some more money from the Ansett administrators. So the actuary decided to put the fund under 'actuarial management' while awaiting the outcome of the court proceedings. But when the trustees settled the court case, there was no hope. The fund would never return to solvency – winding up was the only alternative.

The SIS regulations have rules for the division of assets on winding up – but unfortunately, as it turned out, the rules were quite unworkable. Under the SIS rules, the actuary was required to work out the minimum benefit index, which is calculated as

$$\text{MBI} = \frac{\text{net realizable assets} - \text{benefits for former members}}{\text{minimum requisite benefits of current members}}$$

If the MBI is less than 1, then the assets must be divided so that each former member must receive a benefit which is at least MBI × benefit entitlement, but less than 1.00 × benefit entitlement. Each current member must receive a benefit that is at least MBI × minimum requisite benefit, but less than 1.00 × minimum requisite benefit.

In the Ansett fund, this formula plainly had the potential to favour those who were retrenched early, at the expense of those who remained in the fund until the date of the winding up. For example, suppose that the benefit entitlement for a former member is the retrenchment benefit, say $120; the minimum requisite benefit for a current member is $60.01; and assets are $180. The MBI is just under 100 per cent. The former member (sacked the day before the winding up) will get $120; but the current member (sacked the day after the winding up) will get only $60. Under the SIS formula, the 'last man out' will be disadvantaged, and this seems unfair.

To solve this problem, the Ansett trustees simply made sure that nearly all the members were classified as 'former members' before the date of winding up. For legal reasons, one member volunteered to be the sole remaining member of the fund at wind-up. In the above example, this would mean that the $180 could be divided evenly between both members.

As the actuary noted, the SIS formula was apparently devised on the assumption that the MBI would be only slightly less than 1.00. But in the Ansett case, the MBI became very unstable, and was rapidly approaching negative infinity! The benefit entitlement of former members was much greater than the available assets, and the MRB for the last remaining member was a relatively small number. In fact, as one actuary pointed out, if the last member had resigned before the wind-up, the MBI would cause a 'divide by zero' error and the MBI would be undefined! When the MBI is a negative number, this effectively means that the minimum benefit payable to each member is $0. In other words, the SIS legislation, which is supposed to ensure some equity for members in a fund wind-up, was completely ineffective in the Ansett case.

Many trust deeds give considerable discretion to the trustees, and the Ansett fund was typical in this regard. The trustees were entitled to allocate the assets in any manner they considered to be fair and equitable, after considering the advice of the actuary. They considered two options: *pro rata* in relation to retrenchment benefits; and *pro rata* in relation to vested benefits. On the advice of the actuary, the trustees chose the second option, which is more favourable to the older members of the fund.

FUTURE DIRECTIONS AND CONCLUSIONS

So in the end, the Ansett superannuation fund ended up with a shortfall of about $150 million: on average, members received less than 80 per cent of their entitlements. Is this a satisfactory outcome? Or could we devise a system that provides better protection for employee entitlements?

Other countries have been facing the same problems, and have adopted quite different approaches. In the UK, in the early 1990s, there were a number of cases in which pension funds lost the whole or a substantial part of their assets, and 'public confidence in the integrity of pension schemes was severely shaken'[11] (Pension Law Review Committee, 1993). As a result, the government set up a committee to review the legislation. Roy Goode, the chairman of the committee, argued in favour of increased protection for pension fund members:

> Those who favour the retention of the laissez-faire principle in all its vigour argue that the establishment of a pension scheme is a voluntary act on the part of the employer. Since the employer does not have to provide a scheme at all, surely it must have complete freedom to set the terms of any scheme it chooses to provide. Though such a proposition still has its advocates, it is not dictated by either policy or logic. It is perfectly legitimate to insist that if the employer does choose to set up a scheme, the bundle of benefits offered to the employees as an integral part of the remuneration package should be legally protected and financially secure. (Goode, 1993)

As a result, the government introduced the minimum funding requirement (MFR) in 1997. But unfortunately, the MFR has not been an outstanding success. Under the MFR, funds are required to maintain assets sufficient to cover vested benefits. But in the UK, vested benefits are not lump sums: they are deferred pensions. The value of deferred pension benefits is not fixed: the cost of the benefits will depend upon a number of factors such as future investment returns, inflation, mortality rates and so on. The value can only be estimated by the actuary, and it will fluctuate from time to time as market conditions change. Since the pension liabilities are long term, the value will be very sensitive to the assumptions adopted. Furthermore, UK pension funds have traditionally invested a high proportion of their assets in equities. So both asset values and liability values are quite volatile.

Unfortunately, during the last few years, conditions have been quite unfavourable, and many funds have developed large deficits. This has created problems for many employers, because they were expected to make additional contributions to fund the deficits. Under the MFR, the timeframe for restoring the fund to solvency was quite short (varying with the level of the shortfall). As a result, employer contribution rates became more volatile.

Naturally, the employers protested. They proposed amendments to the valuation assumptions: if the actuaries were allowed to use more optimistic assumptions about future experience, that would reduce the MFR. If the rules were changed to extend the timeframe for funding shortfalls, then this would relieve the pressure on employers. But of course, these changes would also reduce the security for the fund members.

The Institute of Actuaries was asked to review the standards. Stating the obvious, they pointed out:

it is not possible to reconcile a desire to invest pension scheme assets in equities with both stability of employers' contributions and stability of members' benefit security levels.

The MFR was not, in fact, a very strong funding requirement, and this soon became only too obvious to the public.

The Ansett saga raises a number of issues about superannuation solvency legislation, as follows.

What Level of Benefits Should be Protected by Minimum Funding Standards?

Under the Australian legislation, the minimum level of funding only covers the minimum requisite benefits – that is, the benefits arising from member contributions and compulsory SG contributions. These MRBs are often much lower than the benefits promised in the trust deed. When the SIS legislation was introduced, the government decided that benefits arising from compulsory SG contributions deserve a higher level of protection than benefits arising from the employer's 'voluntary' superannuation contributions (Duval 1992).

However, as suggested by Justice Warren's comments (given above), these additional superannuation contributions are not really 'voluntary'; they are not provided by employers as an act of benevolence. They form a component of the remuneration of the employee, in return for services rendered. Shouldn't these benefits be protected? In other countries, including the UK and the USA, the minimum funding standards are designed to cover vested benefits.

What Action Should be Taken when Assets Fall Below the Minimum Funding Requirement?

The SIS legislation says that a fund is in an 'unsatisfactory financial position' when the assets are less than the vested benefits – but under the Australian legislation, the employer does not have any legal obligation to fund the shortfall over any particular timeframe. In many other countries, including the UK and the USA, minimum funding requirements are based on vested benefits. When there is a shortfall, then employers are required to make additional contributions to fund the shortfall within a specified timeframe. In the USA, employers who fail to make the required contributions may be subject to significant tax penalties – providing a strong incentive for compliance.

However, employers may find such legislation burdensome: hence there is often pressure on the regulators to adopt more lenient regulations. Indeed, some employer groups in the USA have been quite successful in persuading regulators to adopt more optimistic valuation assumptions and/or longer amortization periods for deficits. Hence the regulators face a difficult task, trying to balance the need for security of employee benefits against the costs to the employer.

In December 2003, the Australian government published proposals to strengthen funding requirements for defined benefit funds. At the time of writing, the government is considering submissions from a number of professional and industry groups.

Should the Fund be a Priority Creditor when an Employer Becomes Insolvent?

No matter how strictly we enforce minimum funding requirements, it seems inevitable that the system will occasionally fail: employers will become insolvent and funds will be left with a deficit. Should the superannuation fund have a claim over the assets of the employer? And should the superannuation fund have priority over other creditors?

As we have seen, the Australian law is not at all clear about the priority of employee entitlements such as superannuation when an employer becomes insolvent. This uncertainty has undoubtedly contributed to the distress of Ansett employees, as they wait for the legal issues to be resolved – and this is inevitably a slow process.

After the Ansett collapse, the government indicated that there would be a review of the Corporations Law, to consider giving certain employee entitlements higher priority (even ahead of secured creditors). However, there has been strong opposition to this proposal. If employee entitlements get higher priority, other creditors (such as banks) would face greater risks in lending to employers. Hence they would be forced to charge higher interest rates to corporate customers; some companies might face difficulty in borrowing (Oldfield, 2003; Dwyer, 2002).

Similar problems are likely to arise if superannuation shortfalls are treated as high-priority debts in the event of insolvency. Potential lenders would want to have much more information about the level of the shortfall in the superannuation fund; they would also want to assess the risks that the deficit might increase. The superannuation fund's asset mix might have a direct bearing on the employer–sponsor's ability to borrow.

Despite these problems, some other countries (including the UK and the USA) do make explicit provision for defined benefit shortfalls to be counted as liabilities when the employer becomes insolvent (up to specified limits). These laws specify both the method of calculation of the shortfall, and the priority of the debt relative to other creditors.

If superannuation funds do become priority creditors, this will increase pressure for improvements in accounting standards. Financial market analysts are already concerned about the level of deficits in many Australian superannuation funds, because of the effect on the employer–sponsor. If the employer–sponsor is required to make extra contributions to cover the deficit, this may drain profits and depress the share price (Oldfield, 2002). But according to newspaper reports, analysts found it difficult to assess the size of the deficits, because: some companies do not disclose enough information; some companies use optimistic forecasts in valuing their liabilities; and some of the actuarial reviews are out of date (up to three years old) (Oldfield and Buffini, 2002).

Should There be a Guarantee Fund to Cover the Shortfall when the Employer Becomes Insolvent?

In Australia, ultimately, the members of the superannuation fund bear the risk. When the Ansett fund became insolvent, the members of the fund received lower-than-expected benefits.

The risk of loss could be spread across the wider community, by the creation of a guarantee scheme. For example, in the USA, the Pension Benefit Guaranty Corporation (PBGC) provides plan termination insurance. The PBGC is a public corporation which steps in and takes over management of terminating plans. The PBGC becomes trustee of the plan assets; and it becomes a high-priority creditor of the employer–sponsor to the extent of any unfunded liability. It also collects levies from all insured plans, to cover any shortfalls. The PBGC guarantees payments of all basic vested benefits (subject to certain limitations); hence it provides a high degree of security for members.

But the PBGC is currently facing a massive deficit, as a result of major insolvencies in the airline industry and in the steel industry. Some of these companies have consistently underfunded their pension funds for many years – leaving the losses to be covered by other, more responsible employers. To reduce the potential for such moral hazards, the PBGC has, over time, introduced more stringent funding requirements – but employers have often resisted such changes.

The Australian government recently reviewed the prudential standards for superannuation funds, and they considered the introduction of a more comprehensive guarantee system for superannuation funds. However, most of the submissions to the enquiry were against to this proposal – on the basis that it would create an unacceptable moral hazard.

NOTES

1. There are some exceptions, including part-time workers under age 18 and workers earning less than $450 per month.
2. The rules are rather technical. This is a simplified explanation.

3. The value of available assets is the market value of assets, less the costs of realization, less assets set aside to pay benefits for former members of the fund – that is, employees who have left service but have not yet been paid their benefits (SIS Regulation 9.15).
4. Transitional rules apply to employees who started work before 1 July 1992.
5. The Superannuation Guarantee (Administration) Regulations set out the rules for determining MRBs and NECRs. The IAAust gives guidance to actuaries to help determine the MRB; see IAAUST Guidance Note 456.
6. The actuary must inform the trustees if he/she thinks that the fund is currently in an unsatisfactory financial position, or the financial position of the fund is likely to become unsatisfactory (S130). When performing an actuarial review of the fund, the actuary will usually make financial projections three years ahead, as per SIS Regulation 9.31.
7. S130 only applies if the actuary or auditor forms an opinion while performing an actuarial or audit function under the Act. See IAAust Guidance Note 460 for interpretation of this requirement.
8. There was also an accumulation section of the scheme. This covered a small number of members from a pre-existing scheme, who had elected to remain in their accumulation scheme instead of transferring into the defined benefit scheme. Casuals and temporary employees were also covered by the accumulation scheme. Any member was entitled to make additional voluntary contributions or to roll over benefits from another fund – these were invested in the accumulation section.
9. They were entitled to make additional voluntary contributions as well. The voluntary contributions and rollovers into the fund were simply held in an accumulation account and the balance was paid out at exit.
10. It may take several months to complete an actuarial review, so the delay is not out of the ordinary – the legislation allows 12 months (SIS Regulation 9.30(2)).
11. The most notorious losses were incurred by funds associated with the late Mr Robert Maxwell. After the death of Mr Maxwell, it became apparent that he had diverted the assets of the superannuation funds of his employees to prop up his sagging business empire.

REFERENCES

Boyle, J., B. Sandilands and J. Koutsoukis (2001), 'Ansett in danger, warns Singapore', *Australian Financial Review*, 23 June, p. 3.

Deloitte Touche Tomatsu and Institute of Chartered Accountants of Australia (2002), *Governance of Australia's Superannuation Funds*, 31 October, on website http://www.deloitte.com.au/home.asp?Page=/internet/items/item.asp&id=5825

Duval, D. (1991), 'Letter from the Australian Government Actuary to Mr Rob Paton, Convenor of the Institute of Actuaries Superannuation Practice Committee dated 6 October 1992', in *Transactions of the Institute of Actuaries*, 1992: pp. 638–40.

Dwyer, M. (2002), 'Ansett Deal Opens New Chapter on Entitlements', *Australian Financial Review*, 31 January, p. 51.

Easdown, G. and P. Wilms (2002), *Ansett: The Collapse*, Melbourne: Lothian Books.

Goode, R. (1993), 'Defining and protecting the pension promise', *Journal of the Institute of Actuaries*, **121**, Part 1, pp. 161–77.

Institute of Actuaries of Australia, Guidance Note 456 – Preparation of Benefit Certificates Required Under the Superannuation Guarantee (Administration) Act 1992, March 1995.

Institute of Actuaries of Australia, Guidance Note 460 – Prudential Reporting to the Trustees and the Regulator, December 1994.

Institute of Actuaries of Australia, Guidance Note 461 – Funding and Solvency Certificates, December 1994.

Institute of Actuaries of Australia, Professional Standard 400 – Investigations of Defined Benefit Superannuation Funds.

Institute of Actuaries of Australia Superannuation Practice Committee (1992), Solvency Issues, *Transactions of the Institute of Actuaries of Australia*, Volume II, pp. 1011–27.

Lampe, A. (2003), 'Solvency of super funds declines thanks to bear markets', *Sydney Morning Herald*, 28 March, p. 27.

National Union of Workers, 'Ansett Australia – Special Members Report – Superannuation – 20 September 2001', on website at www.nuw.org.au/archive/campaign/ansett/Ansett%20Special%20Members %20Report.

Oldfield, S. (2002) 'Companies brace for superannuation black hole', *Australian Financial Review*, 13 December, pp. 1 and 66.

Oldfield, S. (2003), 'Banks fight worker priority pay', *Australian Financial Review*, 23 April.

Oldfield, S. and F. Buffini (2002), 'Underfunding risk to earnings', *Australian Financial Review*, 13 December, p. 66.

Trustee of the Ansett Australia Ground Staff Superannuation Plan Pty Ltd, Newsletters to members dated October 2001, December 2001, March 2002, May 2002, June 2002, September 2002 and December 2002, available on website www.ansettsuper.com.au/gssp/index.html.

Pension Law Review Committee (1993), *Pension Law Reform*, London: HMSO.

Wood, L. and S. Paxinos (2001), 'Ansett staff hit by super shortfall', *The Age*, 31 October, p. 3.

10. Pension funds and retirement benefits in a depressed economy: experience and challenges in Japan

Masaharu Usuki

INTRODUCTION

Markets can be scary in many different ways. In the USA and UK, for example, the scary markets idea is associated with stock markets which have risen and fallen with high amplitude, and with price earnings ratios which are unprecedented. This has generated a deep uncertainty in the minds of investors and fund managers about the future course of market valuation.

Japan shares some of this history. Japan's stock market boom, however, took place more than a decade ago, and the period since then has been characterized, not by a bust, but by a steady erosion of all asset prices – stocks, bonds, commercial real estate, and housing – which shows no sign of bottoming out. These more recent profiles do not resemble the pattern that has emerged over the last short period in the USA and the UK, where there are signs of stock price recovery, and where residential real estate has boomed.

Japan, of course, is at a different stage demographically from many other developed economies. It is on some definitions the world's oldest economy. The labour force has been declining since the mid-1990s and the population will peak in 2006. These demographic forces are sometimes linked to Japan's economic and financial malaise. It is not clear to what extent, if any, Japan's economic and financial experience over the last decade is a harbinger for younger economies which have yet to confront the full onslaught of demographic transition. But the Japanese experience is scary just because of that possibility. It would indeed be a serious outcome of global population ageing if macroeconomic and financial conditions were to follow the path of Japan.

This chapter discusses how companies have adjusted their pension plans, and how the government has modified its policy stance, to cope with the scenario depicted above. Overall, the responses have meant that the unanticipated declines in asset prices and economic activity have been shared across workers, profits and retirees. This has been possible because of the unique legal structure of pension funds in Japan and the somewhat soft nature of their liabilities.

PENSION PLANS IN JAPAN

Two Types of Defined Benefit Plans

For Japanese employees, both public pensions and private benefit plans provide retirement benefits. Public pensions for employees consist of a fixed component from the National Pension Insurance (NPI) and an earnings-related component from the Employees' Pension Insurance (EPI). For employees with an average earnings record and a spouse, the total of these two benefits is equivalent to 59 per cent of the current average wage after tax.

In addition, employers also provide retirement benefits. There are two types – lump-sum severance payments, which employees usually receive upon

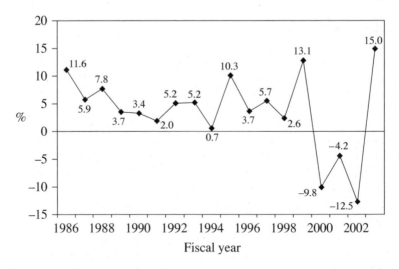

Note: Return in fiscal 2002 is preliminary estimate. Fiscal years start in April and end in March.

Source: Pension Fund Association (2003), 'Basic Material about Company Pension Plans 2003)'.

Figure 10.1   Return on assets managed by EPFs

termination of employment, and old-age occupational pension plans. Originally, all retirement benefits were lump-sum severance payments. In 1956, according to a study by the Ministry of Health, Labour and Welfare, 97 per cent of businesses with 500 employees or more, and 60 to 70 per cent of smaller businesses, had severance payment plans explicitly stated in their labour contracts.

At first, funding for severance payment plans was supplied not from externally accumulated assets, but from book reserves. As severance payments became a general practice, however, an increasing number of large companies began to introduce pension benefits that used externally accumulated assets for funding. As a result, in 1962 tax qualified pension plans (TQPPs) were introduced as a type of defined benefit pension plan, for which contributions were recognized as expenses for tax purposes.

In 1966, when employees' pension insurance was raised from a trivial level to 10 000 yen per month, employers were allowed to establish Employee Pension Funds (EPFs) to undertake the administration and management of the income-related portion of Employees' Pension Insurance. This measure, called contracting out, was adopted to accommodate management's demand to streamline the dual burdens of social security tax and employers' contribution to pension plans.

Regulation of Pensions

As a result of the contracted-out portion, EPFs came to be treated as a quasi-public pension that is tightly regulated. The government stipulated detailed rules for administering and managing EPFs. For example, plan sponsors must distribute at least half of this in the form of an annuity unless pensioners request payment in lump sum. Also, employers must entitle all employees with at least five years of tenure to membership in its EPF, and, for those with 20 years of membership, to rights to receive pension benefits. EPFs must have at least 500 participants.[1] The government also prescribed actuarial assumptions for EPFs to use. The discount rate was fixed at 5.5 per cent per annum from the time of inception in 1966 through 1997 (when this regulation was changed).

In addition, there were two major regulations regarding investment management. One was the legal list of asset allocation, and the other was the exclusive use of trust banks and insurance companies for fund management.

One exception to this strict regulatory framework for EPFs was the minimum funding rule applicable to termination liabilities. The amount of actuarial liabilities was to be calculated assuming continuity of pension plans. The minimum funding rule for the termination liabilities did not come into effect until 1997. Until then, there were no rules to examine the current level of funding, or to ensure sufficient funds were available for benefits to be paid in cases of plan termination.

One reason for this leniency in funding rules was that losses in tax revenue were a larger concern for the government. In the case of EPFs, taxes on employer/employee contributions as well as income generated from pension assets had been deferred because the government tried to discourage excessively large contributions.

Regulations for TQPPs have been similar to, but somewhat more permissive than, those applied to EPFs. TQPPs do not have to provide annuities, and the minimum membership is only 15 participants. Funding rules were also more lenient, with no funding requirement for termination liabilities. With regard to taxes, however, only those on employer contributions were deferred.[2]

Pensions' Role as a Reserve for Severance Payments

By March 2003 there were 1656 EPFs with 10.5 million active participants, compared to 66 752 TQPPs with 8.6 million active participants (see Table 10.1). Taking into account duplication, the total number of participants in TQPPs and EPFs is approximately 15 million, which equals 30 per cent of total employment in the private sector.

Eighty-seven per cent of employers in the private sector provide retirement benefits, which means that 63 per cent of the total workforce is covered by retirement benefit plans in one form or other. The difference in coverage between pension plans (30 per cent) and all retirement benefits (63 per cent) means that 33 per cent of employees are covered only by severance benefits with book reserve funding. Even among large employers with more than 1000 employees, only about half have at least a portion of retirement benefits funded as pension plans, with the remainder as book reserve plans.

Contributions made for pensions are recognized as expenses for tax purposes, and the derived interest on EPF assets is also tax exempt.[3] From the perspective of corporate finance, as in Black (1980), a funded pension system has a more favourable tax treatment than a book reserve system. This tax advantage of pension plans should help generate a higher valuation of plan sponsors' stock.

None the less, management has been less than enthusiastic about introducing a pension system and making contributions for funding liabilities. Possible reasons for this include a desire to lessen the investment risks of depressed asset prices and to retain capital internally for future investment or to prevent the increase in benefit levels from being used to increase benefits.

Table 10.1 Characteristics of employees' pension funds and tax qualified pension plans

Fiscal year ending	Employees' Pension Fund						Tax Qualified Pension Plans		
	Total number of plans	Number of active participants (million)	Asset under management (billion yen)	Number of terminated plans	Number of benefit reductions	Number of plans having returned contracted portion	Total number of plans	Number of active participants (million)	Asset under management (billion yen)
March 1994	1804	11.9	35 416	0	0	0	92 467	10.6	16 071
March 1999	1858	12.0	51 281	18	16	0	85 047	10.3	19 988
March 2000	1835	11.7	55 486	16	52	0	81 605	10.0	21 137
March 2001	1814	11.4	58 017	29	177	0	77 555	9.7	22 358
March 2002	1737	10.9	58 297	59	114	0	73 913	9.2	22 719
March 2003	1656	10.5	57 200	73	} approximately 300	481	66 752	8.6	21 447
March 2004	1580	na	na	64		290	na	na	na

Source: Pension Fund Association (2003), 'Basic Material about Company Pension Plans 2003'.

191

CHANGES IN SURROUNDING CONDITIONS IN THE 1990s

As shown in Table 10.1, the number of TQPPs, EPFs and their participants have been declining since the late 1990s. The environment surrounding defined benefit pension plans has made them more difficult to maintain. Below we examine two factors contributing to this change – lower than expected return on pension investment and changes in accounting rules.

Lower than Expected Return on Pension Assets

Stock prices in Japan peaked at the end of 1989. From 1990 to 2002 the average rate of return for the Tokyo Stock Market Index (TOPIX) was –4.9 per cent. The return has been especially dismal since 1997 and the TOPIX return was –6.9 per cent and 4.8 per cent in 1997 and 1998 respectively. The return reached 31 per cent in fiscal 1999, supported by the global boom in technology and telecommunications stocks, but declined again, recording –26.6 per cent, –16.0 per cent and –27.3 per cent in the three years from 2000.

Looking at other asset categories, the average returns from 1997 through to 2002 on fixed income securities and foreign bonds and foreign stocks were 3.3 per cent, 7.2 per cent and 2.6 per cent respectively. However, the return from the first two assets could not compensate for the losses suffered from stock investment. As a result, the return on EPF funds was –0.8 per cent during that period, and a mediocre 2.0 per cent from 1990 through 2002 (see Figure 10.1). The rate of return has recorded three straight years of negative performance since 2000.

Changes in Accounting Rules Regarding Retirement Benefits

Changes in accounting rules for retirement benefits in 2001 are the single most important factor hindering pension plan sponsors from maintaining retirement benefits, especially defined benefit plans.

In financial statements based on the previous accounting standards, employers' cash contributions were recorded as a periodic expense at the time contributions were made. No pension benefit obligation or provision was recorded as a liability on the balance sheet.

The treatment of severance payments was different. In the book-reserve financed severance payment system, a certain percentage of total benefits was given the status of tax-free book reserves under the tax law, and recognized in reserves for retirement allowances. In this case, expenses during the current period amounted to the increase in the reserve balance from the end of the previous period.

Under the new accounting standards, adopted from the fiscal year ending after March 2001, the accrued liability for both pension and severance payments must be recorded on companies' balance sheets. The difference, if any, between the total present value of this projected benefit obligation and the fair value of assets in pension plans must be recorded on the liability side of the employer's balance sheet as a reserve for retirement allowances.

Examining the results of 1006 companies listed on the first section of the Tokyo Stock Exchange (with a total of 8.3 million employees),[4] we find that, in the fiscal year ending March 2001, when the new accounting rule was applied for the first time, the retirement benefit obligation was 70.1 trillion yen. Against this, the fair value of pension assets was 37.7 trillion yen, or 53.8 per cent of the obligation, leaving a differential of 32.4 trillion yen as unfunded liabilities. A significant portion of these liabilities consisted of transition obligations and actuarial losses that can be smoothed out and recorded over a long period.[5] On the income statement, periodic benefit costs amounted to 10.4 trillion yen. This amount corresponded to 57.6 per cent of recurring profits (before taxes), which means profits would have been 1.6 times without benefits costs (see Table 10.2).

In the next fiscal year (ending March 2002), periodic benefit costs declined by 42.8 per cent to 5.9 trillion yen, mainly because recognition of transition obligations decreased. Benefit obligations, however, grew by 5.7 per cent to 74.1 trillion yen because of the discount rate decline reflecting lower market interest rates. Moreover, negative returns on assets exacerbated the funding status, for which increased contributions could not compensate. As a result, the net shortage of funds increased by 14.5 per cent.

In the fiscal period ending March 2003, projected benefit obligations declined by 6.7 per cent to 69.1 trillion yen. This is mainly because more than 200 EPFs returned the contracted-out portion to the government. However, this put-back reduced the fair value of plan assets at least by the same amount. In the end, the net shortage of funds increased by 23.7 per cent to 40.1 trillion yen.

The large ballooning of unfunded liabilities is mainly the result of the stock price decline from the 1990s and the increase in the value of benefit obligations due to the decline in the discount rate. As is shown in the right-hand column of Table 10.2, the average discount rate decreased from 3.1 per cent in the fiscal year ending March 2001 to 2.4 per cent in the fiscal year ending March 2003.

As of the end of March 2003, the funding ratio was a mere 42 per cent and the shortage amounted to 29.6 per cent of plan sponsors' shareholders equity. Periodic pension costs still recorded 35.1 per cent of recurring profits. It cannot be overemphasized that the disclosure of such liabilities and expenses in financial statements under the new accounting rules has heightened the uneasiness of plan sponsors in their management of retirement benefit plans.

Table 10.2   Financial conditions in plan sponsors' financial statements

Fiscal year ending	Projected benefit obligation A	Plan assets B	Net shortage of funds C = (A/B)	Funding radio (B/A) (%)	Periodic pension costs D	C/ Shareholders' equity (%)	C/ Recurring profit (%)	D/ Shareholders' equity (%)	D/ Recurring profit (trillion yen) (%)	Discount rate (%)
March 2001	70.1	37.7	32.4	53.8	10.4	23.3	179.7	7.5	57.6	3.1
March 2002	74.1	37.0	37.1	49.9	5.9	26.9	334.7	4.3	53.6	2.8
March 2003	69.1	29.0	40.1	42.0	6.0	29.6	235.5	4.4	35.1	2.4
(Year on year increase)										
2001–2002	5.7	–1.9	14.5	–3.9	–42.8	3.6	155.0	–3.2	–4.0	–0.3
2002–2003	–6.7	–21.5	8.1	–7.9	0.7	2.7	–99.2	0.1	–18.5	–0.3
2001–2003	–1.4	–23.0	23.7	–11.8	–42.5	6.3	55.8	–3.1	–22.5	–0.7

Note: Figures are disclosed in financial statements of plan sponsors listed in the 1st section of Tokyo Stock Exchange.

Source: NIKKEI Needs and NLI Research Institute.

RESPONSES OF PENSION PLANS AND SPONSORS

To cope with such increasingly difficult conditions, pension plans and their sponsors have taken several measures. These measures can be divided into three categories: asset management, benefit design, and (partial) termination of pension plans.

Sophistication of Asset Management

On the asset management side, sponsors have tried to upgrade their methods of asset management. As advocated by modern portfolio theory, portfolio and time diversification of risk has been gradually adopted by pension plans. Plan managers have come to believe that diversified and long-term investment in stocks and other assets can increase returns without incurring much additional risk.

By way of example, in just three years from 1996, the per centage of funds allocated to the domestic stock market increased from around 15.7 per cent to 36.5 per cent, as shown in Table 10.3. Usage of specialized investment management firms increased in favour of balanced fund managers such as trust banks and insurance companies.

As the experience of the last five years in Figure 10.1 shows, however, it has been difficult to find a good solution on the asset management side. Stock prices went up globally in 1999, but plummeted thereafter. Doubts were cast not only on the level but also on the existence of the equity risk premium. While investment in fixed income bonds has generated a handsome rate of return, the possibility of capital loss has become very high because the current yield of ten-year government bonds is merely 0.71 per cent at the end of March 2003. Investment in foreign securities was hindered by concern about exchange rate risks. Some large funds have sought to improve their rate of return by investing in alternative assets such as hedge funds, real estate and private equity. As the name implies, it is impossible for these alternative assets to obtain a major share in total assets.

Adjustment of Benefit Design

Because of this deadlock in asset management, employers turned their attention to the liabilities or benefit design side.

Reduction of benefits

In 1997, the government stipulated conditions to allow benefit reductions. These conditions include the approval by two-thirds of plan participants and agreement by the labour union.[6] The most notable pattern has been the

Table 10.3 Asset allocation of EPF (%)

As of the end March in each year	1991	1993	1995	1997	1998	1999	2000	2001	2002	2003
Stocks	18.4	14.9	16.5	26.0	37.1	44.8	54.6	52.2	51.6	41.9
Domestic	13.0	10.0	11.1	15.7	21.5	28.3	36.5	34.0	32.0	25.9
Foreign	5.4	4.9	5.4	10.3	15.6	16.6	18.0	18.1	19.6	16.0
Yen (Straight bonds)	21.7	24.1	21.2	25.0	24.1	22.2	21.5	21.3	21.3	11.9
Yen (Convertible bonds)	3.3	4.5	4.7	5.2	3.5	2.0	1.6	1.3	0.7	0.4
Foreign bonds	5.2	4.8	3.8	5.4	6.1	8.5	7.4	10.3	10.2	23.2
Insurance companies general account	36.9	40.3	42.2	30.6	24.4	17.7	11.1	11.3	12.1	13.9
Real estate	0.6	0.4	0.3	0.3	0.1	0.1	0	0	0	0.0
Money	3.2	2.2	2.8	2.4	2.2	2.5	2.5	2.2	2.7	4.4
Other	10.8	8.9	8.4	5.1	2.5	2.2	1.3	1.4	1.4	4.3

Source: Pension Fund Association (2003), 'Basic Material about Company Pension Plans 2003'.

reduction of annuity amounts by lowering the assumed rate of interest for conversion of severance payments into annuities. Recently, there have also been cases where the reduction is not limited to annuity amounts, but affects the total present value of retirement benefits stipulated in the labour contract.

Another notable development has occurred in a few cases where even the benefits of pensioners are reduced. This reduction is possible provided that two-thirds of pensioners agree, and pension plans reimburse the present value of benefits in lump sum form if any of the pensioners request them to do so.

Introduction of cash balance plans

Recently, an increasing number of benefit adjustments have taken the form of traditional defined benefit plans converted into cash balance plans. As in the USA, with cash balance plans, the balance of benefits in each participant's account increases every year by the sum of service credits and interest credits, the latter of which equals the account balance at the end of the previous year multiplied by the base interest rate. Plan participants receive the balance of that cash value at the time of job termination or as annuities upon retirement.

According to a survey by a research institute affiliated to the Ministry of Health, Labor and Welfare, as an alternative to traditional defined benefit plans, cash balance plans are attracting interest on a par with defined contribution plans. The reason is that cash balance plans help plan sponsors to share interest rate risks with plan participants and pensioners.

In cash balance plans, the benefit formula can be designed to counteract the effect of interest rate changes on the amount of pension benefit obligations. Both the base rate used for the calculation of interest credits and the discount rate used for valuing the pension benefit obligations increase (decrease) as the market interest rate increases (decreases). An increase (decrease) in the base rate accelerates (decelerates) the growth of benefit amount, while an increase (decrease) in the discount rate lowers (raises) the economic value of the benefit obligation as well as the amount of the benefit obligation for accounting purposes. As a result, in the financial statements of plan sponsors, the effect of interest rate changes on the amount of benefit obligations is offset by the change in interest credits in the opposite direction. In cash balance plans, benefit obligations have a shorter duration and are less sensitive to interest rate movements than benefit obligations of traditional defined benefit plans.

In Japan this adjustment mechanism can be applied even to the period of annuity payments. Depending on changes in interest rates, a pension plan can adjust the base rate by which the cash value is converted into annuities. The amount of annuities decreases if interest rates decline.

In sum, the introduction of cash balance plans enables plan sponsors to share interest rate risks with plan participants, especially the downside risk of interest rates.

Introduction of defined contribution plans

The third adjustment in benefit design is the introduction of defined contribution plans, following the passing of a new law allowing their establishment in September 2001.

Again we find a feature of defined contribution plans is that they alleviate the financial burden of plan sponsors. In addition, new defined contribution plans can assume past service liabilities as well as accumulated assets from defined benefit plans. Plan sponsors can be construed to have paid up accrued pension liabilities in EPFs and TQPPs by transferring the same amount of plan assets to defined contribution plans and distributing them to each participant's account. After that rollover, plan sponsors are freed from the investment risks of asset management and from accounting liabilities as well as from volatility in the value of liabilities.

As seen in Table 10.4, out of 632 defined contribution plans existing in November 2003, 376 plans (59.5 per cent) have been introduced for the purpose of the rollover mentioned above. Among large companies with over 300 employees that proportion is 67.5 per cent.

In spite of this feature, as of the end of January 2004, 28 months after the Defined Contribution Law went into effect, only 2007 companies with 659 000 participants have adopted defined contribution pension plans. One reason for the low adoption rate is that the maximum annual contribution is only 436 000 yen if an employer has no other tax qualified defined benefit plans, and 218 000 yen if an employer has any type of tax qualified defined benefit plan. Another reason is that participants cannot withdraw any money from their accounts until the age of 60. Liquidity is thus constrained compared not only with severance payments but also with defined benefit plans in which participants can receive at least a portion of benefits as a lump sum.

Plan Termination

Complete termination

If plan sponsors expect little improvement in financial performance either through sophisticated asset management methods or by adjustment of benefit design, they have no choice but to abandon the pension plan altogether. The number of pension plan terminations is increasing (see Table 10.1). Many plan sponsors say that they can no longer endure the volatility in their benefit obligations and contributions. Plan termination is one of the surest ways to escape from these risks.

Usually at the time of plan termination, plan assets are distributed to participants after the deduction of the amount necessary to pay benefits to current pensioners. While the total amount of retirement benefits in the labour contract does not change, the amount of assets distributed at the time of plan termina-

Table 10.4 Breakdown of company-type DC plans introduced by November 2003

	Total		With more than 300 participants		With less than 300 participants	
Number of plans	632	(100.0)	289	(100.0)	343	(100.0)
Rollover from other DB plans						
No rollover or transfer of assets	256	(40.5)	94	(32.5)	162	(47.2)
Rolled over from	376	(59.5) <100.0>	195	(67.5) <100.0>	181	(52.8) <100.0>
TQPP	230	<61.2>	99	<50.8>	131	<72.4>
Book reserve lump-sum	69	<18.4>	44	<22.6>	25	<13.8>
Combination of above two	57	<15.2>	32	<16.4>	25	<13.8>
EPF	13	<3.5>	13	<6.7>	0	<0.0>
Combination of TQPP and EPF	2	<0.5>	2	<1.0>	0	<0.0>
Combination of lump-sum and EPF	2	<0.5>	2	<1.0>	0	<0.0>
Combination of three	3	<0.8>	3	<1.5>	0	<0.0>

Note: Parentheses denote percentage poins.

Source: Ministry of Health Labor and Welfare.

tion is taken into account in deciding the amount of remaining benefits to be paid in the future. Usually the labour contract is amended so that plan sponsors disburse the remainder of retirement benefits to employees when they leave their jobs in the future.

Put-back of the contracted-out portion

Not as drastic as complete termination, but much larger in number is the partial termination of plans by reverting the contracted-out portion of EPFs. The background to this is the increasing disadvantage for plan sponsors that maintain the contracted-out portion of EPFs. One reason is that the interest rate for calculating the rebate premium the government distributes to pay the contracted-out benefits was set at 5.5 per cent per annum, which has been much higher than interest rates prevailing in the market.

In addition, under the new accounting standards, the contracted-out portion has been included in sponsors' pension benefit obligations. The discount rate used in evaluating these obligations is based on the current market rate, which is far below 5.5 per cent. Thus liabilities recorded in financial statements are 20 to 50 per cent larger than actuarial liabilities.

As another disadvantage of the contracted-out portion, plan sponsors have come to think that the inflexible rules for the design, administration and management of EPFs, because of their quasi-public nature, are cumbersome. They also think that operating costs are burdensome, including those for the computation, collection and distribution of premiums and benefits.

An increasing number of EPF sponsors have voiced their desire to escape from these burdens of contracting out. In answer to these demands, the new Defined Benefit Corporate Pension Plan Law which came into effect in 2002 allows the reversion of the contracted-out portion. After putting back the contracted-out portion, EPFs can be changed into one of two types of defined benefit plans under the Defined Benefit Corporate Pension Plan Law: contract type and fund type.

Reversion relieves the employer of the foregoing burdens. It also enables plan sponsors to record one-time profits on the income statement. This is possible because the reduced amount of benefit obligations for accounting purposes, reduced by the reversion, is much larger than the amount of assets that sponsors are required to pay back to the government. This difference is brought about because the discount rate used for accounting purposes is higher than the rate used for calculating the amount needed to pay back to the government.[7]

Plan sponsors' interest in this scheme is very high. Within 12 months of the new law's enforcement, out of 1600 EPFs, 771 in blue chips such as Toyota, Hitachi and NEC have been allowed to revert the contracted-out portion. In particular, 45 per cent of single-employer and affiliated-employer plans have acquired permission for reversion.

The Effect on the Labour Relationship

It is curious that employees would agree with the change in benefit design, in particular the reduction of accrued benefits and the shift of investment risk through the introduction of defined contribution and cash balance plans. This can be explained by two factors.

First, the entire employment and compensation system is currently being restructured. Many large companies have been trying to reduce the number of employees, although certain conditions must be satisfied to legally lay off employees. Once employees lose their jobs, it is very hard for them to find new ones, partly because the labour market is relatively illiquid and inflexible. In short, employees facing the 'hold-up' problem are forced to make concessions.

Second, it is still disputable whether retirement benefits can be construed as deferred wages. It is legal and very common for an employer to reduce benefit amounts when an employee leaves because of his/her own will or is dismissed because of misconduct or criminal charges. If employees and employers consider that benefit amounts can change depending on circumstances, then agreeing with a reduction and the shift of financial risks is less difficult for them.

CHANGES IN GOVERNMENT REGULATIONS

Along with the foregoing measures taken by pension plans and their sponsors, the government has changed the way it regulates pension plans.

Regulation before the 1990s

As stated in Altman (1992), enhancing the equity, adequacy and security of pensions is the main objective of pension fund regulation. As far as EPFs are concerned, the strict rules explained earlier have succeeded in maintaining the equity and adequacy of benefits.

Rules for the security of benefits, however, were not complete in either type of Japanese defined benefit pension schemes (EPFs or TQPPs). Generally, arrangements for the security of benefit rights include: (1) vesting of benefit rights, (2) separate management of pension assets from employers' business assets, and (3) securing payment by minimum funding rules and plan termination insurance.

It has been mandatory for EPFs to pay pension benefits to participants with 20 years of membership, and to have pension assets managed in separate accounts at trust banks and insurance companies. Otherwise, EPFs and TQPPs have had very few explicit rules for the protection of benefit rights.

We can point out that there was very little need for special arrangements to maintain the security of benefit payments until the end of the 1980s. Both the rate of return on, and the amount of, pension assets were at a comfortable level for plan sponsors, and they did not have to consider the idea of reducing benefits. There were no EPF terminations other than to combine two or more plans. The Termination Insurance Programme for EPFs started in 1989, but no applications were made in the first few years.

Changes in Regulation in the 1990s

Deregulation of asset management
Conditions favourable to plan sponsors took a turn for the worse after the asset bubble peaked in 1990. The first termination of an EFP occurred in 1994. Business conditions continued to decline, especially in the older, well-established industries, and the rate of return on pension assets declined to a very low level.

At first, countermeasures taken by pension plans were mostly in the area of asset management. Deregulation processes for asset management rules from the late 1980s supported these movements. Government completely abolished the legal list to restrict asset allocation in December 1997 and lifted the rule limiting investment management to insurance companies and trust banks. In their place, the prudent person rule requiring duty of care and loyalty explicitly came into effect through ministerial guidance.[8]

Changes to funding rules
It was gradually recognized, however, that changes in asset management practices alone could not solve the financial difficulties of defined benefit plans. In 1997 the rules for funding started to change.

As a first step, EPFs and TQPPs were allowed to determine the actuarial discount rate at their discretion. The government only implied a range for the discount rate every year based upon the average yield of ten-year government bonds issued in the previous five years. Also, the minimum period for amortization of unfunded liabilities was shortened from seven years to three years. These changes enabled plan sponsors to accelerate the amortization of unfunded liabilities.

At the same time, the minimum funding requirement for termination liabilities was first introduced for EPFs. In accordance with that rule, if the value of accumulated assets is less than 105 per cent of termination liabilities of the contracted-out portion or 90 per cent of termination liabilities of total benefits, EPFs must set out a recovery plan incorporating contribution increases to achieve those funding ratios within seven years. Clearly the objective of these changes was to accelerate funding and protect benefit rights.

Notwithstanding, the government took a measure contradicting the protection of benefit rights in 1997. For the first time it explicitly allowed the reduction of benefits under certain conditions: (1) agreement by labour and management, (2) consent by two-thirds of participants, and (3) the existence of hardship in the employer's business conditions.

At that time, because of large unfunded liabilities and increasing contribution amounts, plan sponsors were gradually becoming interested in giving up pension plans. If the government had only set a funding requirement that was difficult for many plans to achieve, the number of plan terminations would have increased. It can be deduced that the government was trying to strike a balance between measures to require sufficient funding and measures to help plan sponsors continue pension plans.

Further relaxation
After 1997, however, conditions did not improve. The economy did not experience a strong recovery, and the stock market downturn continued after a short-lived boom in 1999 and 2000. New accounting rules revealed the widening shortage in funding.

Under these circumstances, the government could not help but take a measure to alleviate the financial burden of plan sponsors. In 1998 pension funds were allowed to suspend the contribution hike if assets at the end of March 2006 were expected to exceed 105 per cent of minimum liabilities for the contracted-out portion.

A further downturn in the stock market from 2001 compelled the government to take several additional measures to loosen minimum funding rules. By way of example, EPFs were not required to implement a recovery plan if the funding shortage was within the range stipulated by the government.

In cases where EPFs are required to formulate a recovery plan, they are allowed to suspend implementation for two years. After the two-year suspension, it is possible for EPFs to take ten years instead of seven for completion. This prolongation is applicable to EPFs that seek to recover funding levels either by reducing benefits or lowering the actuarial discount rate. They can also raise the contribution rate gradually until five years from the beginning of a recovery plan, when the rate is supposed to reach the final level.

Introduction of new types of pension plans
The introduction of defined contribution plans, cash balance plans, as well as defined benefit plans without the contracted-out portion, can be regarded as measures to help pension plans adjust their benefit design.

The Defined Contribution Plan Law came into effect in 2001. The Defined Benefit Corporate Pension Plan Law which came into force in April 2002 has made it possible for EPFs to adopt the benefit formula of cash balance plans.

It has also allowed EPFs to revert to the contracted-out portion and transform themselves into either contract-type or fund-type defined benefit plans. Hence we now have three types of defined benefit pensions (see Figure 10.2). Existing TQPPs must convert to one of the three types within a ten-year transition period.

The introduction of new types of pensions is aimed at supporting the continuation of pension plans. Plan sponsors can transfer investment risks to plan participants in defined contribution plans. In cash balance plans, they can share risks with plan participants. The government has even tried to help them deal with risks in managing assets and liabilities accrued in the past. For example, the government ruled that accrued liabilities in old defined benefit plans could be satisfied by removing the same amount of assets from old plans to these new types of plans.

Possible Policy Debate

All in all, the government has made lenient policies in funding requirements because it has prioritized helping pension plans to overcome and survive these financial difficulties in the long term. Another policy option would have been to require the fast recovery of funding levels and force termination in case pension plans cannot recover the funding. In reality, very few underfunded plans were forced to dissolve, while the minimum funding rule continued to be relaxed. As of March 2001, out of all 1800 EPFs, more than half were underfunded. That is, accumulated assets were short of 0.9 times the amount necessary to pay benefits upon plan termination, and 1.3 times the minimum actuarial liabilities for the contracted-out portion.

These policies may be criticized on two points. First, in the context of

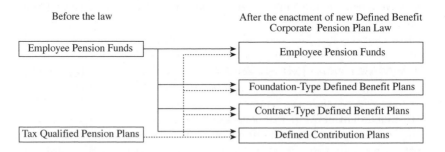

Source: Ministry of Health, Labor and Welfare.

Figure 10.2 Change in corporate pension structure under the new Defined Benefit Corporate Pension Plan Law

prudent regulation, such forbearance policies in respect of troubled financial institutions are said to bring about several inefficiencies. One is the moral hazard of management revealed in excessive risk-taking activities. This occurs if there is a termination (deposit) insurance scheme, as was experienced in the Savings and Loan crisis in the 1980s.

We must note a few reservations before using this analogy. In Japan, with regard to termination insurance for EPFs, if inappropriate management is the cause of underfunding or the funding ratio is below 50 per cent, the insurer can reduce the amount of insurance money to be payable to the insured. Further, examining 21 applications for insurance payment in the past, the insurer rejected ten and did not admit any payment. The duty of prudence as a part of fiduciary responsibilities, which the law requires for plan management, could be effective in preventing imprudent investment. These factors may somewhat prevent excessive risk-taking by pension plan management.

The second criticism of forbearance policies is that if the government leaves underfunded plans, it increases the possibility of benefit reduction and destabilizes the participant's life after retirement because it increases the possibility of benefit reduction. However, if underfunded plans are forced to terminate by the government, no one can replenish that shortage. Participants could not have received the full amount of accrued benefits, since termination insurance can cover only part of them. Under these circumstances, pre-emptive intervention into pension funds is not necessarily more advantageous for participants than forbearance.

Considering the above, policies that accommodate underfunded pension plans might be as worthwhile as policies that force them to terminate. Even if the government had pursued a tighter policy from the 1990s, it is doubtful whether it would have been more successful. A macroeconomic shock could have made it almost impossible for any plan to meet the strict requirements of the government. Forbearance policies might be selected as a second-best option.

SUMMARY AND IMPLICATIONS FOR THE FUTURE

For over a decade in Japan, retirement benefit plans have been struggling in a severe environment. More than a decade after the problem emerged, pension plans in other developed countries seem to be facing similar problems. Without a crystal ball, we cannot foretell to what extent pensions in other countries will follow the fate of pensions in Japan. Here we summarize the experiences of pension plans, plan sponsors and the government, and explain the future tasks they must encounter.

The Experience and Challenges of Plan Sponsors

The phenomenon that plan sponsors had to cope with was that of very low *ex-ante* probabilities. Placing ourselves in the shoes of plan sponsors back in 1990 or 1997, we could not have expected the situation where the rate of return of the stock market would be –4.9 per cent for 13 years or –6.6 per cent for six years. Even if we could forecast the risk-free rate accurately, the probability of such low rates of return is less than 5.0 per cent, using a historical equity risk premium. Only when we make a modest assumption of a 2.0 per cent equity risk premium do the probabilities of the actual return from 1997 to 2002 rise to 11 per cent[9] (see Table 10.5).

Such low probabilities or low risk premia were mostly outside the consideration of plans and plan sponsors. Furthermore, a low rate of return has been brought about by structural change in the economy. The stock market performance and plan sponsors' business conditions deteriorated at the same time. This might be especially true in the deflationary economy. In the equation derived from the simple dividend discount Model,

$$S_t = D_t / (R_f + P - G),$$

stock prices are determined by the dividend at the starting point D_t, risk-free rate R_f, risk premium P, and the expected growth rate of the dividend, G. Usually in an economic downturn, the decline in G is somewhat offset by the decline in risk-free rate R_f. In a deflationary environment, however, this relation becomes less binding. Dividend and earnings growth rates in the foreseeable future fall into negative territory, while the risk-free rate cannot fall below zero. In this case, the decline in G, which reflects deflationary business conditions, influences stock prices more directly. The correlation between stock prices and business conditions rises.

Facing this dual burden of bad business and sluggish return, plan sponsors have been trying to reduce the amount of benefits and to transfer a portion of their liabilities accruing from the past to plan participants or employees. Even so, *ex-post* reduction has the possibility of damaging employees' morale, and the reputation of and confidence in plan sponsors.

For the future, plan sponsors can meet the challenges of dealing with this type of shock in advance. One way is to shift all or part of the investment risks to plan participants through the introduction of defined contribution plans and cash balance plans.

Another measure Japanese plan sponsors have yet to try is risk diversification through diversified investment. Business performance is more correlated to the domestic than global economy, even though business activities of some markets are increasingly globalized. Reducing the exposure to domestic stock

Table 10.5 Ex-ante probabilities of Japan's stock market experience after 1990

| Breakdown | Assumption (A) | | Actual return (B) | | Probabilities of (B) or worse under Assumption (A) in normal distribution (%) |
| | Mean expected return | | | | |
	Total (%)	Standard deviation (%)	Years	Normal average return (%)	
Risk Free Rate (Average 1990–2002) 1.95%	7.39	17.70	Averge 1990–2002	–4.86	0.63
+Risk Premium 5.44% (Average 1953–2002)		(Average 1953–2002)			
Risk Free Rate (Average 1997–2002) 0.15%	5.59	17.70	Average 1997–2002	–6.57	4.62
+ Risk Premium 5.44% (Average 1953–2002)		(Average 1953–2002)			
Risk Free Rate (Average 1990–2002) 1.95%	3.95	17.70	Average 1990–2002	–4.86	3.64
+ Risk Premium 2.00%		(Average 1953–2002)			
Risk Free Rate (Average 1997–2002) 0.15%	2.15	17.70	Average 1997–2002	–6.57	11.38
+ Risk Premium 2.00%		(Average 1953–2002)			

Note: All date are annualized from original monthly data.

Source: Ibbotson Associates Japan Inc.

markets and increasing the exposure to foreign markets could lessen the impact of macroeconomic shocks. With that objective, plan sponsors have to engage investment managers with professionalism and motivate them with proper incentives.

Government Experience

To cope with the difficult conditions of plan sponsors, the Japanese government first tried to ensure and protect benefit rights by strengthening solvency (funding) regulations and the termination insurance scheme. However, the macroeconomic shock was so widespread that it was almost impossible for pension plans to abide by tightened rules. On the other hand, rigid funding rules would surely have led to the dissolution of problematic plans.

The government turned around and accommodated plan sponsors' demands for more lax regulation on funding in defined benefit plans and benefit design. It clarified conditions for the reduction of accrued benefits, including those of pensioners.

It is easy to point out in hindsight that pension benefits would have been better protected if assets equal to termination liabilities had been upheld by the minimum funding rule since the 1990s. As has been explained earlier, such rigid funding policies are yet to be justified. In the Netherlands the regulatory authority's tough stance is now arousing a big controversy.

In the future, as a matter of course, *ex-post* reduction of pension amounts is undesirable for employees. In order to avoid benefit reduction, a strict minimum funding rule should take effect in defined benefit plans, although it may be difficult to thoroughly implement this rule unless we can completely avoid macroeconomic shocks. The lax funding requirement is still applied to new types of defined benefit plans introduced by the Defined Benefit Pension Plan Law in 2002, since most of them are succeeding under funded EPFs and TQPPs. As a precondition to applying a strict minimum funding rule, it might be necessary to make employers and employees thoroughly negotiate over employers' ability to pay pension benefits when there is any underfunding of pension liabilities and/or bankruptcy or other trouble with the employers' businesses.

Finally, the challenge that we believe has relevance to other governments is related to accounting principles. Changes in accounting rules should have nothing to do with the market value of plan sponsors and their pension plans. If the market is completely efficient and valuation in the market corresponds with plan sponsors' intrinsic economic value, changes in accounting rules should have no effect on market valuation.

Accounting matters in reality because market participants were not omniscient and the market was not very efficient. Funding shortages already existed before the change in accounting rules. Both the management and investors of plan sponsors, however, paid little attention until the change in accounting rules in 2001. Once rules were changed, management began to worry about investors' reaction to the amount of unfunded liabilities and periodic benefit costs. Minimizing both the amount and volatility of these has become one of the largest motives for management to abandon traditional defined benefit plans and adopt new types of plans.

Other countries where new accounting rules have been introduced, such as the UK, are experiencing the same situation wherein changes in accounting rules have seriously affected pension fund management. Regulatory authorities of pension funds should pay attention to plan sponsors' accounting disclosure and to the reaction of the market and investors to that. They may well give thought to the idea of integrating actuarial accounting for two purposes: one is to determine the amount of company contribution to a plan, and the other is to disclose information to market participants.

NOTES

1. Plan sponsors of EPFs can be classified into three categories: single employer, multiple employers of affiliated companies, and multiple employers in the same industry or local area. Their minimum number is 500, 800 and 2000 respectively.
2. Employees' contributions, if any, have been classified as a life insurance premium, and 1.0 per cent of the asset value is assessed annually as a separate corporate tax.
3. Although suspended until fiscal 2002, for Tax Qualified Pension Plans and defined contribution plans, a special corporate tax of 1.173 per cent is assessed on outstanding assets.
4. We examine the data on 1006 non-financial companies for which information on retirement benefits both at the end of March 2001 and through 2003 was available.
5. The maximum period for recognition of transition obligations is 15 years, and the maximum period for recognition of actuarial losses is the employee's average remaining service period.
6. The reason for reduction has to be one of the following: change in the labour contract; plan sponsors' distressed business conditions; unbearable hike in contribution rate; and the combination of two plans.
7. In the case of reversion, assets equal to liabilities for the contracted-out portion must be returned to the government, specifically to the Government Pension Investment Corporation.
8. In addition to supporting pension plans investment activities, included in the objective of these deregulation measures was the development of the Tokyo market by the so-called big-bang initiatives of the government.
9. By the calculation based on log-normal return distribution, probabilities of actual stock return are 0.9 per cent and 5.7 per cent, based on a historical risk premium and 5.6 per cent and 14.5 per cent, assuming a 2.0 per cent risk premium.

REFERENCES

Altman, N. (1992), 'Government regulation: Enhancing the equity, adequacy and security of pension benefits', in *Private Pensions and Public Policy*, Paris: OECD.

Black, F. (1980), 'The tax consequences of long-run pension policy', *Financial Analysts Journal*, **36**(4), 21–8.

11. The structure and regulation of the Brazilian private pension system[1]

Flávio Marcílio Rabelo

INTRODUCTION

As compared to retirement income systems operating elsewhere, private pensions in Brazil are scary due to the extreme volatility of the economic and financial environment in Brazil. Almost as scary, however, is the increasing trend towards more and more complicated private pension regulation. This was realized in 2001 with the passing of legislation setting out a new regulatory framework for the private pension system. Since then, regulating bodies of the closed and the open systems, the Council for Complementary Pensions (CGPC) and the National Council for Private Insurance (CNSP), respectively, have been preparing the necessary regulations.

This chapter begins with an overview of the main market trends in the private pension system, emphasizing coverage, the emergence of new products and competitive patterns. It then analyses the impact of the new legislation on retirement income security and furthering the expansion of the private pension system. The taxation of funded pensions and the costs of private pensions in Brazil are covered next. A final section concludes.

STRUCTURE OF BRAZILIAN PRIVATE PENSIONS AND MARKET TRENDS

The structure of the Brazilian private pension system is quite similar to the private pension systems operating in the USA and the UK as it comprises both occupational pensions and personal pension plans. The former are referred to as 'closed funds', and are restricted to the employees of the sponsoring organization, while the latter, called 'open funds', are offered by insurance companies to the general public. Personal pension plans, or open funds may also take the form of group personal pensions (GPPs), also called 'collective open plans', in which case an organization contracts with an insurance company to set up a plan for its employees or members. Occupational pension plans are managed by foundations called Entidades Fechadas de Previdencia Complementar (EFPCs), which have a legal status of their own and whose assets are separated from those of the sponsoring firm.

Occupational Pension Plans

Participation in occupational pension plans, or the closed system, has remained practically the same since 1995, although there has been an increase in the ratio of beneficiaries to active participants. Factors which could explain this stagnation include: the high level of unemployment during these years; the privatization of large state-owned firms; the competition with collective open plans; and the regulatory burden of closed funds.

State-owned firms pioneered the private pension system in Brazil, and these firms sponsored most of the large plans. In the 1990s, many of these firms were privatized and, as part of restructuring by the new owners, large lay-offs were implemented. The other explanations are somewhat related. Insurance companies targeted the corporate market and offered firms favourable terms for establishing their pension plans. Since most insurance companies are controlled by banking groups, pension plans are viewed as another item in the product portfolio. In some cases, lower fees were negotiated to capture a profitable market base for other banking services.

It may also simply be that firms do not wish to go through the process of creating a foundation (EFPC). But one may then raise the question: why not join a multi-sponsored closed pension fund? As will be discussed later, the open and closed pension systems have been regulated quite differently. Many observers feel that the regulatory burden imposed on the closed system is disproportionately high and a major cause of the current situation. This is a worrisome picture given the very low coverage rate, of only 8 per cent of those employed in the formal labour market as of 2000.

In the UK, guaranteed private pensions (GPPs) are the natural choice for smaller companies. Further studies are required to identify the type of firms that are contracting collective open plans for their employees. The Secretariat for Complementary Pensions (SPC) periodically publishes the authorized requests made by sponsoring firms to withdraw their sponsorship of closed pension plans. In the October and November 2002 reports, six sponsoring firms, with plans ranging from 115 to 1601 participants, withdrew their sponsorship and decided to transfer the balances to open pension plans. Such a process may take one or two years to be approved by the relevant regulatory body (the SPC), so it is not known how many such requests have been made. Interviews with former staff of SPC indicate that there is a very large number of these requests. As shown in Figure 11.1, there has been a reduction in the number of sponsoring firms.

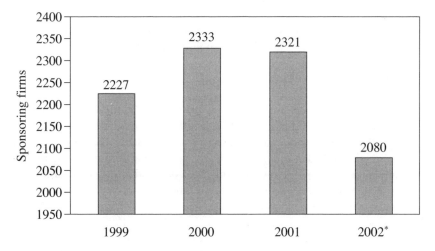

* August. For other years, number refers to situation in December.

Source: SPC/MPAS: *Boletim da Previdência Complementar*, **1** (8 and 13), 2001; Informe
            Estatístico, August 2002.

Figure 11.1   Closed pension plans – number of sponsoring firms

As to the size of the closed pension funds, Table 11.1 shows that nearly 70 per cent of total participants (active and beneficiaries) belong to EFPCs with more than 10 000 members. This is an important matter given the scale economies that operate in the private pensions industry. Less than 4 per cent of total participants are enrolled in EFPCs with 1500 or fewer members.

It is important to distinguish EFPCs with one sponsor from the multi-sponsored EFPCs. The latter are seen as a vital instrument in promoting the expansion of the closed system. There are basically two types of multi-sponsored plans: those established by firms which are part of a business group or belong to a related industry, and those set up by financial institutions. In the latter case, the financial institution earns a profit by selling services and charging investment management fees to the plan sponsors. There are around ten multi-sponsored plans set up by financial institutions, with a total membership (including active participants and beneficiaries) of around 145 000 (or 6.5 per cent of total membership). Table 11.2 presents the growth of the three largest of these plans, which account for 70 per cent of participants. It does not seem, however, that banks are really keen to invest in this business segment, and there are doubts regarding the growth potential of the closed system. Some large EFPCs are also trying to expand their base of sponsoring firms in order to take advantage of scale economies.

Table 11.1   Membership of EFPCs (in 2002)

Total membership	No. EFPCs	No. members	% members	Cumulative %
100 001–150 000	1	142 870	6.3	6.3
50 001–100 000	5	412 750	18.1	24.4
25 001–50 000	12	456 750	20.0	44.4
10 001–25 000	34	544 007	23.8	68.2
5001–10 000	41	288 069	12.6	80.8
2501–5000	71	256 956	11.2	92.0
1501–2500	48	95 681	4.2	96.2
1001–1500	37	47 325	2.1	98.3
501–1000	37	27 225	1.2	99.5
Up to 500	51	12 442	0.5	100.0
Total	337	2 284 075	100.0	

Source: SPC/MPAS.

Table 11.2   Growth of large multi-sponsored plans

	Number of active participants			
	1996	1997	1998	2002
CCF	57 483	57 265	59 443	44 033
MULTIPREV	1 266	7 080	9 185	21 526
BB PREVIDÊNCIA	76	6 346	13 844	29 391
Total EFPCs	1 759 437	1 732 455	1 753 250	n.a.

Note: *August.

Source: SPC.

Access to the closed fund system has been extended to members of profes-sional associations and trade unions. These entities (called *instituidores*) are allowed to create an EFPC, subject to the requirement that the plans are set up as defined contribution plans, and investments are fully externally managed by qualified financial institutions. The minimum condition for an entity to attain the status of *instituidor* is 1000 members or associates and three years of certi-fied legal existence.

The impact of this new law on extending coverage rests largely with the ability of professional associations and trade unions to mobilize their members. Few trade unions have a significant portion of their membership with earnings above the limit required under the private pension system (RGPS).[2] It has also to be said that these plans will face direct competition

Table 11.3   Evolution of EFPC investments*

Year	1994	1995	1996	1997	1998	1999	2000	2001	2002*
R$ billion	46.5	57.5	71.8	88.9	90.8	115.1	130.1	154.6	153.1
% GDP	8.3	8.2	9.2	10.3	10.3	12.5	13.2	14.4	14.3

Note: *Until May 2002.

Source: SPC/MPAS and ABRAPP.

from collective open plans, which have been available for a long time to these same institutions. Given the dismal track record of insurance companies in creating collective open plans for professional associations, there is sufficient reason to doubt the potential of this market for closed funds.

The evolution of the closed pension system's assets in absolute values and as a percentage of GDP is shown in Table 11.3. It is evident that despite a 72 per cent growth since 1994, the assets to GDP ratio is still small when compared to that in OECD countries with developed funded schemes and with

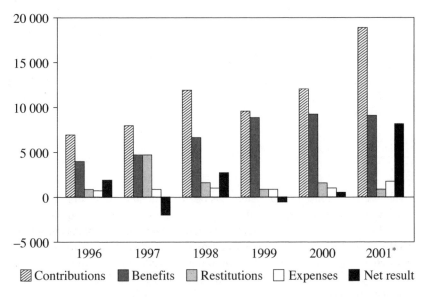

Note: *   Contributions were extraordinarily high this year due to large back payments from sponsoring firms.

Source: ABRAPP and SPC/MPAS.

Figure 11.2   Contributions and benefits of the closed pension system

Table 11.4 Private pension products in Brazil

	Type	Individual collective	Return guarantees	Benefits	Portability	Withdrawal	Fees	Taxation
Closed system	DC or DB	Collective	No (for DC plans)	Annuity (for DB plans) Annuity/ programmed withdrawal (DC plans)	Not yet fully regulated for DB plans	Only when employment relation ceases	No fees. Administrative and investment management charges deduced	Employee contributions are exempt up to 12% of taxable income. Employer contributions are exempt up to 20% of payroll. Investment returns are taxable limited to 12% of employer contributions. Benefits are taxable
Open system								
Traditional plans	DC	Individual	Yes – inflation + 6%	Annuity			Fees on contributions. Investment management costs are also deducted	Contributions are exempt up to 12% of taxable income. Benefits are taxable
PGBL	DC	Individual or collective	No	Annuity	Fully portable	After a minimum of 60 days	Fees on contributions, investments and withdrawals	Same as for closed plans. Investment returns are not taxed in individual plans
PAGP	DC		Yes – inflation	Annuity	Fully portable	After a minimum of 60 days	Same as PGBL	Same as PGBL
PRGP	DC		Yes – inflation + a set index	Annuity	Fully portable	After a minimum of 60 days	Same as PGBL	Same as PGBL

VGBL	DC	Individual	No	Annuity	Among VGBL, VAGP and VRGP	After a minimum of 60 days	Same as PGBL	Contributions are not deductible. Investment returns are not taxed in individual plans. In collective plans, follows the rules for closed plans. Only the portion corresponding to investment returns are taxed when benefits are paid
VAGP	DC		Yes – inflation	Annuity	Same as VGBL	After a minimum of 60 days	Same as PGBL	Same as VGBL
VRGP	DC		Yes – Inflation + a set index	Annuity	Same as VGBL	After a minimum of 60 days	Same as PGBL	Same as VGBL

Notes:
* The individual always has the option to withdraw the whole of this account balance before the set annuitization date.
* These plans ae not yet available. They will be allowed in both individual and collective formats.
** Currently the VGBL has only been regulated in the individual format. It will soon also be allowed in the collective format.
** Given the different tax treatment, funds from VGBL, VAGP and VRGP plans cannot be transferred to traditional pension plans PGBL, PAGP, PRGP and closed plans without the incidence of income tax.

Chile. Figure 11.2 shows the annual variation in contributions, benefits and other expenses of the closed pension system. The net result was negative in two of the last six years and there was only a small surplus in 2000.

Open Pension Plans

The open pension system comprises insurance companies and some non-profit entities. The latter generally do not offer accumulation products, concentrating on pension plans geared towards a lump-sum death benefit (*pecúlio*). They represent about 5 to 6 per cent of the open pension plan market in terms of the volume of contributions.

There are three types of open pension plans: the traditional pension plans, the Free Benefit Generator Plan (PGBL) and the Free Benefit Generator Life Plan (VGBL).[3] Table 11.4 summarizes the features of the current private pension products in Brazil.

The VGBL was created in 2002 and works just like a Roth Individual Retirement Account (IRA) in the USA under which contributions are not tax deductible, investments accumulate tax free and only investment gains are taxed when benefits are paid.[4] It is a defined contribution scheme with no return guarantees on investments and where all contributions must be directed to a mutual fund created for this specific purpose.[5] When purchasing a VGBL, the participant can set the date when benefits will start being paid in the form of an inflation-indexed annuity. At the moment, the VGBL can only be sold as an individual contract. The Superintendent for Private Insurance (SUSEP) is planning to allow the sale of collective VGBL plans to corporate clients, in a similar form to collective PGBL plans. Few insurance companies still offer traditional plans.

Just like the PGBL, the mortality table and the interest rate for annuity conversion from the VGBL are set on the date of purchase. This is a rather specific characteristic of personal pension plans in Brazil. In order to protect themselves from risks, insurance companies use a very conservative mortality table, and set the interest rate at 0 per cent. Six months before the pre-established date for benefit payment, the participant receives a report with the balance and the annuity value according to the original agreed conditions. He also receives a new proposal from the insurance company based on revised parameters. The participant then has the option of withdrawing these funds and paying the due taxes, transferring the funds to another VGBL or PGBL plan, or accepting the new terms offered by the insurance company.

The PGBL and VGBL were designed jointly by SUSEP and the insurance companies to address the major flaws associated with traditional plans in the accumulation phase, including the lack of transparency and complicated rules. As such, both the PGBL and VGBL plans have a simple charging structure: insurance companies may charge a commission as a percentage of contribu-

Table 11.5 Contributions, investments and reserves – open pension system

Year	Contributions	Variation (%)	Investment portfolio	Variation (%)	Technical reserves	Variation (%)
1994	670 382	56.6	3 017 627	17.3	1 600 676	44.0
1995	1 050 181	92.3	3 539 466	69.8	2 306 567	44.1
1996	1 397 918	33.1	4 637 091	31.0	3 133 717	35.8
1997	2 163 893	54.8	6 254 606	34.9	4 645 677	48.2
1998	3 185 200	47.2	8 376 350	33.9	6 965 447	49.9
1999	3 803 716	19.4	12 726 117	51.9	10 394 238	49.2
2000	5 971 661	40.0	17 142 853	34.7	14 837 463	42.7
2001	7 371 057	38.4	23 415 944	36.5	19 635 218	38.5
2002	6 987 366	27.84	29 249 395**	36.50**	26 734 035	39.12**

Notes:
* Total contributions from January to October 2002. Growth compared to same period in 2001.
** Investment portfolio and technical reserves up to 31 October 2002. Growth compared to the figure on 31 October 2001.

Source: ANAPP – Associação Nacional de Previdência Privada.

219

tions and the mutual fund company that manages the specific fund charges a fee on assets.

Unlike the closed fund system, open pension plans have been experiencing high growth in the level of contributions (see Table 11.5). The new products (PGBL and VGBL) already receive 55 per cent of all contributions. In fact the success of the VGBL plans has been amazing. They were designed for those individuals who do not qualify for tax deductions on their contributions and for persons in the informal labour market. Those who have already reached the full limit for contribution deductibility and wish to make extra contributions to a pension plan may also use it. As of October 2002, 11 insurance companies were offering VGBL plans, 293 410 plans had been sold and accumulated contributions reached R$1.64 billion.[6] In this same period (January to October 2002), contributions to PGBL plans totalled R$2.19 billion.

There is particularly strong market concentration in the open pension fund industry. Three main market participants – Bradesco Vida e Previdência, Brasil Previdência and Itau Previdência, account for 65 per cent of contributions in the open pension plan system, including 48 per cent of contributions to PGBL plans, 63 per cent to traditional plans and over 94 per cent to VGBL plans. The dominance of Bradesco Vida e Previdência in the VGBL market is partly explained by the fact that it was the first to offer these plans.

In order to understand this market, one must take a look at the Brazilian financial services industry. This industry is completely dominated by banks. Brazil adopts a universal banking model, similar to Germany, and practically all private savings are allocated in banks. Independent mutual funds and insurance companies hold a very small share of the market. It is thus important to separate independent insurance companies from those controlled by a banking group. In fact, in terms of contributions to the open pension system, the only insurance company that is not controlled by a major commercial bank is Icatu Hartford. The only other independent insurance companies which play a role in the open pension system are AGF Brasil, Sul America Etna and Cigna Previdência e Investimentos. The other foreign independent insurance companies operating in the Brazilian personal pension industry are: Canada Life, Cardif, Metropolitan Life, Nationwide, Mapfre and Zurich. The only way for these independent providers to survive is to offer customized products to niche markets, especially in the corporate sector.

The major problem associated with bank dominance is in the sale process. Bank staff offer pension products simply as another financial product in their portfolio, and may not give the best advice to customers. Given the short deferment period – that is, the period in which the participant is not allowed to withdraw or transfer funds – insurance brokers are not eager to sell PGBLs and VGBLs. It is therefore very difficult for customers to find independent qualified advice. It remains to be seen if the independent players will be able to win a significant market share from bank-controlled insurance companies. Despite this concentration, it has been argued that the open pension system is now a competitive market. Some analysts expect market consolidation in the near term, arguing the market size does not support so many players.

An important concern with the new products is the short period before withdrawals can be made. Present regulation allows insurance companies to set a no-withdraw limit from 60 days to two years, but practically all individual plans use the two months' limit. The consequence is that PGBL and VGBL plans may be sought more for short-term tax planning then for retirement purposes. There is no definite answer as to whether this is the case, but an indication is that insurance companies promote large sales campaigns each December based on the tax savings argument. In 2001, total and partial withdrawals from PGBL plans amounted to R$563 million (20.7 per cent of contributions) and from January to October 2002 the number was R$954 million (43.6 per cent of contributions). These numbers may indeed show that a relatively large group of people are using these plans for short-term financial purposes.

Although the PGBL and the VGBL have offered an adequate solution for the accumulation phase of the open funds, there still remains the problem of annuity provision. The fact is that there are no specialized annuity providers, and an annuity market simply does not exist in Brazil. It may be that Brazil does not have a critical mass sufficient to foster this market. Perhaps, given the long-term mortality, inflation and interest rate risks in an economy as volatile as Brazil's, annuities might not be sound business, or only feasible under terms that are unfavourable to consumers. SUSEP argues that annuities might work better if they included a clause establishing a periodic renegotiation of the terms. The regulating body would have to set strict procedures for this renegotiation in order to protect consumers' rights. Given the preference of 401(k) (an employer sponsored defined contribution pension plan named after section 401k of the Internal Revenue Code subsection that regulates it) participants for lump-sum withdrawals of their benefits instead of annuity purchase, it might be argued that it may be even more difficult to induce Brazilian consumers to opt for annuities.

SUSEP has already set the regulatory framework for the creation of a new family of products that include investment guarantees in the accumulation phase. These are simply variations of the PGBL and VGBL. In the PRGP and VRGP, the consumer purchases an interest rate and an indexation guarantee in the accumulation phase, whereas the Plano com Atualizacao Garantida e Performance (PAGP) and the Vida com Atualizacao Garantida e Performance (VAGP) offer only a price index guarantee. They will also offer a portion of the excess return. Insurance companies are still analyzing what would be the best financial index for the PRGP/VRGP as they want to avoid the use of a price index.

It is important to identify the difference between these new plans and the traditional plans. During the accumulation phase, the new plans can offer an interest rate guarantee (up to 6 per cent) and an inflation index guarantee, just as traditional plans do. The contributions allocated to these plans, however, must be directed to a specific mutual fund, with daily public quotation. This feature means much more transparency in the calculation of the actual excess return since a portion of the excess return is contracted. The fact that all assets are invested through a publicly quoted mutual fund also provides a greater guarantee as to the availability of these assets for benefit payment. This structure allows for a much greater matching of assets to liabilities in these plans.

Unfortunately, the available data do not permit calculation of the number of individuals covered by open pension plans in Brazil. Insurance companies inform SUSEP only of the number of contracts sold, but there is significant double counting in these numbers, since one person may own multiple contracts. Those using open pension plans for tax planning purposes are especially prone to have multiple contracts. The National Association of Private Pensions Providers (ANAPP) estimates the population covered by open pension plans at around 2 million. However, there are no public statistics on the number of organizations that purchased collective open plans. Table 11.6 presents the number of personal pension plans that have been contracted up to October 2002.

REGULATION OF PRIVATE PENSIONS

The supervisory bodies of the closed and the open pension systems have adopted quite different approaches towards regulation. Whereas the SPC included the regulatory and supervisory details in the legislation (Law 109), SUSEP opted for stating only general principles in the law and providing the details through resolutions issued by the CNSP. Given these options, the open system now enjoys a much more flexible and effective regulatory framework. Changes in a complementary law require a qualified majority in Congress and thus takes a long time to be implemented.

Another crucial difference is that since 1995, SUSEP and the insurance companies have established efficient working terms, which has led to the joint development of new products suited to market demands and regulatory procedures. This cooperative relationship, however, does not imply that the regulator was 'captured' by the regulated. In the closed funds arena, dialogue between the SPC and EFPCs has not been constant, and there were periods of quite antagonistic relations.

Table 11.6 *Personal pension plans*

	Number of participants				Number of beneficiaries			
	Total	Retirement benefit	Lump sum death benefit	Survivors' pension	Total	Retirement benefit	Lump sum death benefit	Survivors' pension
Non-profit EAPPs (traditional plans)	1 716 702	215 396	1 274 874	226 432	46 698	32 955	754	12 989
Insurance companies (traditional plans)	3 301 648	1 708 976	633 428	956 848	164 573	151 138	3 469	9 964
PGBL*	1 268 949				5 358			

Note: *Besides insurance companies, two non-profit EAPCs also commercialize PGBLs.

Source: SUSEP.

FUNDING, SOLVENCY AND BENEFIT PROTECTION

The Closed Pension System

One of the government's goals with the new legislation was to impose stricter funding rules on pension funds. The 2001 World Bank Report on Brazilian pensions had questioned the minimum funding levels and the lack of a methodology for their calculation (World Bank 2001, p. 141). The part of the law relevant to this discussion is Section 3, Article 18 of Law 109, which states that 'existing funds of each benefit plan must at all times fully cover existing obligations assumed by the plan'. However, it is generally agreed that this statement is confusing and open to many interpretations. It is by no means clear that it implies a full funding of the Project Benefit Obligation (PBO).

One interpretation is that this was meant to prohibit the retention of funds by the sponsoring firm that occurred under previous legislation. Since that law required that only 70 per cent of the reserves for benefits to be granted needed to be actually funded, sponsors retained the remaining 30 per cent as a sort of loan, which accrued by the actuarial target of the plan. In other words, this was a very inexpensive loan. The above-mentioned statement has also been used as the basis for the SPC demand that past services can only be financed through a contract with guarantees. Alternatively, it can mean that an EFPC cannot allow a participant with past services to be financed. The moment the individual retires, the EFPC must fully fund his reserves. As such, past services would no longer be an appropriate method for financing a defined benefit plan.

In 2002, the CGPC approved a new Resolution (No. 11) which set the technical actuarial parameters to be observed by closed pension funds. The resolution is largely the product of a document prepared by the Brazilian Institute of Actuaries (IBA). The reference mortality table set by the resolution is AT49. Although clearly outdated, it is in some sense an improvement since there are pension funds using even less conservative tables. The fact is, however, that there is no scientific basis for the choice of AT49 for the closed fund population. This is an area where further research is urgently required. SUSEP, for instance, has already produced a reference mortality table for the personal pension plan industry.

A positive feature of the new resolution was to limit the turnover rate to 5 per cent. This is quite important, since this item may have more impact on the actuarial cost of the plan than the mortality table used. There is consensus among actuaries that this is a reasonable limit. A maximum interest rate of 6 per cent was confirmed by the resolution. Such a rate is high by OECD standards, and the use of a lower rate has been suggested. The issue is that, in the last 20 years, real interest rates in Brazil have been much higher, and pension funds hold a large stock of government securities paying inflation plus 12 per cent. The matter of the appropriate long-term interest rate for the calculation of pension costs is further complicated by the lack of long-term treasury bills in the country. Using a 6 per cent interest rate may, in fact, inflate the real costs of a pension plan. One proposed approach is to segregate, in the actuarial calculation, the liabilities and assets that perfectly match. If the plan has a benefit flow of R$1000 per year and a security with an 8 per cent interest is bought that will produce a payment flow exactly equal to the benefit flow, it is perfectly hedged. Notwithstanding this, if the benefit flow is discounted at 6 per cent and the present value of the security is 8 per cent, the plan will have a deficit. The proposal, then, would be to segregate these portions of the liability and assets when doing the actuarial evaluation, since they are perfectly matched. Otherwise, the regulatory body would be imposing an additional cost to the sponsor.

Also of concern is the pricing of the assets in the pension funds. The Brazilian Central Bank introduced a requirement in 2002 that mutual funds must mark to market all their assets. This increases the confidence on the stated prices of the assets that are externally managed. CGPC Resolution No. 4 of 2002 also requires EFPCs to mark to market some internally managed securities, while other categories of securities are to be evaluated by their acquisition costs plus the produced gains. While quite complex, this concentrated effort on a relatively small number of EFPCs could dispel concerns about the actual market prices of assets.

Open Pension Plans

Funding problems apply only to traditional plans, since both PGBLs and VGBLs are defined contribution plans with no guarantees during the accumulation phase. The fact that traditional plans offer a 6 per cent real interest rate guarantee during the accumulation phase raises the question of their proper funding. According to SUSEP, the insurance companies that offer these plans are properly hedged and there is no system-wide solvency risk. The real problem lies with traditional plans managed by the non-profit EAPCs. The funding status of these entities and the quality of their assets are not sound. The situation is not as bad as it might be, since the non-profit EAPCs have sold mostly lump-sum death benefit plans (*pecúlio*). In addition, today they represent only a small fraction of the personal pension industry. Another concern affecting traditional plans is the fact that they mostly employ an outdated mortality table (AT49) for annuity calculation.

A great improvement to the system's funding was brought by SUSEP Circular No. 185 of 2002, which introduced the requirement for an annual actuarial evaluation, and set the minimum technical parameters for this evaluation.

Previously, SUSEP had scarce information on the actuarial situation of personal pension plan providers. Reserves were calculated based on the original assumptions made when the plan was created. After Circular No. 185, insurance companies and non-profit EAPCs had to recalculate their reserves based on the minimum parameters. The reserves that are now reported are far more accurate. SUSEP also produced a reference mortality table for the open pension system. When a provider does not have sufficient information or experience to produce its own table, it can employ the ones developed by SUSEP.

As for assets, an important protection measure was introduced by CNSP Resolution No. 98, which requires that all assets be registered to a custodian. Furthermore, the personal plan provider is required to authorize the custodian to make available to SUSEP all the information regarding the investment of these assets. SUSEP has on-line control of the assets given as guarantee, and has the power to cancel operations with those assets that it has reason to be believe will endanger participants.

Another protective mechanism employed by SUSEP surrounds the fiscal director in the case where an insurance company is being liquidated. If the appointed fiscal director judges that the insurance company will be unable to pay its liabilities, he (she) may order some plan portfolios to be transferred to other insurance companies. As such, the risks of participants of new plans are dissociated from those of the old ones.

Only insurance companies that operate exclusively in the life sector are allowed to sell personal pension plans. The purpose of this restriction is to avoid the contamination of personal pension plans by the risks associated with other kinds of insurance products. What is presently needed are legal measures to safeguard the assets held by the insurance companies, for the purpose of funding plan's reserves from being used to pay creditors in a bankruptcy procedure. Legislation already stipulates that an insurance company's non-operational assets must be equal to its non-operational liabilities.[7] However, this does not avoid the risk of insurance companies misrepresenting the value of their non-operational liabilities. Therefore, additional protection measures of the guarantee funds in the event of bankruptcy are desirable.

One item that is still pending regulation is the establishment of solvency margins for personal pension providers. Insurance companies deemed an initial SUSEP proposal of an 8 per cent of reserves solvency margin excessively high. There is now a tendency to set a margin of 8 per cent for traditional plans and other products with guarantees, and a 1 per cent margin for PGBL/VGBLs. Another ongoing discussion is the creation of a solvency fund, financed by the insurance companies themselves. Large companies have resisted this measure, since they will bear a cost and not benefits from the creation of the fund. However, it is thought that the creation of such a fund may boost consumer confidence, helping to increase sales.

Potential problems related to asset pricing are limited to traditional plans. The new plans must invest their assets in mutual funds regulated by the Brazilian Central Bank and the Securities Exchange Commission (CVM). These funds have had to mark to market their assets since 2002. SUSEP also has a department that verifies if the reported asset prices reflect market reality.

Private Pension Plan Investments

The closed pension system

The rules presently governing the investment of pension fund assets are established by National Monetary Council (CMN) Resolution No. 2829 of 30 March 2001. The main innovations brought by this resolution include: limits on investment in fixed income securities based on credit risk; limits on equity investments to follow corporate governance criteria; a centralized custodian required for all securities held; an independent auditor required for investment management; and the establishment of a risk control and evaluation system (to calculate and inform value at risk). Table 11.7 presents current limits and Figure 11.3 shows the distribution of the consolidated portfolio of the closed pension system.

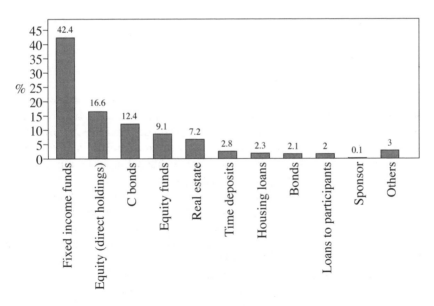

Source: SPC.

Figure 11.3   Distribution of EFPC investments (August 2002)

Table 11.7 *Portfolio limits in the complementary pension system*

Asset class/subslasses	Closed funds			Open funds
	Max. %	DC %	DB %	
Fixed income[1]	100			100
Low credit risk				
Treasury securities, Federal Reserve	100			100
Quotas of mutual funds				100
States and municipal securities	80			80
Certificates of bank deposites (CDBs/RDBs)	80			80
Bonds, real state securities[2]	80			80
Savings, swaps, other	80			80
Quotas of mutual funds				80
Quotas of FACs				80
Quotas of FIEX	10			10
Quotas of creditory rights mutual funds	10			10
Middle/high credit risk[3]				
CDBs/RDBs		30	20	
Savings		30	20	
Bonds		30	20	
Quotas of creditory rights mutual funds	5			
Equity				
In market[4]				49
New market – special		60	45	49

Level 1 corporate goverance	45	35	15
Level 2 corporate goverance	55	40	30
Market (normal)	35	30	15
Participations			
Project finance, investment funds, private equity	20	10	5
Others			
BDRs, gold market	3		3
Real estate[5]	16–8		18–8
Development[6]			
Rent income			
Real estate funds[7]			10
Others			
Loans to participants	10		

Notes:

1 The total drawings, shared obligations or responsibility of an institution may not exceed 25% of the net equity company. There is a 25% limit of the fund net equity in case of inversions by the EFPCs themselves. Also a 40% limit of the fund net equity.

2 Total issues, shared obligations or responsibility of an institution may not exceed 25% of drawer net equity.

3 Total issues, shared obligations or responsibility of an institution may not exceed 15% of drawer net equity.

4 The total investment in the stock of a company may not exceed: (a) 20% of the company's voting capital; (b) 10% of total capital; and (c) 5% of assets reserve.

5 The limit of 16% applies until 2002 and will then be gradually reduced to 8% by 2009.

6 Each investment may not represent more than 25% of the corresponding centerprise.

Source: SPC/MPAS.

The supervisory process and the transparency of the information could be enhanced if proper benchmarks were developed for each asset class and sub-class. The sub-classes for equity investments are rather confusing. Further, the use of governance criteria for setting limits, though a good idea in practice, may generate an artificial market bubble, since very few Brazilian firms have a good rating in this area. Improvements are also needed in regard to risk control and performance evaluation of pension fund investments. One alternative is to place greater responsibility on the Board of Trustees, demanding that they produce a formal document stating that they are satisfied with the fund's investment performance. In this manner, more transparency would be obtained without the supervisory body having to demand more information from the pension funds.

A much-criticized issue is the establishment of different portfolio limits for defined benefit and defined contribution plans. There is no technical background for introducing this differentiation and it should be abolished from the regulation. Brazilian pension funds are still not allowed to make foreign investments. The only exception is those funds that invest in Brazilian foreign sovereign debt bills. It has been suggested that they be permitted to purchase ADRs of Brazilian companies and also foreign issues (debt) of Brazilian companies.

Beyond these more specific critiques of the current legislation, one can question the whole rationale of the regulation of occupational pension fund investments in Brazil. The concept of quantitative portfolio restrictions and the requirement of monthly detailed reports on portfolio allocation do not seem efficient. Since mid-2002, pension funds have been required to send the SPC a detailed report describing the allocation of their portfolio. This is simply a cost that produces no benefit since the SPC does not have the resources to analyse these reports properly. And even if it had, the value of such short-term data to evaluate the soundness of a fund's investment policy is questionable.

What the SPC needs is a risk evaluation model and a law defining the responsibilities and penalties for trustees, actuaries, auditors, accountants and investment managers. There should be a duty on these agents to report unlawful behaviour. What should be demanded from EFPCs is that they keep a reliable record of the investment decision-making process, to determine who took the decisions and how they were made. One of the reasons that make it hard to punish pension fund managers and trustees is the difficulty of establishing clear personal responsibility for harmful investment decisions. A large pension fund recently adopted a very sound policy to deal with this matter. It established published guidelines that have to be followed in every investment decision, and a checklist of items to be observed by the decision makers. In cases where the decision maker decides not to abide by a specific guideline, he (she) must state in writing the reasons for this departure.

The open pension system

Investment regulations in the open fund system differ according to the type of product and the period. Traditional plans must abide by the asset class limitations and diversification requirements established by CMN Resolution No. 2967 (31 May 2002). These limits, as can be observed in Table 11.7, are quite similar to those of the closed fund system. One difference is that this regulation does not apply credit risk criteria for the limits of fixed income securities as is done for the closed funds. There are also lower limits for equity investment.

The new plans (PGBL, PRGP, PAPG, VGBL, VRGP, VAGP) have to respect the 'special conditions' of the above-mentioned Resolution 2967. These conditions require that during the accumulation period, all the assets of these plans must be invested in a mutual fund (FIF) created specifically for this purpose. They may also invest in a mutual fund that purchases quotas of these special FIFs, which is called a FAQ, although the use of this latter vehicle is still pending a circular from SUSEP. The portfolio of these FIFs must comprise only assets as specified under Resolution 2967 and, except for the equity investment limits, respect the limits and conditions set by this Resolution. This implies that these FIFs may not invest in real estate. During the benefit payment period, if the annuity contracted includes the reversal of a portion of the excess return, the guaranteeing asset must obey these 'special conditions', otherwise they may be invested according to the general parameters set by Resolution 2967.

All the new plans can be grouped in the three categories according to the portfolio composition of their FIF: sovereign, fixed income and mixed income. A sovereign fund can only have government securities in its portfolio. Fixed income funds are allowed to purchase private fixed income instruments, and mixed income funds can have in their portfolio any of the securities mentioned in Resolution 2967.

The great advantage of this investment structure is its transparency and the assurance of better control over the assets and their pricing. All FIFs are supervized by the Brazilian Central Bank and the Securities Exchange Commission (CVM), and have to abide by mark to market procedures set by these bodies. Insurance company managers are satisfied with these investment regulations and believe that they conform to the conservative view the great majority of Brazilians adopt regarding their savings.

Supervisory Structure

The main issue in relation to supervision is the question of the single regulator for the complementary pension system. This is quite controversial, as the recent UK experience shows (Davis 2002; Pickering 2002; DWP 2002a and

2002b). It is not clear whether the differences between employer-provided occupational pension plans and personal pension plans provided by insurance companies justify the existence of separate regulators. If this were changed to a single regulator, there would still remain the issue of under which Ministry this body should be subordinated: Social Security or Finance. Presently there is not enough evidence to clearly work out what the best arrangement is. Brazilian policy makers need to analyse with greater care the experience of countries – such as Sweden and Australia – which opted for a single regulator.

PRIVATE PENSION COSTS

The Open Pension System

Since traditional plans are no longer offered, this discussion will concentrate on the PGBLs and VGBLs. The first thing to be noted is that stiff competition in this market, especially the desire of new entrants to capture market share, has led to a strong fall in fees. Three types of fees may be charged: a fee on contributions; a fee for investment management charged as a percentage of the fund's assets, and, more recently, a fee on withdrawals and transfers. The last is probably charged to recover the impacts of CPMF taxation (0.38 per cent of the value of transferred funds from the account where the funds were held). As expected, the charging policy differs between individual and collective open plans. Charges on contributions and on transfers or withdrawals must be outlined in the plan's prospectus. Since all PGBLs and VGBLs must invest in publicly quoted mutual funds (FIFs), the investment management fee is reported in the major newspapers, making this a very transparent charging structure.

In 2001, SUSEP conducted a study on fees charged by individual PGBLs. Fees on contributions varied from 0 per cent to 5 per cent and investment management fees from 2.5 per cent to 3.5 per cent. In many individual plans the value of the fees on contributions falls according to the value of the accumulated reserves and period of participation. SUSEP believes that investment management fees may fall with the increase of total assets in these funds and with the forthcoming rule changes allowing PGBLs and VGBLs to invest directly in an FAC.[8]

For the collective open plans, it is common practice for insurance companies to waive the fee on contributions for medium to large sponsors. The maximum investment management fee that providers have been able to charge recently is around 1.5 per cent to 1.8 per cent. This is somewhat higher for the smaller sponsors. The average fees are reported to be around 1.5 per cent to 1 per cent, although there are a few collective plans charging less than 1 per cent. Table 11.8 takes a look at the reported investment management fees of all PGBL funds. It does not distinguish, however, funds that receive investments from collective and individual plans. These fees can be considered low when compared to those practised by 401(k) providers in the USA. In addition, it is worth noting that these asset management fees are not very different from those charged by fixed income mutual funds for investments under R$50 000.

A comparison of these fees with those levied in the compulsory individual account systems introduced in a number of other Latin American countries is not simple given the different charging structures. In Chile, Argentina, Peru, Bolivia, Colombia, El Salvador and Mexico, individual account providers use a front-loaded fee on contributions. In Brazil, however, although there is a fee on contributions, the major cost component is the asset management fee. The comparison therefore requires the conversion of these different structures to an equivalent asset management fee. James et al. (2001) undertake this exercise based on the Chilean case. Based on an average level of a 15.6 per cent fee on contributions, they show that the equivalent asset-based fee could vary from 0.45 per cent to 33.37 per cent, depending on workers' working and contribution history. The longer the worker stays in the system, the smaller will be the equivalent asset management fee. Their guess is that an average annual expense would be 0.94 per cent. Bravo (2001), however, states that the contribution fee for the same period is around 21 per cent of contributions (after deducting that part of the fee earmarked for survivors' and disability insurance). He estimates that for workers who have contributed for less than 15 years, the management fees are above 4 per cent of their funds.

Table 11.8   Asset management fees of PGBL funds

Asset management fee (%)	PGBL fixed income		PGBL sovereign		PGBL mixed	
	No.	%	No.	%	No.	%
Below 1	0	0.0	0	0	1	0.9
1.00	6	6.8	2	40	1	0.9
From 1.01 to 1.50	34	38.6	2	40	15	12.8
From 1.51 to 2.00	25	28.4	1	20	46	39.3
From 2.01 to 2.50	8	9.1	0	0	29	24.8
From 2.51 to 3.00	12	13.6	0	0	22	18.8
From 3.01 to 3.50	3	3.4	0	0	2	1.7
From 3.51 to 4.00	0	0.0	0	0	1	0.9
Total	88	100.0	5	100	117	100.0

Source: Gazeta Mercantil (7–8 December 2002).

Whatever the correct assumption, it seems that fees charged in the Brazilian open fund market compare favourably with those of Chile. Furthermore, given that the Brazilian system is voluntary, and the contribution period may be shorter, an asset management fee would be much more favourable to the consumer. It must also be noted that competition in this market is much more vigorous in Brazil than in any of the comparator countries. This may lead to greater fee reductions in the future.

TAXATION OF PRIVATE PENSIONS

Since 1983, the EFPCs had been battling the Brazilian Income Revenue Service (SRF) in the courts on the issue of tax immunity for closed pension funds. The SRF wanted to tax closed pensions during the accumulation phase. This was rather confusing, since it had already granted, in 1995, tax deferral for contributions and investment returns of open pension funds.

This issue was finally resolved in 2002 with the decision that all funded pension schemes would have their investment returns taxed at the normal income tax rate of 20 per cent. They were, however, granted the option to adhere to a special taxation regime (the RET) that sets a limit to the amount of this tax. Pension plans, open and closed, that opt for RET will pay an income tax limited to the product of employer contributions and the difference between the sum of income tax and net profit social contribution (CSLL) rates, and 80 per cent of the maximum marginal tax rate for individuals. Since the former is equal to 34 per cent and the latter to 22 per cent, the maximum tax paid under RET is 12 per cent of employer contributions to the plan. Simulations suggest that the impact of this tax is about 5 to 6 per cent of the balance of a defined contribution account, given equal employer and employee contributions over a 35-year period.[9]

To opt for RET, however, the pension funds had to cease all litigation with the SRF regarding taxes and pay the due amounts (with a pardon for interest and penalties). This condition affected only the closed pension funds. It is estimated that as a result of this measure, the government collected around R$9 billion by September 2002.

Although the impact of the RET regime does not seem to be very significant, it maintains the fear of instability in the tax treatment of private pensions. It must be remembered that the 12 per cent on employer contributions rule may be automatically changed if marginal rates for corporate and individual income are modified. It would certainly assist the further development of funded pensions in Brazil if the government granted full tax deferral, as is the practice in most OECD countries. It is estimated that R$700 million are collected annually as a result of this tax.

The greatest tax burden now for funded schemes is the Financial Transactions Provisional Contribution (CPMF). This tax commenced in 1998 as a transitory tax to help finance investments in health. It is charged on every financial transaction at a rate of 0.38 per cent. Every time money is withdrawn from an account, this tax is charged. When a pension fund sells a security to purchase another, it must pay CPMF. It can be argued that, just like banks, pension funds should be exempt from CPMF when they are investing assets which guarantee the benefit plan. Contributions made by the employer to the pension fund should also be exempt from CPMF.

Another issue is the taxation of VGBL plans. Although modelled on the Roth IRA (offered in the USA), VGBLs have a less generous tax treatment, since the portion of the final account balance corresponding to accrued earnings is taxed when distributed. A solution would be to specify the concept of qualified distributions: those withdrawn after a minimum period of time (such as five years, as in the USA) since the contribution was made and when the participant has reached a minimum age (such as 59½ years, as in the USA). Such distributions would then be subject to no income tax.

CONCLUSION

It seems very likely that future pension reforms in Brazil will follow the path of the USA and the UK instead of that of other Latin American countries. This would imply a gradual reduction of the importance of the public pension system and increasing reliance on the private pension system as a source of retirement income. Presently the coverage of the private system is small, although personal pension plans have been growing at an impressive rate since 1995. Coverage of occupational pensions, however, has remained stagnant. The government therefore must direct its policies in this area to maintain the growth of personal pensions and foster a new growth phase for occupational pensions.

On the basis of the US and UK experience, Brazilian authorities should seriously consider if current tax incentives are sufficient to foster the expansion of private pension coverage. Recent developments have gone in the opposite direction. It appears that in seeking greater participant protection and attempting to curtail abuses of tax incentives, regulatory authorities in many countries have construed a regulatory framework that is far too complicated and imposes undue costs on private pension providers. Unfortunately, this is exactly what has happened in Brazil in regard to occupational pension funds (closed funds). There is the great risk of 'devaluing the regulatory currency'. The occupational system clearly demands a new regulatory approach based on appropriate risk evaluation models and cost–benefit analysis.

NOTES

1. The author would like to thank the following persons for their collaboration with this report: Luiz Peregrino and Beatriz (SUSEP), Eduardo Bom Ângelo (ex-President of Cigna); Fuad Noman Filho (ex-President of ANAPP and Brasilprev); Osvaldo Nascimento (President of ANAPP and Itaúprevidência); Paulo Ferreira (Tillinghast); Devanir da Silva (Superintendent, ABRAPP); Ana Carolina (Mattos Filho Lawyers); Ricardo Weiss (BNDES); Edson Jardim (W.M. Mercer) and Newton Conde (Watson Wyatt).
2. RGPS is the public pension system that covers the working population with the exception of public employees (including the military). The latter have their own public pension system (the RPPS).
3. The VGBL is classified as a life insurance product for tax purposes.
4. The Roth IRA has a much more favourable tax treatment as there is no taxation on benefits. There is always the risk in the case of the VGBL of taxing inflationary gains, which, depending on inflation, may significantly hinder the performance of these plans.
5. The law allows the investment of VGBL plan assets in the same mutual funds (FIFs) used by PGBL plans. This is exactly what providers are doing in order to benefit from scale economies and reduce the incidence of the financial transactions tax (CPMF).
6. Throughout this chapter all values will be expressed in reals, since strong fluctuations in the exchange rate may distort the analysis.
7. Non-operational assets are those that are not given as a guarantee to the reserves of benefit plans and non-operational liabilities are those not related to the payment of plan benefits (they correspond to labour and tax liabilities).
8. AFAC is a mutual fund that invests in quotes of other mutual funds (FIFs). This measure, which is still pending regulation, will lead to fewer expenses with the financial transactions tax (CPMF).
9. Simulations by the author and Watson Wyatt Brazil.

REFERENCES

Bravo, J. (2001), 'The Chilean pension system: A review of some remaining difficulties after 20 years of reform', paper presented at the International Seminar on Pensions, Hitotsubashi University, Tokyo, Japan.
Davis, B. (2002), *Report of the Quinquennial Review of the Occupational Pensions Regulatory Authority (OPRA)*, Department for Work and Pensions (DWP), London, UK.
Department of Work and Pensions (DWP) (2002a), *Simplicity, Security and Choice: Working and Saving for Retirement*, presented to Parliament by the Secretary of State for Work and Pensions, London, UK.
Department of Work and Pensions (DWP) (2002b), *Simplicity, Security and Choice: Technical Paper*, London, UK.
James, E., J. Smalhout and D. Vittas (2001), 'Administrative costs and the organization of individual account systems: A comparative perspective', World Bank Policy Research Paper No. 2554, Washington, DC, USA.
Pickering, A. (2002), *A Simpler Way to Better Pension: An Independent Report*, Department of Work and Pensions, London, UK.
World Bank (2001), *Brazil: Critical Issues in Social Security*, Washington, DC.

Index